POCKET
ENCYCLOPEDIA

HOME
DECORATING

POCKET
ENCYCLOPEDIA

HOME DECORATING

Contributing authors
John McGowan · Roger DuBern

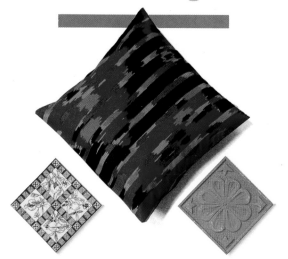

DORLING KINDERSLEY
London · New York · Stuttgart

A Dorling Kindersley Book

First published in Great Britain in 1991
by Dorling Kindersley Limited,
9 Henrietta Street, London WC2E 8PS

Designed and edited by Swallow Books,
260 Pentonville Road, London N1 9JY

A CIP catalogue record for this book is available from the British
Library

ISBN 0–86318–533–9

Typeset by Bournetype, Bournemouth
Reproduced by Colourscan, Singapore
Printed in Singapore by Kyodo Printing (Co) Pte Ltd.

CONTENTS

Introduction Page 6

INTRODUCTION

Obtaining a professional finish when decorating is easy if you take the trouble to find out how to do each job properly and arm yourself with the correct equipment and materials. The cardinal rules are to take your time and to work carefully; do not cut corners and never skimp on any part of the job. Decorating is no longer cheap; all materials are expensive. However, by doing a thorough job you will save money in the long run. The room will stay looking good for far longer than if you skimp. If you rush at it, ignoring the rules and then settle back into an armchair before the paint has dried, you will probably have created an eyesore which will be hard to live with. In no time at all, you will find yourself having to start again from scratch, spending more money – but this time doing it the right way!

This book is an invaluable addition to your decorating toolkit; it will enable you to produce top-quality results with any task, from painting a door to laying a carpet. It does not matter whether you have had any previous experience; you will find that the easy-to-follow, concise, step-by-step instructions will give you the confidence to complete any job successfully. Even those unavoidable technical terms that confuse and baffle the inexperienced are explained fully in a simple glossary. In addition, there are a host of handy hints and tips to help you to avoid all the traps and pitfalls which would otherwise spoil a job and cause delays.

The book has been planned carefully to take you through each aspect of the main decorating jobs: painting, wallpapering, tiling and laying floor coverings. Finally, it offers invaluable guidance on those important finishing touches – shelving, dressing a window and soft furnishings – providing a total guide to refurbishing a room.

One of the most frustrating aspects of practical work is finding that you have not got the correct piece of equipment for the job. This means having to stop work to find the vital tool. It is even more annoying then to discover that you have not got a particular item and that the shops are all closed. To help you to avoid this major inconvenience, there is a complete list of the items that you will need for each job at the beginning of each chapter. You will find that, where necessary, precise details are given for each tool.

One of the best ways to learn about decorating is to find out the cause of poor results in any previous decoration. A fault-finding guide is given, where relevant, which explains what may have gone wrong with your earlier efforts.

Drilling equipment
A hand drill (top) can be used if you do not have an electric one. The bradawl (above) is used to make starting holes in flat surfaces for screws.

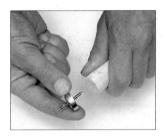

Making blinds
The steps show the various stages of making up curtains and blinds, and the different methods of hanging.

Curtains
A wide range of both unlined and lined curtains is dealt with. The most suitable types of fabric for each style of curtain are listed, and their compatibility with types of lining material. Accessories such as curtain tracks and poles are also illustrated and discussed.

The chapter on painting begins by explaining the differences between the various paints, from primer to emulsion and gloss, and how to estimate the quantity needed for a particular job. Both the protective and decorative aspects of paint are discussed, and the effects that colours can have on a room. The key to perfect painting is found in a correctly prepared surface: stripping old paint, filling cracks and holes in walls, woodwork and metalwork are all outlined before we move on to techniques for applying paint correctly. Finally, the tricks of applying decorative textures and finishes are fully explained.

The chapter on wallpapering stresses the importance of choosing the right type of paper and pattern for a particular job – and also helps you to

Equipment
The equipment illustrated is accompanied by brief descriptions of the variations where necessary, and their suitability for the different types of job.

Fixtures and accessories
Fittings and accessories for all types of furnishings are also included. Clear directions show how to make them up.

Sewing equipment
A wide selection of equipment suitable for both the amateur and the professional is illustrated, and the uses of the various items are described. The step-by-steps are illustrated with contrasting colour thread for clarity.

Wallpapering
The concise and easy-to-follow step-by-step instructions enable you to tackle the job with confidence.

Soft furnishings
The wide variety of bedcoverings is supplemented by features on related items, such as hems, frills, seams and edgings. The profusion of different types of patterned fabric is also illustrated and discussed.

Hacksaw (above, top)
This implement is useful for cutting either metal or wood, especially when creating shelves.

Paintbrushes (above, bottom)
The well-prepared do-it-yourself enthusiast will have a variety of brushes for all types of jobs.

solve that common dilemma of how many rolls to buy. Hanging wallpaper and ceiling paper can only be accomplished if you are able to reach every part of the room safely and easily, so this chapter also shows you how to set up a secure working platform, both on flat surfaces and on stairs. The preparation of a room is covered in detail, including how to strip off old paper and make the necessary repairs to create that vital smooth surface. Finally, the techniques for measuring, cutting, pasting and hanging the paper are illustrated, with special emphasis given to tricky areas such as windows, light fittings and radiators. To round off the chapter, textured wall coverings – hessian, silk, grasscloth, and so on – are described and illustrated, together with the special techniques that are required for hanging them correctly.

Techniques
The various techniques for achieving a professional finish are not only illustrated, but also explained in the text.

Table linen
Styles of tablecloths, napkins and table mats are included, together with decorative techniques such as quilting and appliqué, which can not only provide a professional touch, but also change an otherwise ordinary item into an heirloom.

The third chapter explains the secrets of successfully tiling floors, walls and ceilings. Every type of tile is dealt with – ceramic, cork, mirror, brick, plastic, quarry, vinyl and marble – together with individual details such as tile sizes and how to estimate the quantities that you will need. Again, the correct preparation of walls, floors and ceilings is discussed, and there is a section on how to plan the tiling for a well-balanced effect. This is followed by advice on the techniques for fixing or laying each type of tile.

The fourth chapter deals with other types of floor covering, such as carpet, vinyl and wooden flooring, emphasizing the all-important business of preparing floorboards and concrete floors perfectly, to ensure that your new floor covering gives long-lasting wear. All the stages in fixing carpets (including stair

Cutting equipment
Guidance is given about how to store your cutting equipment safely, and how to take care of it so that it will have many years of useful life.

carpets), wood and sheet vinyl are covered, and are backed up with essential advice on choosing the best floor covering for any situation.

Storage and shelving is the basis of a room's furniture, and Chapter Five concentrates on this. The various methods of fixing all types of shelves are shown with, of course, precise instructions for putting them up soundly. The chapter ends with a brief look at other storage units.

Curtains, blinds and soft furnishings provide the finishing touches to a room, and these are covered in the last two chapters. Whether you are fixing curtain rails, need to know about fabrics, making lined or unlined curtains, choosing and hanging blinds, or fixing pelmets, you will find all the information you need.

Tools and equipment
Each chapter contains clear illustrations of all the necessary tools that you will need for the job.

Tiling
The steps clearly show what equipment you need for tiling, and how to use it.

Thimbles, pins and threaders
Thimbles are a must when you are working with heavyweight fabrics, or with dense materials, such as leather. Glass-headed pins in different colours help you to see where the pins lie in the fabric as you sew. The threader is an extremely useful instrument.

The book concludes with a section on making up articles of household linen – sheets, pillowcases, valances, quilts, tablecloths and cushions.

Nowadays it is vital that we, as householders and purchasers of an enormous range of products, do all that we can to help protect our environment and to conserve world resources. We can play our part by using environment-friendly products in our home decorating jobs and, wherever possible, making use of recycled materials – old timber being a prime example. When buying products, do check that aerosols are ozone-friendly and that wood preservatives are water-based. Familiarize yourself with the latest water regulations, since they are there to protect the quality of our water supply.

Fret saw
If you need to cut intricate or awkward shapes, a fretsaw is ideal for the purpose.

Using the materials
Even if you have never used the materials before, the step-by-steps make it clear what to do.

Trimmings
There is a wealth of trimmings available for all types of soft furnishings – tassles, braids, piping, frills and fringes. This variety is reflected in the optional extras to the main items illustrated throughout the text.

CHAPTER ONE

PAINTING

Good paintwork is to a house what a good complexion is to a human face. It reflects the general condition and attitudes of the owner, it provides a background for more striking features and highlights, and it lends an individual quality to the whole appearance.

Modern materials give better and faster results than ever before and a competent repainting will last for many years with new, hard-wearing paints. Although paints are now sold under various descriptions, such as vinyl silk or satin finish, emulsion is still used for walls and ceilings and gloss for woodwork and metalwork. It is still usually cheaper to paint than to paper.

Preparation of surfaces before painting is all-important, since untreated cracks and flaws will rapidly appear through new paintwork and may even be exaggerated.

Any time "saved" in preparation is counter-productive, for you will treble your working time by soon having to strip off new paint to redecorate properly.

Tools and equipment

Cheap tools produce poor results. However tempting it is to save money, this is always a false economy, because good-quality equipment lasts longer, even improving with age, is more satisfying to use and, most importantly, produces a finer finish. Before using any equipment, check that it is thoroughly dry and not rusty, as rust creates indelible stains. Clean tools thoroughly and store them in a cool, dry, well-ventilated place.

Roller and tray

Scraper

Shavehooks

Paint pads

Hot-air gun

Gas blowtorch

Chemical stripper

Rollers and pads
These allow large areas to be covered quickly and easily, but are more suitable for emulsion than for oil-based gloss paint. Solid emulsion is supplied in a block, but liquid paints need a roller tray for an even coating. For a smooth finish, use a roller with a short pile; for a lightly textured look, a medium pile; and for a deeply textured finish, a long pile. Paint pads are lighter than brushes and rollers, and are ideal for

applying water-based paints to ceilings and walls. Small pads can be dipped directly into a paint tin, but larger ones require the use of a tray.

Brushes
A range of brushes will be needed for painting an average room. The smallest, a ¾in (19mm) cutting-in brush with angled bristles, is useful for painting window frames. A 1in (25mm) size is also suitable for window frames and mouldings, a 2in (50mm) for skirtings, and a 3in (75mm) for flush doors and similar large, flat areas of gloss.

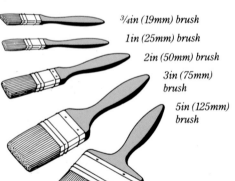

¾in (19mm) brush

1in (25mm) brush

2in (50mm) brush

3in (75mm) brush

5in (125mm) brush

Strippers and scrapers
To soften old paint, you will need either an electric hot-air gun, a gas blowtorch or a chemical stripper, and two scrapers to strip the paint off flat surfaces – one narrow and one broad. For clearing window frames and mouldings, a shavehook with a combination of straight, convex and concave sides is the most versatile kind.

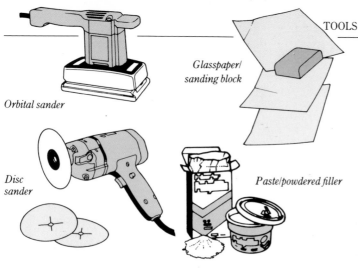

Orbital sander

Glasspaper/ sanding block

Disc sander

Paste/powdered filler

Sanders and fillers
To repair cracks and dents, a filling knife, filler and tray are all that are needed. Glasspaper comes in grades from 00 (fine) to 3 (coarse), and the medium or fine grades are the most useful. A cork, wooden or rubber block used as a "hand hold" for abrasive paper will ease the work on flat surfaces. For large areas, electric finishing sanders help to speed up the work.

Fault-finding

Painting faults can always be traced back to an error in preparation, poor working conditions or incorrect application. Inadequate cleaning and abrading of surfaces, over-brushing or over-thinning of the paint, and overloading the brush are some of the most common mistakes made by amateurs.

If a coat of gloss fails to retain its sheen, you may have left insufficient drying time between coats. Over-brushing and over-thinning of the paint may also give this result. Where a previous coat of paint is still visible, either the wrong undercoat was used, or there are insufficient undercoats. Again, over-brushing,

over-thinning or over-stirring may also dilute the paint and produce this effect. On woodwork, paint will peel if the surface is not correctly prepared; with emulsion, dirt and dust or distemper may be the problem.

All these problems can be cured by allowing the paint to harden for a week, then rubbing it down with glasspaper and cleaning the surface before applying fresh gloss or emulsion.

For blisters on woodwork, cut out the bubble and fill it with fine surface filler. Sand down and dust off before applying fresh gloss. If the blistering is excessive, strip the paint off and start again.

Lack of light will make some white paint yellow, and some red pigments will bleed into a new coat, so apply a barrier coat in between.

Specks and pimples
Specks and pimples are caused by dust in the paint. A badly sanded surface may also leave a speckled finish.

Runs and wrinkles
Runs, sags and wrinkles form if the paint is applied too thickly, or if it has not been adequately brushed out.

Blisters
Blisters are caused by painting on a damp surface or on to old, soft, or lifting paint. Heat may also be a cause.

Brushmarks
Brushmarks may be caused by a poor-quality brush, painting too thickly, or not sanding an old surface.

Paints and varnishes

Paint serves a dual purpose – to decorate and to protect a surface. Paints are available for both interior and exterior use, but it is outside that protection is of paramount importance. Paints can be divided into three categories: preparatory paints, such as primers and undercoats, top coats, including gloss and emulsion, and special-purpose paints, such as masonry and floor paints. Most paints are made up of three ingredients: pigment, which provides colour, a binder, usually a resin, which causes the pigment to stick to the surface, and a liquid, either oil or water, which combines the two. Thus top coats are divided into oil-based paints, which are available in gloss, eggshell and matt finishes, for use on wood and metal, and water-based paints or emulsions, which come in matt, satin or silk finishes, for use on plaster, paper and brick. Varnishes also decorate and protect a surface, but provide a transparent covering. So, unlike paint, they are used solely on bare wood, allowing the pattern of the wood grain to show through.

Choice of paint is the first major decorating decision, and it is worth taking time to choose the most suitable colour. It is also important to select the right type of paint for each job, to avoid repeating the work before you are ready for a change.

It is a good idea to buy a colour test pot and try it out on the area first. This will give you an idea of what it will look like. Use non-drip paints if possible; they are more economical because they have better covering rates than other types of paint.

Masonry paint on brick

Eggshell on lining paper

Primer, undercoat and gloss on wood

Paints

There are several types of preparatory paints which are applied to the surface before the top coat. Primers create a uniform surface on wood and metal. Aluminium primer-sealer (not to be confused with aluminium paint) seals off stains, such as water damage marks. Undercoat is designed to obliterate all other colours and to provide a good surface.

Top coats are divided into emulsion, gloss and eggshell. Emulsion is a water-thinned paint, used for walls and ceilings. It dries quickly and is available in both matt and sheen finishes. Gloss is a solvent-based paint, used on wood and metalwork. It can be purchased as a non-drip (thixotropic) paint. Eggshell produces a sheen finish and helps to conceal faults. There is also a range of new paints which need no undercoat or primer, and special paints – enamel, textured and masonry paints.

Varnishes

Varnishes are widely used to give protection and also to enhance the decorative properties of wood. Polyurethane varnish seal is used for wood and gives either a matt or gloss finish. You can also buy seal and stain combined, in a variety of colours. There is a range of tough varnishes, sold as yacht varnish, which are suitable for exterior decorative wood. Cellulose lacquer is also tough, fast drying, and available in clear and coloured finishes.

Preservatives such as creosote are available for exterior timber, and there are also other types in a limited range of colours.

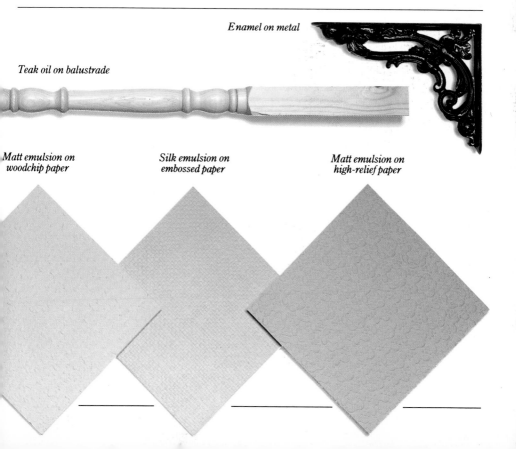

Enamel on metal

Teak oil on balustrade

Matt emulsion on woodchip paper

Silk emulsion on embossed paper

Matt emulsion on high-relief paper

Choosing the right paint

Buy a well-known make, or an "own brand", in one of the superstores or trading groups. Unknown, cheap paints, particularly emulsions, usually give an inferior result and are often not very durable.

It is best to estimate the quantities you will need and to buy the full amount in one batch to be sure of consistent and good colour. This is particularly important if you are having the paint custom-mixed by the supplier. Paints of the same type can be mixed, provided they come from the same manufacturer. If you are mixing your own paint, make a note of the quantities and names of pigments used.

The small area of colour on a manufacturer's colour chart rarely gives a clear idea of how the paint will look in a room. The combined effect of the colour on the walls and the ceiling may intensify the shade as much as 50 per cent above the paint colour chart. Always consider the colour of the paint in relation to the rest of the scheme of decoration.

Whichever type of paint you use, always use the correct type of preparatory paint. This is as important as choosing the right top coat. Use primers to seal porous surfaces such as unsized plaster, and to act as a key on metal surfaces. There are different types of primer for wood, man-made boards, plaster, brick, concrete and metals. Use undercoat on primed surfaces; this will reduce the number of top coats you have to apply. Remember that you should never use emulsion paint on metal surfaces because they are water-based paints and will cause rusting.

When to use emulsion paint

Of all the top coats, emulsion is the easiest to apply. On new plaster surfaces it is usual to use a thinned paint-and-water coating as a primer. On previously painted or papered surfaces, it is advisable to apply the paint sparingly, recoating, if necessary, to ensure that the paint covers well and seeps into any crevices. Emulsion is not ideal on bare wood, since the water content raises the grain, producing a rough finish. Use it on internal walls and ceilings.

When to use oil-based paint

Gloss needs to be more thoroughly brushed out than emulsion and should be applied in thin coats to avoid runs. Non-drip (thixotropic) gloss paint, however, is laid on in a thick layer, without much brushing. The gloss is simply a protective finishing coat, so previous colours must be obliterated by layers of undercoat. Use gloss on exterior and interior wood and/or metal. Generally, gloss paints do not need to be thinned, unless they are being used in a spray gun.

Enamel needs to be brushed on extremely carefully, since the high gloss finish will show up irregularities. Like emulsion, it needs to be built up coat by coat, allowing each layer to dry.

Choosing the right varnish

As with paints, it is best to choose a well-known brand to be sure of a quality finish. If you are treating exterior wood, it is particularly important to choose a protective, exterior-quality product. Varnish will last longer on mahogany-type woods than on coarser woods, such as oak and Western red cedar. If you plan to add a coat of varnish over a stain, check that they have compatible chemical bases.

COPING WITH LEADED PAINTS

Lead is no longer used in paint. However, some old paintwork may still contain lead. If you think this may be the case, make sure that you take the following precautions:

● Do not use a blowlamp, as it creates toxic fumes when the paint is heated.

● Do not use dry sandpaper, as it creates dust.
● Put debris in the dustbin, do not burn it.
● Use gloves for protection, and make sure that you wash your hands afterwards.

If you use spray paint, try to find CFC-free aerosols as far as possible.

SUITING THE PAINT TO THE SURFACE

Different areas of a house require very different treatment. Never cut corners on the preparatory work. Some areas, such as children's furniture, need virtually no preparation and only one or two coats of paint. Others, such as exterior woodwork, may need much preparation – knotting, primer and undercoat – before applying several top coats, so plan carefully before you start.

Ceilings
Pre-paint: primer-sealer; diluted emulsion
Top coat: emulsion (on papered or unpapered ceilings)
Textured paint (on unpapered ceilings)

Children's furniture
Pre-paint: none
Top coat: enamel

Doors, windows, architraves, stairs, skirtings
Pre-paint: knotting; primer; undercoat
Top coat: gloss or eggshell

Exterior walls
Pre-paint: diluted top coat/ stabilizing primer
Top coat: masonry paint/ exterior-grade emulsion

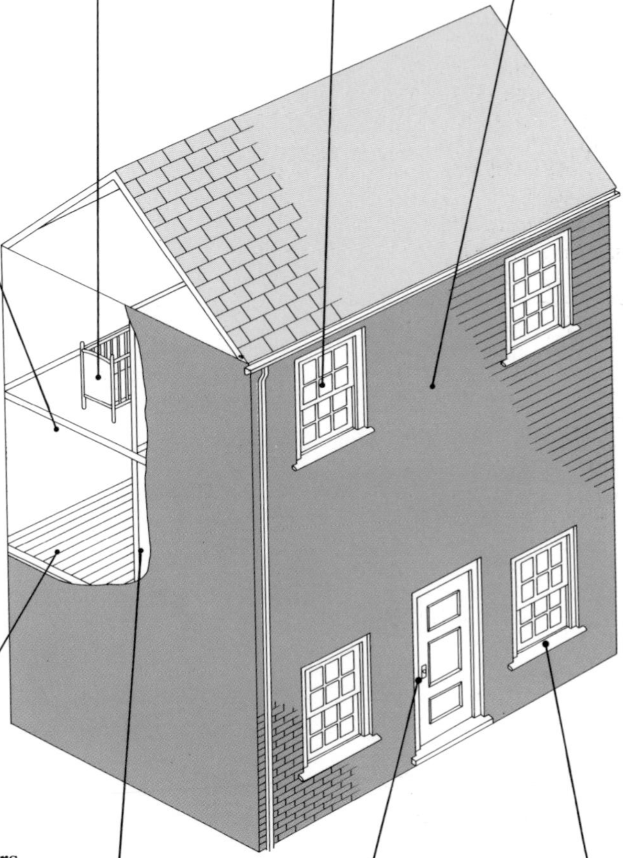

Timber floors
Pre-paint: knotting; primer; undercoat
Top coat: stain/varnish/ floor paint

Internal walls
Pre-paint: primer-sealer; diluted emulsion
Top coat: emulsion/ eggshell

Metalwork
Pre-paint: primer (on clean, bright metal); undercoat
Top coat: gloss

Exterior wood
Pre-paint: knotting; primer; undercoat
Top coat: gloss (several coats)

The effects of colour on a room

Colour has the power to transform a room. It can raise and lower ceilings, it can expand and reduce walls, it can disguise and highlight individual features and it can soothe or excite. A dark room can be lightened with a sheen that reflects light, and warm, dark colours can make a large, cold room feel more cosy. Your decision may be influenced by existing furnishings, and in many rooms the paintwork may need to act as a neutral backdrop to more vibrant accessories. Remember that when applied, the accumulated colour will intensify the shade of the colour chart, as many home decorators have discovered too late!

Diminishing a large room
Colour can influence the apparent size and shape of a room. Light shades will bring space to a small room and dark tones foreshorten a large one. A low ceiling will appear higher if it is painted a paler shade than the walls. To disguise the room shape even more, apply a single dark colour over the ceiling and walls, then break it up with spotlights (above). Complementary textures and the judicious addition of strong colour, as illustrated here, will also ensure that, for the most part, the eye focuses on the lower half of the overall scheme of decoration.

Enlarging and lightening a small room

As a dark colour can help to make a large room look more cosy, so a lighter colour can enlarge a smaller space. A pale, receding background shade will lighten and open out a dark, poky room (left) and will help to conceal pipes, radiators and irregular window shapes. The effect is enhanced by a co-ordinating colour effect. The use of paintings or prints can also give additional weight to the overall effect. Cool shades, such as the frosty blue, monochromatic colour scheme below, lends a cool feeling of light and space to a sunny room. Sparkling white woodwork and silver chrome accessories add to the effect, giving a clean, modern air to an otherwise traditional room.

Establishing moods

Those who demand a stimulating home environment probably enjoy strong primary colours, broken up with neutrals. Others who need a restful, relaxing atmosphere may prefer natural and more muted tones. The aspect of the room should also be considered when selecting paint colour. A burnt orange shade (above) gives warmth to a large room with harsh light coming through the windows. It is complemented by the matching tones of the furnishings.

FURNISHINGS

When planning the colour scheme for a room, it is important to take the furnishings into account. All the examples on this page make the furnishings a complementary or focal part of the overall design in very different ways.

Furnishings include carpets, curtains and chair coverings. If you cannot invest in a whole new suite of furniture, loose covers or throw-overs can do the job just as well and much more cheaply. They are also versatile, easy to clean and can be changed much more easily than fixed coverings. Remember that it is not only colour and tone that can lend originality and vibrancy to your home, but also the textures, weaves and patterns of the fabrics that you decide to use.

Planning

New decoration will only be as good as the planning and preparation of the work. The first step in any redecoration job is to decide on the extent of the initial structural and repair work required, before estimating time, costs and quantities of materials needed. This work will depend on the age and condition of the house.

In a post-1950s house the timber is unlikely to be well seasoned, so when central heating is installed, the woodwork may split, shrink and warp away from the walls, causing cracks that need filling. Many modern homes, however, do have the advantage of low-maintenance accessories, such as plastic gutters and downpipes, and anodized aluminium windows that do not need paint.

Different problems arise in older houses. The walls, usually solid, encourage damp which must be cured before decorating can begin. The lath and plasterwork in ceilings and walls deteriorate over time, so cracked plasterwork will need to be repaired or replaced before painting or wallpapering. A thick layer of paint is likely to have built up on the woodwork over the years. If the paintwork tends to chip badly, strip it back to the bare wood. Preparation can mean more work than decoration.

Estimating quantities

To estimate the amount of paint you need, first calculate the area of each surface to be covered by multiplying the height or length by the width. Take all your measurements, then total your surface areas.

When measuring the area of walls, include windows and doors as part of the surface, unless they are significantly large. This will allow a little extra paint in case the walls prove highly absorbent. A wall measuring 6ft (1.8m) high by 11ft 6in (3.5m) wide has a total area of $69ft^2$ ($6.4m^2$). If it was to be painted in vinyl silk emulsion with a covering rate of $90ft^2$ per pint ($15m^2$/litre), the area, $69ft^2$ ($6.4m^2$), divided by the covering rate, $90ft^2$ ($8.4m^2$), would give the number of pints (litres) required: ¾ pint (0.42 litre) per coat. Windows are difficult to estimate, but as a guide, allow $21ft^2$ ($2m^2$) for a small window, $43ft^2$ ($4m^2$) for a medium-sized window, and $54ft^2$ ($5m^2$) for a large one. Allow for any alcoves and chimneys.

Ceilings
Multiply the widths of two adjacent walls and allow for alcoves.

Walls
Measure the height and width of each wall, without deducting window and door areas. Add the multiples for the total area.

Doors, windows and skirtings
An average window measures $43ft^2$ ($4m^2$). Doors measure $43–21ft^2$ ($4–2m^2$) per side including frame and trim. For skirting, multiply the length by the height.

Covering rates of paints

The covering power of paints varies with the type of paint, the porosity of the surface and the thickness of the coat applied. Non-drip gloss and "jelly" paints, for example, will not cover such a large area as liquid gloss or emulsion, but since the coating is thicker, fewer coats may be required. Most varnishes will go further than paint, while primers will not stretch as far. Bare plaster and textured surfaces absorb more liquid, so it is often more economical to add water to a first coat than to apply an extra top coat.

The type of paint, the colour and the surface determine the number of coats to be applied. You will need an extra coat, for example, when covering a dark colour with a lighter one, but not when using a dark final colour. When decorating previously unpainted wood, use primer and an undercoat before one or two coats of gloss. If painting over old gloss, you may need to apply one or two coats of undercoat to leave a good base for the gloss. A third coat of emulsion is sometimes needed to obliterate a dark background. Glossy emulsions may also need an extra coat. The table (right) gives specific coverage areas.

Paint type	Covering area (ft²/pt and m²/l)
Universal primer (wood)	43–49/7–8
(metal)	55–67/9–11
(plaster)	30–55/5–9
Aluminium primer-sealer	67–80/11–13
Acrylic primer/undercoat	92–98/15–16
Alkali-resistant primer	55–67/9–11
Primer-sealer	61/10
Stabilizing primer	37–74/6–12
Metal primer	55–67/9–11
Undercoat	92/15
Gloss (liquid)	104/17
Gloss (non-drip)	74/12
Silk finish (oil-based)	74/12
Eggshell finish	92/15
Emulsion, matt (non-drip solid)	86/14
Emulsion, vinyl silk	92/15
Aluminium paint	74–86/12–14

POINTS TO REMEMBER

• Make sure that you have enough paint for the job before you start work.
• Prepare the ceilings first, then the walls, and finally the wood and the metalwork. Be sure to paint each coat in the same order.
• Test the paint on a small area of the wall or ceiling before buying the full quantity. Manufacturers often make test cans for this purpose.
• Use the undercoat that is recommended by the manufacturer for the colour you have chosen for the top coat of gloss.
• Fill any cracks and make sure that you remove all the dust before you begin painting.

ESTIMATING TIME

Home decorating invariably takes longer than you think. Remember, however, that your skill and experience, the care you take in your workmanship, the speed at which you work and the number of hours a day you actually work, including meal breaks, will all influence the total time needed to complete the work. Try to arrange three to four uninterrupted hours for each session and, if possible, avoid changing from natural to artificial light. Remember to allow more time for any extra coats, and build in a little extra time for cleaning brushes and equipment at the end of each session. When totting up the total number of days needed to complete the whole room, allow for the time needed for the paint to dry between coats. As a rough guide, emulsion takes about four hours to dry, but gloss should be left overnight.

You should also take into account the time spent fetching supplies of paint and other decorating materials. This can take half a day or more in itself, particularly if you have to travel to a large do-it-yourself store. Shopping in the store can also take a good deal of time, particularly if you go at the weekend, when these stores can be very crowded. These points apply not just to painting, but to any type of home decorating project – for example, tiling, wallpapering, shelving and flooring.

Stripping old paint

It is not always necessary to strip off old paint, for if the gloss on woodwork is sound and smooth, it will form an ideal base for fresh paint. Old whitewash and distemper on walls can often be removed by washing, but if the paint is loose and chips off easily, it is better to strip it off. Test the surface with masking tape; if it pulls paint away, strip the affected area. Most of the methods for stripping paint that are described on these pages apply equally well to stripping varnishes.

Choosing the method

Dry scraping is hard work and can leave score marks, so unless the paint peels off readily, it is best to use heat or chemicals to loosen the coat. Heat stripping is the most economical way of clearing a large area, but a gas blowtorch may scorch the surface. Chemical strippers are especially useful on intricate surfaces. They can be used on emulsion, cellulose and most oil-based paints. Take care to follow the manufacturer's instructions.

Using a gas blowtorch

 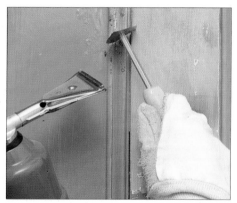

1 *Hold the torch about 6–8in (15–20cm) from the surface, starting at the top. Play it across the paint until it melts. Do not use a gas blowtorch with lead-based paints, as they release toxic fumes.*

2 *With a sharp scraper, peel the paint off into a tin tray. Sweep the flame over the remaining paint until it slides off, taking care not to scorch the wood. Use a shavehook to scrape paint off mouldings.*

Using a chemical stripper

1 *Dab the liquid on thickly with an old brush.*

2 *After a few minutes strip off the softened paint.*

3 *Remove remnants with wire wool and white spirit.*

Using a peel-off stripper

1 *Apply a thick layer of paste with a filling knife, and leave it to eat through the layers of paint. This usually takes several hours.*

2 *After a few hours the layer can be peeled off, leaving a clean sub-surface. Always wear protective gloves when removing the stripper.*

Hot-air gun
Operating like an immensely powerful electric hairdryer, a hot-air gun blasts out a stream of heat which will melt the paint in its path. Direct the gun at an area of paint, and when it softens, after a few seconds, peel off the coat with a scraper. For stripping paint around windows and awkward areas, special nozzle attachments are available (above). Although effective, some hot-air guns are noisy and heavy to use.

SAFETY TIPS

With chemical stripper:
- Always wear goggles, gloves and protective clothing to avoid skin burns, and do not smoke.
- Cover nearby furnishings.

With heat stripper:
- Keep buckets of water to hand in case of fire.
- Never place your fingers in the air stream.

- Catch burning peelings in a tin tray, never in newspaper.
- With a hot-air gun, think about any extra attachments you may need.

How to fill cracks and holes

Time spent filling cracks and holes will be well rewarded in the final result. Standard interior-grade cellulose fillers are suitable for most inside plaster or wooden surfaces to be repainted. They come as ready-to-use paste in tubs or tubes, or as a powder to be mixed with water to a creamy consistency. Most small holes can be simply built up with filler and smoothed off. Corners in walls can be easily chipped when moving furniture. Apply thin layers of filler, and when the surface is slightly raised, allow to harden, then sand down. Small, superficial chips in otherwise good paintwork can be filled with a fine surface filler, which is worked into the surface and spread with a broad filling knife, then sanded to produce an ultra-smooth finish. Badly crazed plasterboard ceilings can be concealed with thick, textured paint, which stretches with the normal movement of the ceiling.

How to apply filler

1 *Score the crack with the side of a filling knife to widen the cavity for the filler.*

2 *Brush away any debris, then dampen the crevice with a water-soaked brush.*

3 *Pack the prepared filler tightly into the crack and smooth it down with a knife.*

4 *Leave for a few hours to harden, then rub with glasspaper for a smooth finish.*

Preparing ceilings

First remove any light fittings that may impede the work, turning off the mains first and sealing any exposed wires afterwards. Then assess the condition of the existing paint and plasterwork. If it is sound, wash down the surface with diluted sugar soap and rinse thoroughly with clean water, taking care not to allow any drips to penetrate fixed light fittings.

If the paint is discoloured by nicotine stains, apply a coat of aluminium sealer paint. Dried water stains, caused by a leaking roof or pipes, will show through emulsion, so these need to be coated with an oil-based primer-sealer. Kitchen ceilings are often coated with accumulated grease, which will prevent the paint from sticking if it is not removed. Likewise, soot or dust deposited on the ceilings above coal fires must be thoroughly cleaned off to prevent it from discolouring subsequent layers of paint.

Fill any superficial cracks with cellulose filler. In an old house, if distemper remains, scrape off the flakes and either wash off the rest or coat the ceiling with primer-sealer before repainting. If paint dust has accumulated, seal with a coat of stabilizing primer.

Loose ceiling paper should be stripped off, but any which is firmly attached can be left and painted. When removing paper, always wash off any remaining adhesive. If existing paper bubbles when washed, make a small slit when dry and restick the edges. Remember that a ceiling may have been papered because it is badly cracked though structurally sound or, in the case of a plasterboard ceiling, because the joints are conspicuous. Therefore, ceiling paper in good condition is best left alone.

Preparing walls

More preparation is needed if a wall is to be painted than if it is to be concealed with wallpaper. Even a small hairline crack will show through paint if it is not filled and carefully smoothed first. Where an otherwise sound wall has become a network of small cracks, try covering it with lining paper or plain wallpaper.

Make sure that the wallpaper is completely dry before you begin overpainting.

A new plaster wall should be left to dry for several weeks before being sealed with a primer or a thin coat of emulsion prior to painting, and fresh plasterboard should be given a coat of plasterboard primer-sealer. A previously painted wall must be washed thoroughly from the bottom up with diluted sugar soap, then rinsed.

CLEARING THE ROOM	FILLER
• Extract anything you may need from drawers. • Move small pieces of furniture into another room to protect them. • Take down all curtains and pictures and store them carefully. • Remove handles from doors and windows, jamming them open where necessary. • Move the large furniture to the centre of the room and cover with a dust sheet if possible, or with pieces of newspaper. • Roll up the carpet and take any rugs or mats to another room. • Cover the floor with a plastic or cloth dust sheet and secure it at the corners. • If necessary, vacuum the floor and wipe any dust from surfaces to be painted, to prevent dirt from spoiling the finish.	Always store unused filler in a cool, dry place and use an old piece of board and a scraper for mixing. Ensure that the filler powder is thoroughly mixed before applying it. To avoid waste when preparing paste, try not to make up more than you can apply within the setting time marked on the packet (usually about 30 minutes). Unlike cellulose filler, resin-based fillers will not shrink as they dry and harden. This means that they can be applied flush with the surface, instead of proud, and will produce a smooth surface with less abrasion. To avoid having to clean a messy mixing container after using filler, either use the ready mixed variety, or line the mixing container with a plastic bag. When you have finished the job, you can just throw the bag away.

Preparing bare wood

Whether it is brand new or stripped of old paint, all bare wood to be painted needs a coating of primer, undercoat and gloss. To ensure a smooth finish, the surface should first be rubbed down with glasspaper or a power sander. Rough surfaces may call for coarse paper, but a final smoothing with a fine grade will ensure a good finish.

After any cracks are filled with filler or stopping, knots in the wood will need a coating of shellac to prevent the resin from staining the paintwork. To seal the pores in the wood and to provide a sound, stable base for undercoat, a coat of primer is applied. Most woods will take a standard white or pink wood primer, but particularly resinous woods need aluminium primer. Universal primer may be used, although purpose-made products give a better result.

Since undercoat is heavily pigmented for hiding power, always select the colour recommended by the manufacturer for use under the chosen gloss. You may find that it is necessary to apply more than one coat of undercoat in order to leave a smooth finish for the gloss coat.

Preparing wood for gloss

1 *Sand and wipe the surface clean, then brush a layer of shellac on to wood knots.*

2 *Leave to dry for a couple of days. Then brush on the primer to provide a stable base.*

3 *Allow to dry, then apply at least one coat of well-stirred undercoat (more if necessary).*

Wood-coloured stopper

Where wood is to be given a clear varnish or lacquer finish instead of a coat of paint, waterproof stopper, which comes in a variety of wood colours, can be used. One type of stopper comes as a putty-like material; another, which also dries to a natural wood colour and can later be stained to any shade, is sold as paste and separate hardener to be mixed together. Both stoppers should be worked well into the surface with a filling knife and allowed to set before sanding down and applying an oil- or spirit-based stain. Take care not to spread the stopping into the grain beyond the immediate split or nail hole. Small gaps that tend to form in window frames and at joints can be packed with stopper and pushed down with a finger before smoothing off with

Applying stopper
Work the stopper well into the surface.

a damp cloth. Always use an oil-based stopper on chipboard, since it is very porous.

Dents can also be treated by using stoppers to build up the surface. Make sure that the stopper is of the appropriate colour.

Preparing metal

Rust is the enemy of ferrous metals (those that contain iron and steel) and must be kept at bay with a rust-inhibiting primer and a sound coat of gloss. Even small chips in the surface paint can allow moisture to seep below the paint film and encourage corrosion, especially in window frames.

First locate the areas of rust and remove all traces with an emery cloth or a wire brush. For larger areas, a wire cup brush or wheel fitted to an electric drill will save time, but always protect your eyes with safety goggles. Holes caused by rust can be repaired using a glass fibre repair kit, which can be bought in most DIY shops.

Rust re-forms rapidly, even overnight, so apply rust-inhibiting primer immediately. Zinc chromate is the most useful primer, since it can also be used for aluminium and galvanized surfaces, but red lead and zinc phosphate are also suitable. Non-ferrous metals such as aluminium and copper should be washed down with white spirit, abraded and primed.

Treating rust

1 Scrape off any rust and flaking paint with a wire brush. Inspect the area carefully to ensure that no trace of rust remains.

2 Before the rust has time to re-form, seal the metalwork with primer, giving vulnerable points an extra coat.

PREPARING PAINTWORK

● Before applying a fresh coat to existing paintwork, the surface must be free from stains, dirt and dust, or the new finish will look pimpled and will soon start to flake.

● Remove surface dirt by brushing, washing or vacuuming and use a pointed handle or knife to clear dust particles from awkward corners.

● When washing down the area, use sugar soap, washing soda, a proprietary cleaner or a mild detergent, and prevent water from dripping down behind electric fittings.

● Before painting window frames from inside, always ensure that outside frames are thoroughly clean so that dirt is not picked up on the brush. Wipe down sills and other wooden surfaces with a lint-free rag moistened with white spirit.

● Where the old paintwork is chipped or cracked, sand it down with glasspaper to make a smooth surface for the new coat of paint. Remember to clean the area thoroughly to remove all dust.

● To ensure that the old paintwork provides a good surface for the new paint, abrade the surface with coarse glasspaper to create a key for the new coat.

How to apply paint

Emulsion and other water-based paints will usually brush straight from the can, but half-full cans of oil-based paints develop a skin. Lift off the layer of solidified paint, then stir thoroughly. Non-drip paints, however, should never be stirred. Gloss and emulsion paints demand slightly different techniques, as shown below. Thixotropic paints, designed to go on in one coat, should be brushed sparingly. There is no need to scrape off surplus paint, but try not to load too much paint on to the brush initially. Before applying a second coat of paint, dust the surface with a lint-free rag to ensure that no specks spoil the finish. Complete each surface in one session to prevent dried paint lines from forming.

Brushing on gloss

1 *Dip the end of the brush into the paint and wipe off the excess. Avoid dipping it too deep, or the paint will trickle down on to your hand.*

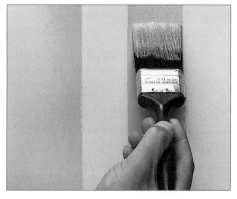

2 *Begin with two or three short downward strokes in the direction of the grain. Change direction to spread the paint, then work with the grain again.*

3 *Reload the brush and paint another strip, leaving a gap the size of the brush width. Then paint across to fill the area between the strips.*

4 *Brush vigorously over the whole area, laying off with vertical strokes. When dry, sand each coat with fine glasspaper to make a key for the next coat.*

Brushing on emulsion

1 *Select a wide brush for quick application. Coat it generously with paint and apply it in horizontal bands about 2ft (60cm) wide.*

2 *With matt emulsion, finish off with criss-cross strokes. With silk or satin emulsion, which dry faster, lay off with light, upward strokes.*

Using a roller or pad

The fastest way of applying emulsion is with a roller. A roller is also less likely to leave marks than would a brush.

Pour some paint into the well of the roller tray, dip in the edge of the roller and run it up and down the slope of the tray to ensure an even coating of paint on the sleeve of the roller. The first coating on a dry roller will take a little longer to achieve, until it soaks up the paint.

Run the roller over the surface in a random, criss-cross fashion. Take care to fill any gaps and keep the joins well merged. Be careful not to overload the roller or to jerk it, or a spray of paint will spatter the area. Be particularly careful near woodwork if you are not going to repaint it, otherwise the roller will spray paint over the unprotected surface. Finish off the edges with a small brush.

When using a paint pad, dip the pad lightly into the paint can and wipe away the excess on the side. You can also use a special applicator to load the paint evenly on to the pad. Smooth on the paint in random directions. Reload the pad with paint as soon as you notice the layer begin to become too thin.

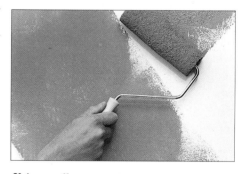

Using a roller
Start with random, criss-cross strokes.

Using a paint pad
Smooth on the paint in a random fashion.

Painting flat surfaces

The first consideration when preparing to paint a large area is the light. Try to avoid starting in natural light and finishing in artificial, or you may find yourself covering the same area twice. You should also complete ceilings and individual walls in one session, since if you stop mid-wall for a meal-break or for the night, the dried paint line will show conspicuously through the final finish.

Before applying emulsion, close the windows to stop the paint from drying too quickly so that you have time to join up the wet edges of each section. When the room is finished, open the windows to accelerate drying time. For ease of working, try to get as close as possible to the ceiling. Bare walls need a diluted coat of emulsion to prime the surface before applying a first coat, but pre-painted surfaces need no primer. If the paint does not cover well, do not try to thicken the coat, but leave it to dry and apply an extra coat. For a perfectly smooth finish, you may need two or three coats.

While painting, keep a damp cloth handy for removing dust or blobs. As a general rule, paint a room from top to bottom, so that disturbed dust does not fall on to wet paint and so that drips can be painted over later. If using a roller, complete corners with a small brush.

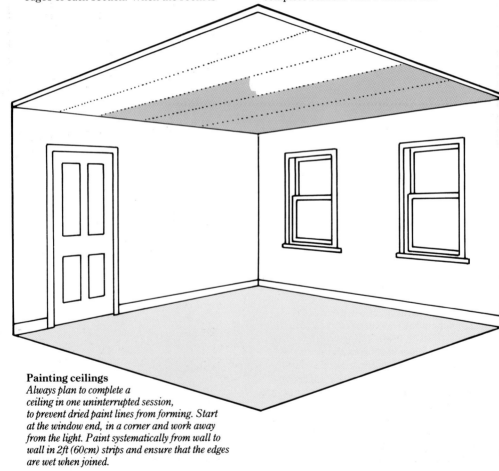

Painting ceilings
*Always plan to complete a
ceiling in one uninterrupted session,
to prevent dried paint lines from forming. Start
at the window end, in a corner and work away
from the light. Paint systematically from wall to
wall in 2ft (60cm) strips and ensure that the edges
are wet when joined.*

Painting walls
Start at the top corner of a wall nearest the window.
Cover the wall in broad, horizontal bands and work
down to the skirting board. Cut in with a narrower
brush around windows and door frames.
If using a roller, first coat the edges
with a narrow brush.

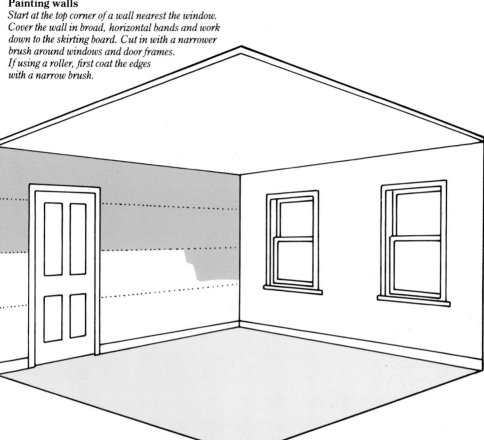

Painting skirtings

Painting skirtings can be a tedious and time-consuming job. However, it can be made easier if you tackle it in the following way.

Use a 2in (50mm) brush and a piece of old card. Rest the card on the top of the skirting, or tuck it down between the skirting and the wall. This prevents the paint from smudging on to the walls.

At the corners, dab a lightly loaded cutting-in brush into the crevice and draw away the excess paint. To protect the floor, slide a piece of hardboard below the skirting.

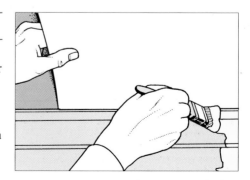

Using card to protect the walls
Insert card between the skirting and the wall.

Using ladders

A variety of convertible step ladders is now available, which will either slide or swing out into a straight ladder, for using against the wall. Make sure that your ladders are safe. Ensure that the connections will not allow the ladder to slip when extended and check for loose screws and jammed parts. If you are buying a new ladder, the aluminium types illustrated here are generally lighter and cheaper than the old wooden sort. Always ensure that the ladder reaches at least 3ft (1m) above the highest level at which you wish to stand, and never stand above the third highest rung. Face the ladder as you climb and do not lean over too far to either side while painting. For larger areas, such as stairwells and ceilings, use a secure, stable working platform (page 49).

A clip-on shelf
This serves as a useful platform for equipment.

Non-slip ladders
Ladders which stand on two levels are useful on stairs, provided there are suction pads on the feet.

Convertible ladders
The sections can be rearranged to form a straight ladder, or a self-supporting type capable of opening at a variety of angles.

Painting radiators

Radiators should always be painted when cold and allowed to dry thoroughly before the heating is turned on again, or the finish will be impaired. A strong smell usually emanates from a newly painted surface when heated, but it soon fades. Old radiators may need to be treated for rust and primed, but new ones are delivered pre-primed, ready for undercoat and gloss. Any copper pipes connecting with the radiator can be painted in the same way. Shield the wall behind them with card.

Use a 1in (25mm) brush for a panelled radiator and a crevice roller or brush for tricky areas. Work carefully to avoid runs and do not paint the connections, or they may prove difficult to undo if the radiator needs to be removed. Ordinary paints are usually satisfactory, but avoid paints with a metal pigment, since this will reduce radiating power.

Painting stairs and stairwells

The stair area should be painted last, since halls and landings are likely to be scuffed when moving furniture from room to room; also, as the nucleus of the house, it forms the main colour link between individual rooms and upper and lower floors. First set up a secure working platform for reaching even the least accessible parts of the stairwell. Remove carpet and fittings, clean the entire staircase and cure any faults such as creaking and uneven stairs, cracks, dents or splits. Follow the usual order of work, beginning with the landing ceiling, then the walls of the stairwell, working from the top down, and finally the stairs, banisters and the handrail. Throughout the work, keep the movement of doors and people to a minimum until the paint has dried, to reduce dust. If the wood is to be varnished and its colour changed, first fill any holes or splits and coat it with a woodstain.

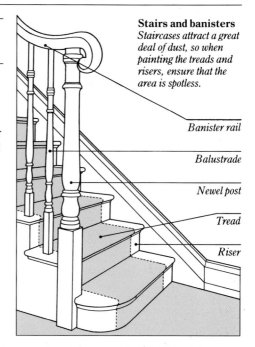

Stairs and banisters
Staircases attract a great deal of dust, so when painting the treads and risers, ensure that the area is spotless.

Banister rail

Balustrade

Newel post

Tread

Riser

Painting kitchens and bathrooms

Steam and condensation are the main problems to be solved when redecorating these rooms. Good ventilation in the form of efficient extractor fans will help to minimize the effect of moisture, and a layer of emulsion on walls and ceilings will provide an easily washable surface, especially if it has a slight sheen. Anti-condensation emulsion paints containing insulating material are now available to help offset some of these problems. These paints come in a wide range of colours. Avoid gloss on walls and ceilings, since it exaggerates condensation and irregularities. Copper pipes can be given a coating of undercoat and gloss, and will not need primer. Normal gloss will withstand temperatures of up to 194°F (90°C), although white and pale colours may yellow at over 158°F (70°C). Alternatively, a metallic paint can be used. Metallic paints are corrosion and heat resistant and give lustre to both hot and cold pipes.

Avoid water-based paints, since they tend to soften and crack when heated. Never paint connections of fitting nuts on pipes; they could prove difficult to undo if they are sealed with a layer of paint. If you are repainting sound paint, simply wash down the surface and abrade it to make a key for the new paint.

PAINTING EXTERIOR WALLS

- Start at the top of the house and work down.
- Divide the house into sections, using natural breaks as demarcation lines. Begin with fascia boards, gutters and eaves, then tackle the walls and downpipes and finish with the windows and doors.
- Work in horizontal strips one block at a time.
- Do not apply masonry paint in frosty weather, as it may damage the paint.
- Porous surfaces, such as masonry and pebbledash, absorb about 50 per cent more paint than wooden surfaces.
- Try to work in the shade and move around the house in the same direction as the sun.

Painting doors

Always remove handles, keyhole plates, hooks and other door furniture before painting, to avoid smudges and runs and to speed up the work. Store them carefully with their screws and loosely refit between coats to allow doors to be opened and closed. Clean keyholes and the top edges of doors thoroughly so that specks are not picked up on bristles and spread over the surface. Complete any necessary repairs, such as fixing hinges and sanding down a sticking door, before painting.

Aim to paint doors after walls and windows but before skirting boards and in one continuous session to prevent dried paint lines from forming. Doors need a gloss or oil-based silk finish for protection against normal wear and tear; they represent the largest area of gloss in most homes. An undercoat is necessary – even if the existing paint surface is sound and the new colour is darker than the old. Use two undercoats, however, when covering a dark or strong colour with a paler shade, and sand between coats. There is no need to paint the top edge of a door, unless it is visible from stairs above. However, a painted edge will collect less dust than bare wood. If the door is to be painted in different colours on each side, paint the hinge edge the same colour as the outer face and the lock edge the same colour as the inner face if the door opens into the room.

Following the sequence shown below, paint first with vertical strokes, then cross-brush to fill in the gaps. Lay off with upward strokes.

Panelled doors
1 *Use a 1in (25mm) brush to paint the mouldings.* 2 *Paint the panels with a 2 or 3in (50 or 75mm) brush.* 3 *Paint the vertical centre sections.* 4 *Cover the top, middle and bottom horizontal bands.* 5 *Complete the vertical outside sections and edges, and finally the frame.*

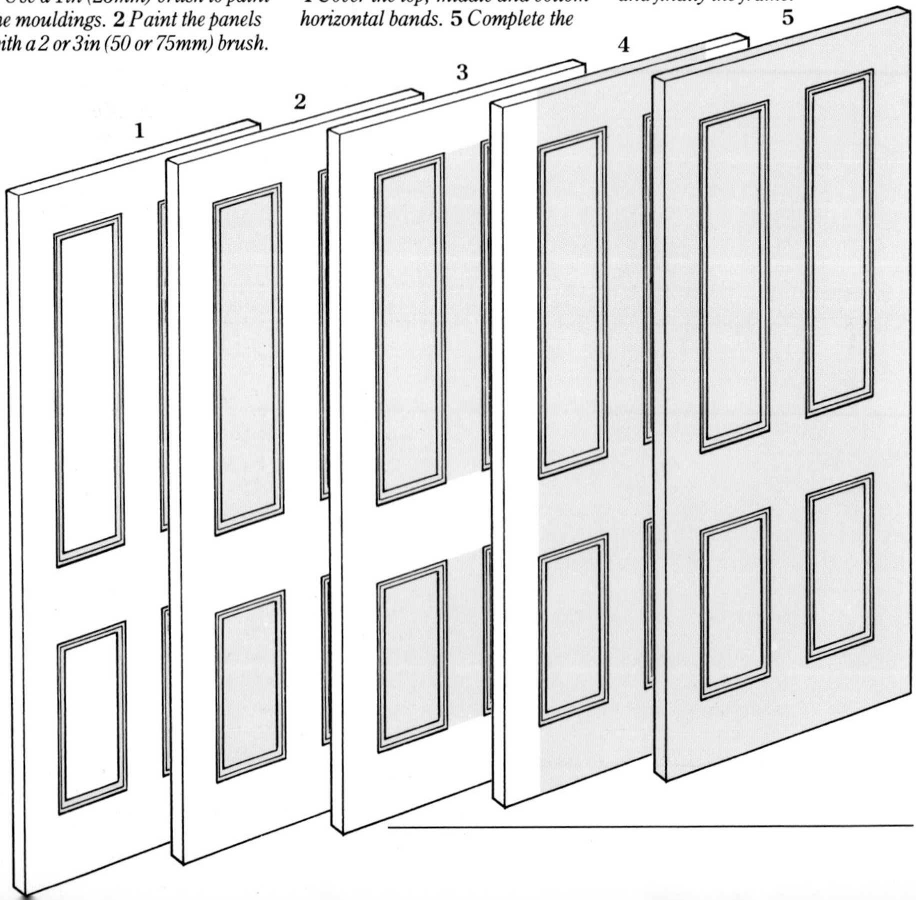

Painting panels and edges
Always paint the panels (left) from the top down, and do not overload the brush, or the paint may run. Gloss is the most liable to run of all paint types. When painting edges (above), use a small brush: this will prevent paint ridges from forming. The top edges of doors do not need to be painted unless they can be seen from above. For when to paint the panels, see the working sequence on the opposite page. Sand each coat with fine-grade glasspaper to make a key for the next.

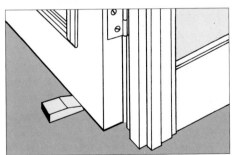

Jamming the door open
Jam a flush or panelled door open by tapping a wedge under it. This exposes both the hinge and handle edges for painting, and avoids the risk of your being trapped in the room when you have removed the door handles. Allow each coat to dry thoroughly before closing the door, otherwise the wet paint will cause the door to stick to the frame.

FLUSH DOORS

To cover the area quickly, use a 3in (75mm) brush. Start at the top corner of the hinge side and work in 9in² (60cm²) sections until you reach the bottom corner on the handle side. Begin with vertical strokes, then cross-brush to spread the paint and lay off with light, upward strokes before moving on to the next section. When painting the edges, take care not to allow the paint to build up into ridges and, where possible, take the paint over the corners. You will find a small 2in (50mm) brush easiest for the edges. Try to avoid the common mistake of applying too much paint to the top of the door and too little to the sides. Work quickly so that the edge of each 9in² (60cm²) painted section can be covered before it dries. Flush doors have a larger area of flat surface than panelled doors, so make sure that you take extra care when applying paint, since any runs or drips will be very noticeable.

Painting windows

Window frames, which suffer both condensation and changes of temperature, are subjected to the worst conditions of all interior woodwork. Repair any damage and prepare the surface before painting. Paint any openable windows as early in the day as possible to allow time for them to dry. You will need a 1in (25mm) brush and, if you choose, a paint shield.

The order of working for individual parts of a window is determined by its construction. For the best results, follow the order given below for sash and casement windows and always finish painting in the direction of the wood grain.

Cutting in

It is worth practising the cutting-in technique to get a fine line on glazing bars, frames and edges. Place a loaded brush about ⅛in (3mm) from the edge and carefully push it towards the join. Press lightly down and draw the brush swiftly along to make a long, clean line. If you do not feel confident about using this method, use a paint shield or masking tape instead (opposite). The effect will be the same.

Sash windows
Follow the order of painting shown (right and below). **1** *First open both sashes so that there is an 8in (20cm) overlap. Paint the bottom meeting rail of the top sash and the accessible vertical sections.* **2** *Almost close both top and bottom sashes and paint the rest of the top sash.* **3** *Then cover the bottom sash, leaving it to dry thoroughly.* **4** *Almost close the sashes (use matchsticks to prevent them from sticking) and paint the frame.* **5** *Finally, paint the exposed parts of the runners, taking care not to get paint on the sash cords, and then paint the sill.*

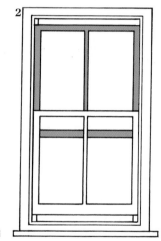
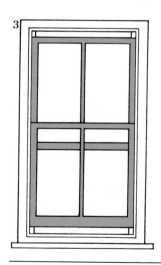

Casement windows
1 First remove catches and handles and store in a safe place. If one window is fixed, begin with the one that opens, painting the rebates. 2 Then do the crossbars, starting from the top ones if necessary. 3 Then move on to the crossrails, again starting from the top. 4 Go on to the sides and the edges. 5 Finally, paint the frame and sill. Always paint the sill last, otherwise paint will get on to your clothing. Also leave the stay until last, to allow the window to be adjusted during painting.

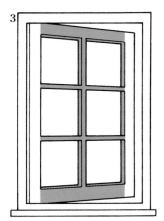

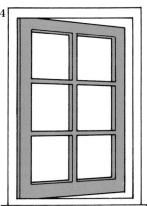

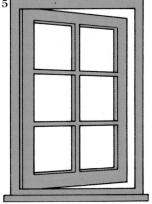

Tips on keeping paint off glass

To guarantee a neat edge around window panes, try protecting the glass with a paint shield as you work, or apply masking tape before you begin. Press the tape firmly down to prevent paint from creeping under the edges, and remove it before the final coat of gloss is dry to avoid peeling a layer of paint off the frame. Always allow the paint to overlap slightly on to the glass, to prevent moisture from seeping through the join between the putty and the glass and causing the wood to rot. Splashes can be scraped off when dry with a razor blade and white spirit.

Neat edges for window panes
Masking tape protects the glass as you work.

Textures and finishes

A wide range of attractive paint finishes can be achieved by brushing, sponging, rolling, or dabbing a design into a coloured glaze, or by stencilling on a shape, while textured paints can be rollered or combed into a raised pattern. These effects need no special skill and in many cases can be completed more rapidly than a standard painting job.

Decorative finishes
No specialized tools are needed beyond normal painting equipment, but you must use the correct paint for the base coat and the right glaze. For the ground coat, an oil-based paint with an eggshell finish produces the best results. Ordinary emulsion can be used, but it is more absorbent and so produces a less crisp finish. Glazes can be shiny, matt or transparent. Transparent oil glazes can be bought that may be tinted with universal stainer or artists' oil-colours. Alternatively, a glaze can be made up from one part linseed oil, one part turpentine, one part drying agent, a little whiting and some colour. Extra whiting will reduce the sheen. A third type of glaze is made from oil-based paint, thinned with white spirit.

Textured paints
Textured paints create a subtle decorative finish and can be used to cover a badly cracked surface. Some are also flexible, so that if a ceiling or wall "moves", the cracks remain covered. They are available in both a ready-to-use and powdered form for mixing to a gluey consistency. Some automatically leave a raised pattern when applied, while others are textured by hand after application, with combs, brushes or rollers.

Dragging

A fine, striped pattern is achieved by "dragging" a brush through a superficial coating of transparent oil glaze. First brush on the background coat and allow it to dry. Then brush on an even coating of coloured oil glaze in a broad band. While it is still wet, run the dragging brush down through the glaze to score straight lines. Then glaze and drag the next band of wall. You may find it easier to work with another person, one applying the glaze while the other uses the dragging brush.

This is one of the most elementary of woodgraining techniques, giving the surface the appearance of raw silk, although it will also bring out any irregularities and faults in woodwork. Always drag the brush in the same direction as the woodgrain, and drag away from corners on panels so that pools of glaze cannot form there. Treat mouldings first and leave them to dry. Curving lines and cross-hatching can also give an unusual and attractive effect. You can buy traditional "dragging" brushes, but an ordinary decorating brush will produce the same effects.

Dragging
To achieve a straight line down a high wall, bring the first stroke down as far as you can, then drag the brush up from the bottom to overlap the first one. Vary the position of the joins to hide them.

Sponging

A mottled or stipple pattern can be created with a large natural sponge and a little patience. Unlike dragging and ragging, sponging usually involves adding colour to a neutral background, instead of removing patches of colour. First apply a coat of paint to the wall and leave it to dry for 24 hours. Then pour some thinned coloured glaze into a shallow bowl. Dampen a sponge, dip it lightly into the glaze and dab on to a sheet of newspaper to absorb the excess. When the pattern becomes a delicate speckle on the paper, begin work on the wall. As the design begins to fade, refill the sponge with glaze. Allow the coat to dry, then fill in any gaps. For a softer effect, apply a second glaze colour to the wall.

Sponging
Lightly sponge the second glaze colour over the first, changing direction and position frequently to avoid repetition of patterns.

Ragging

The tucks and creases of a bundled-up rag, the woven design of hessian, or pieces of old net curtain can create interesting textured patterns. When the base coat is dry, apply an even layer of glaze to a small area of the wall, brushing thoroughly to even out the coverage. While the glaze is still wet, lightly roll a clean, lint-free, bundled-up rag in random directions on the colour until a pattern forms. Use a dabbing and pushing action with a slight twist for a clear design. Apply the glaze to the next patch and continue, allowing a small overlap of pattern each time. Replace the rag when it starts to lose its effect. This job can be done by two people, one painting the glaze, the other using the rag. If the colour dries too quickly, moisten it with a damp sponge. Ragging looks best on walls and ceilings, where the distinctive patterns can be fully appreciated.

Ragging
The glaze should be stippled or sponged before applying the rag, to hide brushmarks.

APPLYING TEXTURED PAINTS

Ensure that the surface is clean, dry, sound, and free from flaking paint and distemper. If you are applying self-texturing paint, it will automatically create its own texture as you roller or brush it on. With ordinary textured paint, apply a coat first, then work the textured pattern into the smooth layer of paint. A variety of effects can be created with different implements, such as a plasterer's comb, a swirl brush, a stipple brush and patterned rollers. Experiment on a piece of board before committing the pattern to the wall, to avoid time-consuming errors.

Stencilling

Stencils allow for more individual variations than other decorative finishes. Stencilling kits are available, complete with plates and brushes, but it is not difficult to invent your own design and cut out your own stencil. Draw or trace a picture on to graph paper, scale it up to size, and then transfer the pattern to a piece of stencil board or acetate. If you are using board, tape the picture on top with a piece of carbon paper behind and trace the outline with a pencil. If you are using acetate, insert the design underneath the transparent sheet, tape it down and trace the outline on to the acetate with an isograph technical pen. You can then cut along the lines with a scalpel. Tape the stencil to the surface to be decorated and fill in the colour with a stencilling brush. To avoid errors, try out the design first on eggshell-covered hardboard.

Stencilling
Use a stencil brush to apply the colour.

Painting a mural

As with *trompe l'oeil* (opposite), the only limit in mural painting is your imagination. Murals are normally thought of as being applied to walls, but floors, ceilings and furniture can also be decorated in this way. The preparation is simple, and the materials can be purchased in any DIY shop.

You can achieve very bold designs with stark outlines, or more muted and subtle effects. Landscapes, abstract designs and human compositions are some varieties that you may want to consider. If you do not feel confident about making your own design, try working from photographs or paintings.

First design your image on grid paper, then divide the wall into the same number of squares, but enlarged in proportion to fill the allocated space. Sketch the outline on the wall, floor, ceiling or furniture in pencil, one square at a time, then fill in the colours, using masking tape and a thin brush for the edges.

Using masking tape
Fix masking tape to the outlines, then apply the colour (right). Start with the paler shades and let each section dry before moving on to the next. Brush on the paint thickly to reduce the number of coats required. Finally, remove the masking tape, fill in any gaps in the colour, and apply a thin, black line to the edges (far right).

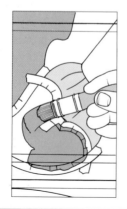

Painting furniture

When preparing surfaces, be meticulous in removing all dirt and loose paint. It is particularly important to do this for painting furniture, since it is in everyday use and defects can easily be seen. Small items can be prepared by spraying them with layers of cellulose paint, although this produces a brittle surface which may crack. Rub down between coats and fill cracks and holes with nitro-cellulose filler.

The decorative paint effects described on this page and previous pages can easily be used to decorate furniture as well as walls. Any item, from a picture frame to a wardrobe, can be given a sponged, stippled, dragged or rag-rolled finish, or a more complicated effect can be produced, like the bird's-eye maple pattern shown. Decorated furniture can provide an interesting and inexpensive contrast to plain walls and furnishings.

One of the simplest paint effects is called spattering, for which you will need a fairly thin glaze and a thick brush. You will also need a second brush or strip of wood. Tap your glaze-laden brush hard against the other brush, while holding both brushes over the surface to be

painted. This action will cause droplets of colour to spatter across it. You will find that a finer spatter can be achieved if you dip a round fitch or artist's brush in some thinned glaze, holding it over the surface to be painted with one hand while you "tickle" the bristles with the forefinger of the other.

Bird's-eye maple

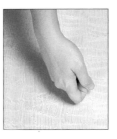 

1 *Tint the base coat with yellow ochre, and the graining colour with raw sienna and burnt umber. To make "creased ribbons", drag a dry brush across the glaze. To create "eyes" dab your knuckles into the wet glaze.*

2 *Leave for 15 minutes if using an oil glaze. The graining is created by using a burnt-sienna-coloured crayon or a fine artist's brush. Draw the graining lines while the glaze is wet. Make the lines wander around the dots.*

Stippling

1 *Stippling produces a subtle finished effect. Apply a base coat which is several tones lighter than, or a different colour to, the glaze. Prime the stippling brush well with a small amount of glaze before use.*

2 *Wipe off any excess glaze with an old rag to prevent the colour from building up. Work quickly in sections, stippling over the joins. Do not allow the glazes to become tacky, or you will not be able to blend them easily.*

TROMPE L'OEIL

The decorative effects you can produce by the use of *trompe l'oeil* are limited only by your imagination. You can create the illusion of another dimension on a flat surface, or improve badly proportioned features. Panelling, beading, fabrics, landscapes and animals are just some possibilities.

Try a *trompe l'oeil* panelled effect on a flat door. Paint it first with white gloss. For the recessed panels, use a white silk emulsion finish tinted with raw umber to produce a greenish-grey colour. Use masking tape to keep the lines straight. To give the illusion of shadows, add darker lines to two sides of the panels.

CHAPTER TWO

WALLPAPERING

Modern wallpaper is no longer simply
paper, but includes a wide choice of
synthetic and fabric materials, designed to
wash, wear, strip and hang more easily
than old-fashioned papers. Vinyls and
washable papers are as easy to clean as
paintwork, and "dry-strip" papers, which
can be removed without water, make
preparation quick, clean and simple when
redecorating. Improved designs, colours
and finishes have introduced a wider range
of choice, and most manufacturers change
their collections every two years.
Once you have decided on the type
of wall covering, measure the areas
carefully, double-check the figures and
calculate quantities. Choice of pattern and
colour will, to some extent, be determined
by local availability, existing furnishings
and costs. Prices vary widely for the same
paper, particularly as it is often cheaper to
buy paper in stock than to order, so it is
worth ringing round the stockists.
Unlike painting, wallpapering can be done
gradually and will conceal minor cracks.
Thorough preparation, however, is
important to ensure a smooth finish.

Tools and equipment

A full set of wallpapering tools is not a large investment, particularly as some general household items form part of the collection. The only expensive piece of equipment you might need would be a steam stripper for removing difficult papers, and this can be hired.

Choose overalls with pockets large enough to hold brushes, scissors and a sponge. A kit of decorating tools should last a lifetime. Just ensure that, at the end of a job, everything is cleaned of paste in warm, soapy water and thoroughly dried.

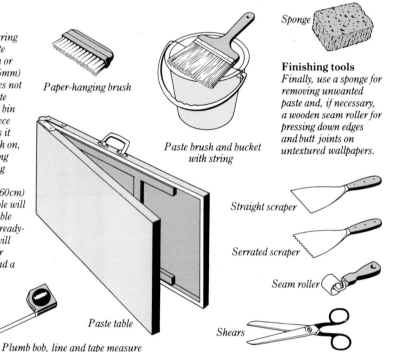

Pasting tools
Essential wallpapering tools include a paste brush or an old 4in or 5in (100mm or 125mm) paintbrush that does not shed bristles, a paste bucket lined with a bin liner and with a piece of string tied across it for resting the brush on, and a paper-hanging brush for smoothing down the paper. A 6½ft × 2ft (2m × 60cm) fold-away paste table will provide an invaluable work surface. For ready-pasted paper, you will need a plastic water trough, a bucket and a damp sponge.

Paper-hanging brush

Sponge

Paste brush and bucket with string

Finishing tools
Finally, use a sponge for removing unwanted paste and, if necessary, a wooden seam roller for pressing down edges and butt joints on untextured wallpapers.

Straight scraper

Serrated scraper

Seam roller

Paste table

Shears

Plumb bob, line and tape measure

Measuring tools
For marking an accurate guide line before hanging, you will need a plumb bob and a pencil for walls, and a chalked stringline for ceilings (or walls). When measuring out the paper, use a steel tape, a 2ft × 3ft (60cm × 90cm) folding boxwood rule or alternatively a straight-edge ruler.

FAULT-FINDING

If there are bubbles below the surface of newly pasted paper, this is because the paste has not been properly brushed out. If the paste is still wet, peel back the paper and rebrush. If dry, cut a cross through the bubble with a sharp knife and paste down the flaps.

If the paper will not stick to the wall, this may be due to a damp or unsized porous wall, the wrong paste, insufficient paste, or not leaving the glued paper to soak for long enough.

Loose edges are caused by either insufficient paste or insufficient brushing. Apply more paste and press down the edges with a seam roller. If the pattern does not match, rehang the paper.

Scraping and cutting tools
You will need a straight and, possibly, a serrated scraper for removing wallpaper, and a pair of shears about 10in (25cm) long for making straight, accurate cuts. A sharp trimming knife and a smaller pair of household scissors are also handy when you are making intricate cuts around complicated shapes.

Setting up workstations

Always set up a safe working platform before attempting to decorate ceilings and stairwells. In most houses this can be improvised using a combination of ladders and boards. The exact arrangement will depend on your staircase, but the system shown below can be adapted for most stair shapes. If the stairwell is particularly high, however, hiring a narrow scaffold tower may be the best solution. When using step ladders, always ensure that they are fully open and that the shelf is pushed well down. When climbing ladders, remember to empty pockets of scissors and knives.

Stairs and stairwells
Put a step ladder on the top landing and lean a straight ladder against the head wall with its foot firmly lodged against a stair riser. Then link them with boards. For the lower levels, put a step ladder in the hall and form a platform with planks resting on a ladder step and a stair.

Wrap cloth around the tops of the ladder to protect the wall and to prevent it from slipping.

For spanning gaps of over 5ft (1.5m), use two planks doubled up and secured together with nails or strong tape.

Always lean a long ladder into a stair so that it lodges firmly against the riser.

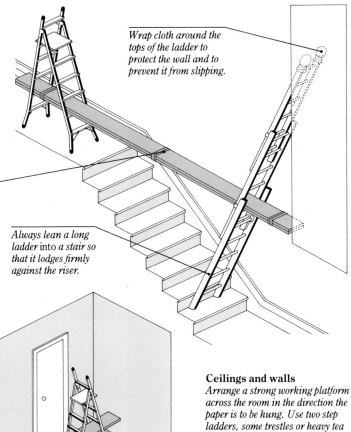

Ceilings and walls
Arrange a strong working platform across the room in the direction the paper is to be hung. Use two step ladders, some trestles or heavy tea chests, and a plank or a series of boards which span the complete room from wall to wall. In this way, the platform will only need to be moved once for each wall. Make sure that you can reach easily, since stretching is dangerous.

A single plank spanning more than 5ft (1.5m) will need additional support.

Ensure that ladders are fully opened to avoid jarring or toppling.

Wall coverings

Modern wall coverings fall into three main categories: paper, plastic and fabric. Within these three groups, the range of decorative styles and practical properties can be overwhelming, so to limit choice, it is usually best to consider practical details first.

The most resilient materials are usually plastic – they will withstand wear and tear, scrubbing and scuffing. Some also have insulating and water-resistant properties. Wallpapers, whether designed to be painted after hanging or not, are less hard-wearing; however, they can help to disguise an imperfect surface. Some papers and fabrics, such as silk, are purely decorative.

Colour, pattern and design influence the style and proportions of a room (pages 54–5), so it is important to choose with great care.

The colour and style of the furniture to be used in the room is also important; choose the wall covering that will best complement it.

Price may also influence your decision. The range is wide, from the cheapest printed paper to expensive silks, and it is worth "shopping around" for the best prices. It may not be possible to cover an entire room in an expensive fabric, so consider using one or two rolls as a panel against a less expensive but harmonizing backcloth. Remember that rolls on display are generally cheaper than papers ordered from a pattern book.

Most wall coverings are supplied in rolls 11yds (10m) long by 1¾ft (52cm) wide, but wider rolls are sometimes available. You will usually find details of the sizes specified in the manufacturer's pattern book.

Types of paper

When selecting wallpaper, it is important to match the colour, pattern and texture to the size, shape and general style of individual rooms. It is, however, equally important to choose a suitably practical material for the job. Some areas, for example, will need resilient papers, others demand easily sponged surfaces. Ease of hanging may also influence your choice, particularly if you lack experience.

The hardest papers to hang are the thin, cheap types which tear easily when wet with paste, particularly when pulled around corners. Medium, heavyweight, washable and vinyl papers are stronger and tolerate rougher handling. Paste smudged on the decorative side of the paper can leave a stain, so the easily wiped vinyl-coated papers and paper-backed vinyls can be an advantage in this respect.

Since they are non-porous, these papers are ideal for steamy rooms, such as kitchens and bathrooms, while heavy vinyls, which resist stains and scuffs, are suitable for hallways, stairs and landings.

Ready-pasted wall coverings save the time and trouble of mixing and applying paste (pages 62–3). Equally easy to use is a tough polyethylene material which is hung directly from the roll after first pasting the wall.

Lining paper is usually hung beneath the wall covering as a sort of "paper undercoat", and will camouflage the outline of carefully filled areas. There are several grades of lining paper, including off-white for normal use under wallpaper and a smoother, pure white type for use where the walls are to be painted later. A cold wall that has been prone to condensation should be lined with expanded polystyrene (page 69). This "warms" and insulates the wall and smooths a poor surface.

TIPS ON BUYING WALL COVERINGS

• Check that you receive the exact design you ordered from the supplier.
• Check that all rolls have the same batch number.
• "Shade before hanging" on the label means that there may be some colour discrepancy within the same batch. If there is variation, hang darker colours nearer the window and avoid using differing shades on the same wall.
• Avoid thin, cheap papers, as they tear easily after pasting.

PAPER AND FABRIC WALL COVERINGS

The chart below illustrates the extremely varied range of textures and types of wall covering. From the gleam of metallic foil to the glow of woven fibres, and from the luxury of silk to the light-heartedness of simple prints, there is something to suit every taste and pocket.

From the outer strip inwards:
Metallic foil
High-relief paper
Hand-printed paper

From the outer strip inwards:
Off-white lining paper
Expanded polystyrene
Ready-pasted paper
Foamed polyethylene
Relief vinyl

From the outer strip inwards:
Standard wallpaper
Woodchip paper
Plain embossed paper
Flock paper

From the outer strip inwards:
Grasscloth
Woven fabric
Silk
Hessian

Lining papers

Lining papers come in different weights and types, depending on what they are to be used for. Plain white lining paper is specially made to provide a smooth surface for painting. Off-white lining paper is used as a base for wallpaper and comes in three weights: lightweight, for use on non-absorbent surfaces, such as gloss-paint when a standard wall covering is to be used; medium weight, for normal surfaces; and heavyweight, when a thick wall covering or a vinyl is being used. Brown lining paper is used under extra heavy coverings such as flock wallpaper.

Reinforced, linen-backed lining paper is a heavyweight, white paper, backed with fine linen scrim. It is used for very uneven surfaces and those subject to movement, such as tongue-and-groove boards.

Expanded polystyrene is used for sealing a wall that is prone to condensation. It also helps to smooth a poor surface before adding the wall covering, and can provide a certain amount of insulation against cold and noise.

Wallpapers

The range of standard wallpapers is vast, with patterns and colours to suit all tastes. These smooth, untextured papers are usually not expensive, but they are the least resilient of all wall coverings.

Embossed papers come in a variety of textures, from basketweave to imitation plaster. Some types, known as duplex, are composed of two layers of paper. These heavy papers are supplied plain and are designed to be painted.

Woodchip is another plain, heavy paper which is designed for painting. It is useful for disguising small imperfections on a surface. It consists of a heavy paper base covered in wood chips, creating a pleasing texture suitable for any size and shape of room.

There is a range of wall coverings that have pronounced relief patterns, which can be random patterns, or can imitate stone, pebbles, tiles or plaster daub. Designed to be painted, these high-relief papers are good for concealing lumpy surfaces.

Hand-printed papers are printed by block or screen methods rather than by machine. Available from specialist suppliers, roll widths and lengths are not always standard.

Flock papers may have either a paper or vinyl base, with a pattern of fine pile on the surface. They need to be handled with care so that the surface does not become stained with paste. Vinyl-based types are more durable, easier to clean, and some are ready-pasted.

Borders and friezes can add a touch of colour and variety to an otherwise plain decor and, if skilfully placed, can make a ceiling look higher or lower. Supplied in thin ribbons of printed paper, they are often designed to co-ordinate with wallpaper ranges. Friezes are usually hung just below ceiling level, and borders are positioned around walls or doorways.

CHOOSING THE RIGHT ADHESIVE

It is vitally important to choose an adhesive compatible with your wall covering, or it may ruin your decoration. So it makes sense to choose your wall covering before you buy your adhesive. Do not be tempted to buy only one kind of adhesive for a variety of wall coverings: it will probably be a false economy. As a general rule, the heavier the paper, the thicker the paste.

For vinyl and heavyweight papers, there are, in addition to powders, a number of ready-mixed pastes used straight from the tub. For vinyls and other impervious materials, it is essential to use a paste which contains fungicide, on both the top covering and the lining, to prevent mould from growing under the surface. Fungicides are poisonous, so always wash your hands after using these pastes. Some materials, such as hessian and grasscloth, demand a special heavyweight paste. With fine materials, such as silks, it is better to paste the wall rather than the fabric, because you risk splashing the right side of the material with adhesive if you paste the fabric itself; it also makes the fabric more unwieldy and difficult to handle.

Plastic wall coverings

These include papers with a plastic coating, and vinyl, polyethylene and foil varieties.

Washable paper has a thin, transparent vinyl coating which makes it easy to clean and resistant to stains, so it is ideal for kitchens, bathrooms and children's rooms. However, it is difficult to remove once hung. Some types are available ready-pasted.

Vinyl paper is not to be confused with washable paper, although it can easily be cleaned by scrubbing with a soft brush. It must be hung using an adhesive containing fungicide. It consists of a thick layer of vinyl bonded on to a paper backing.

Ready-pasted paper has a backing pre-coated with water-active adhesive. It is dipped in water before hanging. This ensures an even layer of adhesive and avoids the awkward and messy job of pasting the paper. Washable vinyl and woodchip papers come ready-pasted.

Foamed polyethylene is hung by pasting it to the wall. It is a lightweight material, resembling printed fabric. It is warm to the touch and, because there is no backing paper, it is easy to strip.

Foamed vinyl is designed to be painted. It is tougher than embossed paper and cannot be spoiled by pressing out. The pattern is raised or embossed by a heat process after printing. This provides a relief effect while retaining a smooth backing.

Relief vinyl is produced by using modern photographic techniques to give realistic imitations of different types of tile. It is an inexpensive substitute for the real thing.

Metallic foils are metallized plastic film, finely embossed with coloured patterns to reflect the light. A smooth wall is essential, since the shine highlights any defects.

Comparing types of wall covering

The durability of wall coverings varies. Vinyls and some of the thicker fabrics stand up well to wear and tear, while thin papers and delicate fabrics are more vulnerable. The emboss on a duplex paper is more resilient than a standard single paper, since the embossed texture is added in the factory while the two papers are still wet with adhesive.

Some materials are also easier to clean than others. Papers divide into three sorts: spongeable types (which can be gently sponged clean); washable types (which can be washed with a wet, soapy cloth); and scrubbable types (which withstand washing with a mild abrasive). Fabrics are more prone to staining than papers, and vinyl less so.

The thicker and washable materials are the easiest to handle. Foamed polyethylenes and foamed vinyls, for example, hold their shape well when pasted and, as the backings are smooth, they use far less paste than the traditional embosses. When pressure is applied to the pattern (when you are securing the edges with a seam roller, for example), the foam will flatten but recover, whereas an emboss will remain flat.

The most luxurious finishes are usually the most expensive and often demand a slightly different hanging technique (pages 58–9), Greater care is needed to keep paste off the surface and avoid expensive cutting mistakes. Once hung they usually have a long life.

PASTING

Coverings with a paper backing are usually easier to hang than those without and can be pasted like normal wallpaper. Most paper-backed wall coverings expand when pasted. It is therefore important to allow the paper to "soak" for a few minutes until expansion is completed before applying it to the wall.

Some wall coverings are available pre-pasted, and the adhesive has to be activated by immersing the wall covering in a water trough. A compromise has to be made by the wall covering manufacturers as to how much paste is applied, and on some impervious surfaces there may be a surplus of paste which will have to be wiped away.

When applying adhesive paste to conventional wall coverings, make sure that you use the correct method (pages 62–3).

Textured wall coverings

Texture in furnishing fabrics influences the atmosphere of a room. Shiny surfaces, such as foils, reflect light and are cool to the touch and to the eye. Lustrous finishes, such as silks and satins, are elegant and cool but soft. Heavier, matt textures, such as hessians, tweeds and linens, absorb the light and give a warmer, more muted and relaxed effect. Many materials also act as heat or sound insulators and most wear better than paper.

Wall coverings are made in a wide range of textures and are sold by the roll or by the metre. Hessians, grasscloths and paper-backed types come in 36in (91cm) widths. Silks, foils and unbacked types come in 27in (69cm) and 30in (76cm) widths.

Hessian

This resilient fabric is available with or without a paper backing and in a wide range of colours and patterns. It can also be painted with oil-based paint or emulsion. It is useful for hiding imperfections in walls and for use in areas prone to condensation. However, it should not be used where it is likely to get dirty, as it is difficult to clean.

Paper-backed hessian is pasted and hung like traditional wallpaper with a layer of adhesive on the back. With unbacked hessian, paste the wall before hanging the lengths. Flatten each strip into place with a roller and take care not to pull the material or it will stretch and leave an uneven surface. Overlap successive strips and complete all the walls before trimming, in case the material shrinks. Trim top and bottom with a sharp knife against a wide-bladed scraper. Make neat seams by cutting through each overlap with a very sharp knife against a steel straight-edge. Remove the off-cut and press down the join.

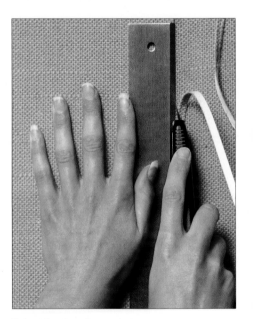

Trimming hessian
Use a very sharp knife to trim seams neatly.

TEXTURED COVERINGS AT A GLANCE

- Hessian is normally sold in 36in (91cm)-wide rolls and is usually hung by pasting the wall. The paper-backed version is easier to handle.
- Grasscloth is a fragile fabric consisting of natural grasses woven into a fine cotton warp and bonded on to a paper backing. It must be hung carefully and with a special adhesive.
- Silk is available plain or patterned, stuck to a paper backing. It is important not to get paste on the face of the material as it stains easily.
- Woven fabrics are sold purpose-made with a paper backing. Alternatively, furnishing fabric can be cut into lengths and applied to a pre-pasted wall.
- Cork is available mounted on to a painted paper backing. It must be hung carefully with a special ready-mixed adhesive.
- Foil can be bought either with a ready pasted backing or without. As with other types of ready-pasted wallpapers, the paste is activated by dipping the foil wall covering into a trough of water. Foil accentuates any irregularities, so should only be used on walls that are perfectly smooth.

Silk

Luxurious and long-lasting, silk suits a sophisticated decor. It is very delicate, so take great care when handling not to stretch or crease it. To prevent adhesive or water marks from staining the silk, apply the paste to the wall, making sure that there are no bumps in the adhesive, or these will show through.

Measure the lengths required, allowing 2in (50mm) for trimming. Cut carefully, using a sharp knife against a straight-edge. Always double-check your measurements to avoid costly mistakes. If you need to divide a length around a corner, you may find it easier to make a rough cut with scissors before scoring through with a knife for a neat and perfectly straight edge. Smooth on to the wall with a soft roller and make neat seams as for hessian.

Foil

Made from metallized plastic film on paper backing, foil provides a reflective surface. This makes an ideal covering for bathrooms, but only on walls that are perfectly smooth, as foil exaggerates irregularities. Two types are available: ordinary and ready-pasted. With the ordinary type, each length is pasted with a foam roller. The ready-pasted type is immersed in water to activate the paste. Hang the foil from the top down and smooth it on to the wall with a clean sponge. Take care to match the pattern accurately and to get the design straight, since mismatching will be obvious. Trim the top and bottom edges, then butt the joins and, finally, flatten them with a seam roller.

Finishing the join
Use a seam roller to ensure neat butt joints.

Grasscloth

Oriental in origin, this woven fabric is made from natural grasses woven with cotton and glued to a paper backing. To hang grasscloth, paste it as normal, but cover the face of the pasting table first with a strip of lining paper, to protect the fabric. Do not fold the cloth or it will leave a hard crease line. Apply lengths to the wall and smooth them down with a clean roller. Using a piece of card, crease a trimming line at the ceiling and the skirting. Only when the adhesive is dry should you trim each length with a sharp knife, using a steel straight-edge. Like hessian, grasscloth is often difficult to clean, so it should not be used where it might easily get dirty, such as in kitchens.

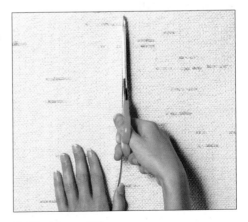

Cutting grasscloth
Cut slowly and use sharp scissors for a neat line.

SUITING THE WALL COVERING TO THE ROOM

When choosing wall coverings, it is important to consider the suitability of the paper or fabric for the room. Each room has its own problems and needs; it may be prone to condensation, for example, or it may need to be insulated against cold or noise.

Certain rooms, such as kitchens and children's rooms, need paper that is washable and hard-wearing. The range of wall coverings now available means that you can choose for both practicality and decorative effect.

Hall/landing
Vinyl
Washable paper
Woodchip paper
Embossed paper
High-relief paper
Relief vinyl

Bedroom
Standard paper
Flock paper
Embossed paper
High-relief paper
Fabrics

Children's room
Washable paper
Woodchip paper
Standard paper
Foamed polyethylene

Bathroom
Metallic foil vinyl
Relief vinyl
Foamed polyethylene
Washable paper

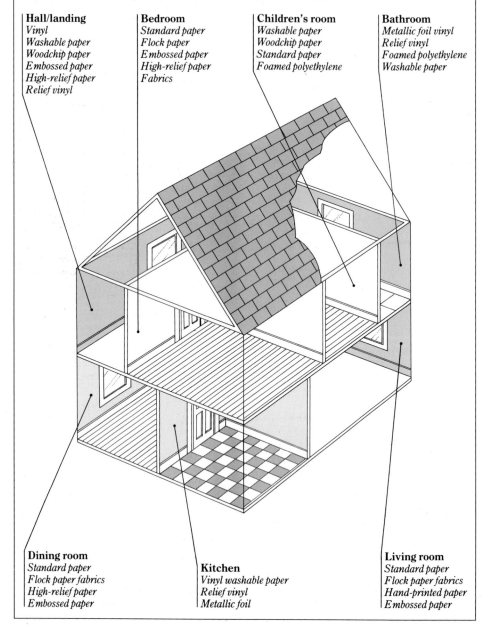

Dining room
Standard paper
Flock paper fabrics
High-relief paper
Embossed paper

Kitchen
Vinyl washable paper
Relief vinyl
Metallic foil

Living room
Standard paper
Flock paper fabrics
Hand-printed paper
Embossed paper

Estimating quantities

Wallpaper quantities can be calculated more accurately than paint, since there are fewer variable factors. Measure the height of the room, not including skirtings, and add 4in (100mm) to allow for trimming. Use the chart to calculate the number of rolls required and remember to add on 10 per cent for waste, especially with a large or "drop" pattern. When completing a room, note down the number of rolls used as a guide for next time. Standard wallpapers come in rolls of approximately 33ft × 1¾ft (10m × 53cm). Lining paper rolls are usually slightly wider than ordinary wallpapers, and they are available in both standard and economical large roll sizes.

CALCULATING THE NUMBER OF ROLLS

Measurement around walls including doors and windows	Number of rolls required for given heights from skirting in feet/metres							
	7½ft (2.3m)	8ft (2.4m)	8½ft (2.6m)	9ft (2.7m)	9½ft (2.9m)	10ft (3.0m)	10½ft (3.2m)	Ceilings
30ft (9.1m)	4	5	5	5	6	6	6	2
34ft (10.4m)	5	5	5	5	6	6	7	2
38ft (11.6m)	5	6	6	6	7	7	8	2
42ft (12.8m)	6	6	7	7	7	8	8	3
46ft (14.0m)	6	7	7	7	8	8	9	3
54ft (16.5m)	7	8	9	9	9	10	10	4
58ft (17.7m)	8	8	9	9	10	10	11	4
62ft (18.9m)	8	9	10	10	10	11	12	5
66ft (20.1m)	9	9	10	10	11	12	13	5
70ft (21.3m)	9	10	11	11	12	12	13	6
74ft (22.6m)	10	10	12	12	12	13	14	7
78ft (23.8m)	10	11	12	12	13	14	15	7

POINTS TO REMEMBER

- Always buy the type of adhesive recommended for the wall covering you have chosen.
- Check batch numbers on rolls before unwrapping them.
- Always paper ceilings before starting on the walls.
- Finish any paintwork before you start papering.
- Wear overalls or an apron with large pockets for holding scissors, a smoothing brush and other equipment.
- Follow the instructions given on pages 64 and 65 for where to start wallpapering on walls and ceilings, to help you to achieve the best results.

Choosing patterns

Complicated patterns are usually best avoided by the beginner, especially in a room with lots of alcoves and corners. Simple, repeat patterns are equally problematic, since the eye will quickly pick up any mismatching. These usually fall into two types: straight "set" patterns which have horizontal repeats, and "drop" patterns with diagonal repeats. "Free match" designs, however, match automatically.

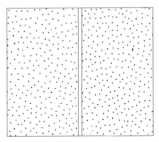

Free match pattern
Pattern matching is easiest when the pattern is small and random.

Set pattern
Horizontal patterns are unsuitable for sloping ceilings.

Drop pattern
A vertical pattern will emphasize uneven corners.

Colour and pattern for effect

Pattern, like colour, influences the mood and shape of a room. Florals, for example, tend to be restful, while geometrics may create a more stimulating atmosphere. Designs can be used to play visual tricks: vertical lines help to "raise" a ceiling, while horizontal lines "lengthen" a room; three-dimensional geometrics give the impression of depth, whereas small designs give a feeling of space; and large motifs diminish the size of a surface. Motifs have the power to focus interest on a feature or disguise irregularities when they are taken over an entire room. For the best effect, avoid having too many patterns in one room, do not combine florals with geometrics and always set off a pattern with a plain background, floor or furnishings.

Floral patterns
Fresh spring colours lend warmth and character to a bleak, angular room (left). Large sprigs have the effect of opening out a room and raising a ceiling, particularly when arranged in vertical strips. If the pattern is carried on to the blinds or furnishings, the warming and softening effect increases. In a small room with irregular shapes – an attic, for example – a miniature floral in random sequences would be more suitable, since a regular line will highlight crooked walls or ceilings.

A printed collage
Menus, wine labels, newspapers and magazines will form an unusual wall covering. A collage is best pasted on to a small area to form a feature in a bathroom (below), or a child's bedroom.

Geometric patterns
These instantly give a room a clean and modern feel – particularly suitable for a bathroom (right). Ideally, the lines should complement any other verticals and horizontals. The angles of the room must be straight or the lines will exaggerate any irregularities. A tiny motif within the geometric pattern will help to soften lines, and one or two colours should also be repeated in other parts of the room. Plain, bright-coloured accessories are shown to best advantage.

Motifs and colour schemes
The pattern used in the conservatory above has been chosen to reflect the purpose of the room. The co-ordinated effect has been achieved by picking up the main colour of the pattern throughout the room and matching accessories to the white background.

Preparation and pasting

The finished look of any decorating job depends to a very large extent on good preparation. This includes not only removing all traces of the existing paint and paper and ensuring a clean, firm surface, but also cutting materials correctly to size and covering the pasting surface in an even and methodical manner. It is important to set up a workstation that will enable you to reach all parts of the room safely and easily (page 49).

Stripping off old wallpaper

Any existing wall covering should be stripped off to leave bare walls, since joins, peeling, blistering or a strong pattern in the old paper may show through the new paper. The fresh adhesive may also pull the old covering away from the wall, together with the new paper you have just hung. The key to stripping wallpaper is to take time and care over the job. The paper should not be scraped off too vigorously or lumps will be gouged from the plaster, leaving more holes to fill in later. Be patient with stubborn areas and continue soaking and scraping until the paper loosens. Standard wallpapers are removed by sponging with warm water until the paper is soft enough to scrape off. Easy-strip papers are simply peeled off their backing paper. Washable papers which will not come off easily may need to be removed with a steam stripper.

Stripping normal wallpaper

1 *Remove wallpaper by soaking with warm water, using a large brush or sponge. Thicker papers may need an extra soaking.*

2 *Once the paper is soaked, you can begin scraping. Keep the scraper as flat as possible to avoid gouging the plaster.*

PREPARING SURFACES

When all old paper has been removed, wash down the walls with hot water to remove any traces of old paste and to loosen any final nibs of paper. Then fill any holes or cracks. When a wall covering comes away easily – assuming it is not an easy-strip type – it indicates a flaking, dusty or damp surface. Scrape away any flaking paint, then check and cure the cause of any dampness in the wall. Apply a coat of oil-based primer-sealer to provide a sound surface for the new wall covering. If papering over sound paintwork, wash down the wall thoroughly first with soap and water. It is a good idea to apply a coating of glue size. Either buy size or use diluted wallpaper paste.

With thinner materials, such as foils, thorough preparation is even more important than with traditional wallpaper, because they emphasize faults. It is best to hang lining paper and then, if the covering is semi-transparent, apply a coat of neutral emulsion before hanging.

Stripping vinyl wallpapers

1 *Easy-strip wall coverings are removed by releasing the edge of the paper with your fingernail or a stripping knife and pulling carefully upwards, not outwards, to avoid ripping the backing.*

2 *Underneath vinyls you will find a layer of backing paper. This can act as lining paper for the new wall covering. If, however, the backing paper comes away in places, it must be removed completely.*

Stripping difficult papers

  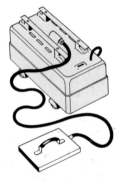

1 *Washable and overpainted papers are made to withstand water, so first score the surface using a wire brush serrated scraper to break down the surface before soaking.*

2 *A steam stripper is simple to use and creates less mess than soaking and scraping. Steam generated by the machine passes through a plate held close to the wall. This loosens the paper, which is then scraped off.*

A steam stripper
This enables you to strip wallpaper from a large area more quickly than soaking and scraping and with relatively little effort. It is worth hiring one if you have a lot to do.

APPLYING GLUE SIZE

Glue size is a gelatinous sealant that prevents a wall from absorbing water from the paste. Diluted paste will serve the same purpose. Although it is not always necessary, a coat over a wall will ensure that the wall covering sticks well. It also leaves the surface slippery, which makes it easier to slide the paper over the wall when you are aligning and butting up adjoining lengths.

Special formulations of glue size can be obtained, although it is now customary for diluted wallpaper paste to be used as size. Normally, a weak mixture

of paste is made up according to the instructions on the packet and applied generously with a large brush. Within minutes it will be dry and papering can begin.

Use size even if you are using ready-pasted wall coverings. If you are preparing a newly plastered wall, or a new plasterboard wall, for paper, make sure that you seal the surface with a coat of oil-based paint or shellac, then apply a coat of glue size. However, you should make sure that the plaster has dried properly before sealing it.

Measuring and cutting

Measure the height of each wall at both ends and in the middle to give you a maximum length for your strips of paper and allow an additional 4in (100mm) before cutting. This gives an extra 2in (50mm) at both ceiling (or picture rail) and skirting for neat trimming. Measure ceilings in the same way and allow an excess of 2in (50mm) on ceilings for trimming on to the side and window walls. Unroll a few feet to check which way up the pattern should be. Trim off the end of the roll and either cut off

lengths as you go, or, to speed up the job, cut several lengths, so that one length can be soaking while you are hanging another (but mark consecutive numbers on the back and make a note of which end is the "top"). When cutting to match use a steel tape measure to mark out lengths, then use wallpaper shears to cut your paper. When using a plain or a random-patterned paper, work from one roll of paper and cut equal lengths. With a diagonally matching "drop-pattern" paper, work from two or three rolls at a time to minimize waste in pattern matching. Drape lengths over a table and align them carefully before cutting.

Measuring out lengths
When measuring out lengths of wallpaper, use a steel tape measure, and allow at least 4in (100mm) of paper for trimming.

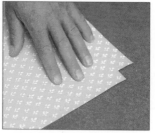

Set patterns
Cut equal lengths of set patterns from the same roll of wallpaper, and allow a small margin for trimming where necessary.

Drop patterns
Always match up drop patterns carefully before you begin measuring and cutting the lengths of paper for pasting.

Pasting and folding

After each length of paper has been cut, it should be given a good coating of paste, then folded and left to soak before hanging. Paste should be mixed until all lumps are dissolved and allowed to stand for a couple of minutes. If using thin paper, extra water must be added for a more dilute mixture. To ensure a good covering of paste, coat the brush generously, then paste systematically and in good light. Dry patches will form "bubbles" when the length has been hung.

Soaking
If no exact guidance is given on the label, the best approach is to soak long enough to ensure that the paper is supple before it is

hung. To "soak" the paper, simply leave it on a clean, dry surface after you have applied the paste and continue pasting more lengths. Always make sure that you keep the soaking time constant between the different lengths to avoid variations in stretching.

BATCHES

Never skimp when ordering paper, since running out can cause considerable problems. Although you may be able to buy another roll with the same design, the colours in the pattern might be a remarkably different shade, which will show in bright light. Check that each roll you buy bears the same batch number. To avoid running out, consider buying a spare roll of paper on a sale or return basis, but remember to keep the cellophane wrapper intact, otherwise you will not be able to return it.

Pasting and folding

1 *Paste the central portion of paper, then the long edge nearest to you.*

2 *Brush the paste over to the opposite long edge, spreading the paste evenly.*

3 *Fold the pasted half over on to itself, not on to the unpasted paper.*

4 *Paste the second half, then fold it over and leave the whole strip to soak.*

Folding long lengths

When pasting a long length of paper, arrange the pasted sections into folds, pasted-side to pasted-side. Do not allow paste to smudge on to the decorative side. Be careful not to crease the folds, since this will leave unsightly marks.

Concertina folds
These folds make handling easier when working on ceilings or stairwells, or when hanging lining paper.

Marking guide lines on ceilings and walls

Corners, door architraves and window frames rarely form true verticals. So the first step when papering walls is to mark a vertical line as a guide to hanging the first length. Suspend a plumb bob on a chalked stringline from the top of the wall and snap it to leave a vertical line. Draw a new guide line on each wall, and keep checking the alignment as you work. Straight guide lines on ceilings are made by measuring equal distances from the wall at each end of the ceiling and snapping a chalked stringline between the two points. The starting point for hanging ceiling paper is generally parallel with the main window, so that, as with painting, you will be working away from the light.

Using a plumb bob and chalkline
When the plumb bob stops swinging, press the chalkline into the base of the wall and pluck it to leave a vertical line.

Where to begin on ceilings
Begin parallel with the main window. Draw your first guide line to allow about 2in (50mm) of paper for trimming.

Where to begin on walls
*Work outwards from **A**. Paper the first side wall, window wall, other side wall, then the far wall. Or start at **B**, paper the rest of the window wall, side walls, then the end wall.*

Chimney breasts
If the paper has a large pattern, centralize the motif on the chimney breast (right). If it has a random design, mark a vertical line at the centre of the chimney breast and hang a length each side, using two full widths (far right).

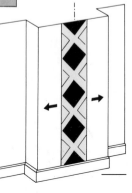

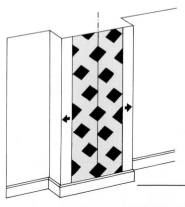

Hanging lining paper on walls

Lining paper is hung horizontally, so each length must be as long as the wall's width. Joining short lengths is not advisable, since it is difficult to get a perfect join.

Mark a guide line for the first length (opposite), start at the top of the wall and work downwards to the skirting. The first length should overlap on to the ceiling by about 1in (25mm) before being trimmed off. Each length should also overlap around the corner on to the next wall by about ½in (12mm). As you work down the wall, subsequent horizontal lengths should butt up closely to the previous length. Any overlaps, except in corners, should be avoided, since these will be evident when the top covering is hung later.

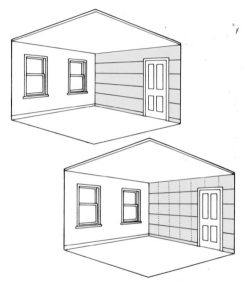

Where to begin lining on walls
Lining paper should be hung in horizontal layers on walls (top). If the surface is bad apply a double layer of paper, known as cross-lining (above). Hang the first layer vertically and the second horizontally.

Hanging horizontal lining
Unfold the paper and smooth it on to the wall.

Patch lining

Where only a small part of the wall needs to be lined, try patch lining. Hang enough lining paper to cover the poor area with an overlap of a few centimetres, but do not stick down the edges. Allow the paste to dry, then tear off a rim of paper to leave a softened feathered edge to the patch. However, do not add small, straight-edged pieces to a damaged length, as the joins will show.

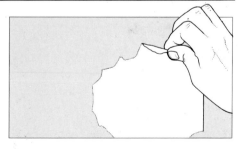

Patching damaged lining
Tear around the patch for a soft line.

How to hang wallpaper

The secret of successful wallpapering is to be thorough, methodical and careful when matching patterns. When decorating, ceilings should be papered first to prevent paste from splashing on to finished walls and woodwork. If the surfaces are in a poor condition, you will probably need to hang lining paper on both ceilings and walls (pages 64–5) before applying your top wall covering. Having lined the surface, cut and pasted lengths, established a starting point and marked straight guide lines, the paper is ready to hang. The first length is lined up against the guide line, smoothed into place, then trimmed. Subsequent lengths are carefully brushed into place to form good pattern matches and neat butt joints.

Applying the paper

1 *Standing square to the wall, unfold the top half of the paper. Position the edge against the vertical guide line. Leave a 2in (50mm) trimming edge at the top.*

2 *Run the wallpaper brush firmly down the centre of the aligned length. Brush outwards to expel any air bubbles and smooth the paper neatly on to the wall.*

3 *Align the lower half of the paper, then run the back of the shears along the paper at the ceiling angle.*

4 *Carefully peel back the paper again and trim along the crease with the wallpaper shears.*

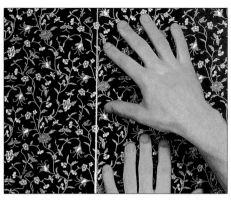

5 *Smooth the trimmed paper back on to the wall with the wallpaper brush. Hang the second strip of paper.*

6 *Align the length from the top of the wall, matching the pattern. Smooth the joins with a seam roller.*

Mismatching

It is almost impossible to complete a normal wallpapering job using patterned paper without some mismatching. The awkward points are usually corners, and around doors, windows and fireplaces. When deciding where to end the papering, choose a point which will not be too obvious. At the edge of a door or window, for example, use a part of the pattern which blends with the other strips ending there, but does not match them exactly. Accurate matching above doors and above and below windows requires using parts of full-width strips, which is very wasteful. Corners are hardly ever perfectly straight and will often be mismatched, although it will be a great deal less noticeable.

BUTT AND DOUBLE-CUT JOINTS

Butt joints are a widely used method of ensuring that the strips of wallpaper stay together as they dry. Hang the first strip, and then, when hanging the second, slide it by hand towards the first until they meet. Continue pushing until a tiny ridge forms. This ridge will disappear as the paper dries and shrinks slightly. This method is not necessary with vinyl papers.

Double-cut joints are made by overlapping the strips and then cutting through both of them with a very sharp knife. The same method is used when hanging hessian (page 58).

A third method of joining strips of wallpaper is to overlap the strips. Begin next to a window and work away from it, particularly when you are working with patterned paper. Although the overlapping method is quite commonly used, it gives a much less professional finish than either butt or double-cut joints.

Carrying pasted paper

To carry pasted paper easily and safely, drape the length over one arm, with the two ends uppermost. This arrangement will prevent you from smearing paste on to your clothes, will enable you to mount the ladder easily with the paper, and will ensure that the length is not crushed. Long lengths of folded paper can be supported on a roll. Make sure that the ladder is adjusted properly before you ascend.

How to carry a length of pasted paper
When carried in this way, with the pasted sides together, ends upwards, the paper will be easy to unfold against the wall when you are ready to hang it.

Hanging lining paper on ceilings

It is advisable to use lining paper on previously painted or distempered surfaces or on new plasterwork. Without a lining, wallpaper may crease and stretch on uneven surfaces, paste may take a long time to dry on gloss surfaces, and gaps may form through shrinkage.

Lining paper is normally hung at right angles to the top covering on both ceilings and walls, so that the joins in the two layers do not coincide. Use the same paste as for the top wall covering, but hang the lining immediately, since there is no need to let it soak. Leave it to dry for 48 hours before pasting on the top covering. When learning the art of paper hanging, it is worth practising with lining paper, even if you paint rather than paper over it.

Applying the lining paper

1 *Set up a safe working platform and mark a guide line on the ceiling. If you have an assistant, have him or her stand by with a clean brush to support the paper.*

2 *Align the first portion of the pasted paper with the guide line. If you are working alone, use a spare roll of paper to support the rest of the paper while you work.*

3 *Keep the remainder of the length close to the ceiling and smooth down the paper to eliminate air bubbles. Mark a crease line with a scraper at the edges.*

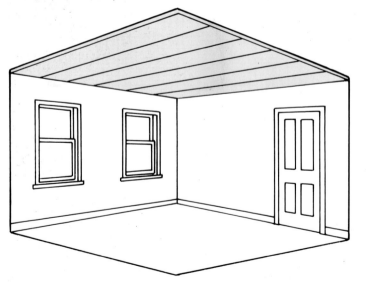

Lining a ceiling
Prepare the ceiling (page 60) and mark a guide line for the first length of paper (page 64). The first length of lining paper is usually hung at right angles to the main window. In this way, the lining will lie at right angles to the top layer of wallpaper, which is usually hung parallel with the window (page 64). Begin lining in a corner and allow about 2in (50mm) of paper to be turned on to the window wall for trimming. Also allow an extra 2in (50mm) for trimming on to the side walls.

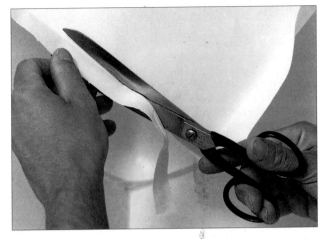

Cleaning shears
For neat trimming, stand paste-clogged shears and scissors in a jar of hot water from time to time. This will dislodge the adhesive and so guarantee that you get clean cuts. If the paste hardens, it may need to be washed off in clean, soapy water.

Trimming lining paper
Trim along the crease line with a pair of sharp, clean shears. If the walls are to be prepared, leave a ¼in (6mm) margin of paper on each wall. Successive lengths are hung in the same way, ensuring that the edges of all the lengths are neatly butt-jointed (page 67).

Hanging expanded polystyrene

This "paste-the-wall" lining material can be hung in horizontal or vertical layers, though it is easier to hang it vertically. Just plan ahead to ensure that the joins fall between the joins in the wall covering. Handle the material carefully, as it is likely to crack or crumble.

Brush heavy-duty wallpaper paste on to the wall over an area to be occupied by one length of the material, and allow it to dry thoroughly. Position the end of the roll close to the ceiling, then unroll the polystyrene down the wall, keeping its edge aligned with a vertical guide line drawn on the wall (page 64). Smooth out the polystyrene, using a wallpaper brush or a paint roller. Take care when trimming the bottom of the length into the skirting board, as the material will crack easily. Press it gently into the top of the skirting to mark off a trimming line and cut before smoothing it down. Butt joint successive lengths and smooth down the joins gently with a seam roller. Do not try to take polystyrene around corners, as it will crumble.

Trimming polystyrene lining
At skirtings, gently press the polystyrene into the angle, mark a cutting line, and trim with scissors or a knife.

Hanging ready-pasted paper

Ready-pasted paper has a coating of dried paste on the back which is activated by immersing the paper in water. Either buy a plastic water trough with the wallpaper or use any container which is long and deep enough to take a loosely rolled length of paper.

Cut a length of paper, then roll it up loosely, with the pattern facing inward, to ensure that the water reaches all areas of paste on the backing. Make sure that the "free" end of the paper is the top edge to be fixed at the ceiling, then immerse the paper in the water for a full minute. Take hold of the top edge of the paper and slowly pull it upwards, allowing the water to run back into the trough. Then smooth it on to the wall using a clean, damp sponge, working from the centre to the edges, and sponge away any paste which may appear at the edges. If a wall has been lined with expanded polystyrene, hang lining paper before applying ready-pasted paper.

Activating the paste
Carefully pull up the top edge of the roll, allowing the water to drain back into the trough.

Borders and friezes

Borders and friezes add an inexpensive finishing touch to a newly decorated room. Although traditionally fitted at ceiling or picture rail level, they can be used to good effect as a vertical wall surround, or to trim a sloping ceiling, for example. A decorative strip can reduce the apparent height of a tall ceiling, elongate a short room, co-ordinate disparate colours, or enliven a quiet room. Borders and friezes look best against a neutral background, but can be used on patterned paper if carefully co-ordinated. Apply them at least 48 hours after hanging wallpaper.

A softening effect
In a simple, neutral room (left) a soft frieze adds a warm and friendly touch, particularly if it picks up a colour in the furnishings. In a room without pattern, a frieze can become a feature.

A co-ordinated effect
On a vibrant wall, the border needs to link with either the pattern or the colour of the wallpaper for a properly unified effect (right).

Papering arches

Paper the outer wall first and turn a 1in (25mm) margin of paper into the arch. Make small, triangular cuts in the edge. This will allow the paper to follow the curve of the arch without tearing. Fold the flaps around the corner and smooth them down. Paper the inside of the arch in two pieces, the exact width of the arch, working from the bottom to the apex of the arch and making a neat butt joint at the top.

Papering arches
Carefully align the edges of the paper with the arch.

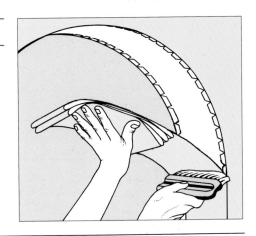

Papering corners

Joins are less noticeable if they fall in a corner, so unless a width of paper conveniently ends in a corner, you will need to cut it into two strips. Internal and external corners are treated in much the same way. When less than a full width is needed to reach a corner, you should measure from the edge of the last length into the corner. Turn the paper face down to mark off the width needed and double-check that the strip is being cut from the correct edge, or the pattern will not match. Pencil guide marks to indicate which edges are to fall in the corner. When the first strip is in place, the off-cut is hung on the new wall. Make sure that its edge is covering the join.

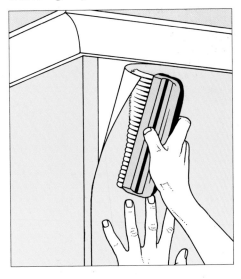

Internal and external corners
Vertically divide a strip of paper between the two walls, allowing a small overlap. Paste the first strip. Mark vertical lines on the next wall before pasting the off-cut. If the paper is patterned, check that the patterns match before smoothing down the paper.

Papering stairwells

The height of most stairwells poses the problem of how to reach the tops of the walls and how to handle very long lengths of paper. The first essential is therefore to set up a safe workstation (page 49).

Although it runs against the normal procedure of working away from the light, it is easiest to hang the longest length first and work away from it in both directions.

When measuring lengths, mark the paper to allow for the slope of the stairs. Allow each length to hang below the longest drop. Carefully crease the paper along the skirting, then trim to fit. After pasting, fold each length concertina-style for ease of handling (page 63) and, if possible, enlist a helper to support the length of paper as it is hung.

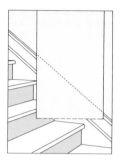

Measuring for the stair angle
Allow for the slope of the stairs when measuring lengths, so that the paper falls below the longest drop. Crease the paper along the skirting and trim.

If you use a ready-pasted paper, always roll each length twice in the trough to ensure that water reaches all parts of the dried paste on the back of these long strips of paper. First immerse the length, pattern outwards, in the trough, so that the bottom end extrudes, then reroll it until the end which will lie at the top of the wall emerges.

Papering around fireplaces

The way to tackle a fireplace surround depends mainly on the mantelshelf. If it reaches right across the chimney breast wall or to within about 1in (25mm) of the corners, treat the wall above and below the shelf as two separate areas. Hang the paper down to the mantelshelf and make a neat horizontal cut. Then hang the lower half of the length and make a neat butt joint where the pieces meet (page 67). Bear in mind that they will be at eye level. If the mantelpiece spans only a part of the wall, hang the length as one piece. Brush on the top half of the paper and cut along the rear edge of the mantelshelf. Then cut carefully around the contours of the fireplace surround, using sharp household scissors for intricate shapes. Smooth the paper into place with a brush. When papering chimney breasts, try to make joins and overlaps on the side, recessing walls.

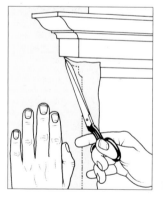

Cutting contours
Use sharp household scissors for intricate cuts.

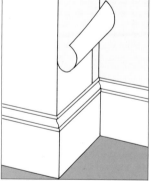

Joins and overlaps
On chimney breasts make joins on the side walls.

PAPERING AROUND RADIATORS

Some radiators can now be tilted forward for decorating, but most are fixed. Either remove the radiator or tuck enough paper behind it to leave a "fully papered" look. Cut a slit to allow for the wall brackets and push the strips down behind the radiator. If the paper is visible below the radiator, butt joint the strips at the base of the wall and trim carefully along the top of the skirting board. For a description of a butt joint, see page 67.

Papering around light fittings

First switch off the electricity supply at the mains. Modern, flush-fitting sockets and switches are simple to trim around neatly. First loosen the cover plate, then hang the length of paper up to the electrical fitting. Cut a hole in the paper, about ¼in (6mm) smaller than the size of the plate. Then smooth the paper on to the wall and replace the plate.

Some older-style sockets and switches are fixed in a block. Press the paper against the switch and make small cuts, radiating from the centre of the fitting to about ½in (12mm) beyond its edges. Brush the paper around the block and trim the flaps. With ceiling roses, make a series of radial cuts instead.

Light switches
Make a cut to each corner, outwards from the centre, then trim along each edge with a sharp pair of scissors.

Light sockets
Make a series of radial cuts from the centre of the socket to the edge, and trim off the tongues with a trimming knife.

Papering around windows and doors

The shape of the window surround will determine the papering technique. In a window reveal, paper the inside walls first, cutting the paper to align exactly with the edge of the outer wall. Then hang a length on the outer wall, with a small margin overlapping into the papered reveal, and match the pattern carefully.

The trickiest rooms to wallpaper are attics and lofts where there are unusual angles. Where dormer windows have triangular-shaped wall reveals, turn a 1in (25mm) margin of paper from the outer wall into the reveal. Cut pieces to cover the reveal walls precisely and overlap the margin. When papering wide picture windows, first cut, match and hang the middle strips above and below the window, then hang the side strips as with other types of window. Adjust the middle strips slightly to minimize any mismatching. Then smooth the paper with a brush, and trim.

Papering doorways
Hang complete lengths until less than a full width of paper is needed to reach the door frame. Cut out an L-shaped piece of paper, leaving about 2in (50mm) excess all around for trimming. Hang the paper from the ceiling down to the top of the frame and trim along the line. Make a diagonal cut about 1in (25mm) long, working away from the top corner of the frame to allow the rest of the length to be smoothed into place. Crease the paper along the top of the frame, then cut. Crease the paper along the vertical, then trim.

Papering around windows
Paper the inside walls first (right) as described above, cutting the paper to fit. Alternatively, paper the outer walls first, cutting away excess paper. Leave a small overlap on the vertical side, brushing the flaps into the recess of the window, top and bottom. Trim at the window edge. Finally, paper the sides of the recess. Set it back ¼in (6mm) to prevent the paper from fraying.

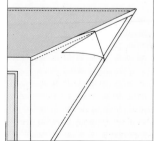

CHAPTER THREE

TILING

Tiles are resistant to water, heat and most
household chemicals. They are hard-
wearing, easy to clean and demand little
maintenance. Although time-consuming,
the laying of tiles requires no special skill,
particularly with modern adhesives and
lightweight tiles. In many cases tiles prove
easier to fix than sheet flooring or wall
coverings and, since they may be bought in
smaller quantities, result in less wastage.
Beyond the wide range of ceramics, tiles
are now produced in a variety of materials.
Cork, brick, mirrored glass, vinyl,
polystyrene and steel tiles offer new
textures and can be fitted in much the
same way as ceramic. Transfer, mural and
mosaic tiles have opened up new individual
design possibilities, and heat-, frost-
resistant and other special-purpose tiles
have broadened their practical value.

Tools and equipment

For a good result, the correct tiling tools are essential; they cannot be improvised. Always ensure that you have the correct adhesive and grouting (if needed) for the type of tile and situation, and in sufficient quantities. A flexible waterproof sealant is useful for filling gaps around baths or sinks. Plastic spacer lugs are also available for ceramic wall tiles that are not already self-spacing.

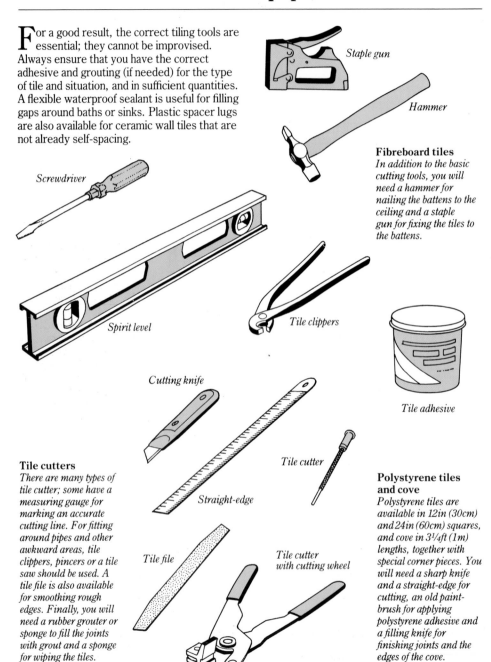

Staple gun

Hammer

Screwdriver

Spirit level

Tile clippers

Cutting knife

Straight-edge

Tile file

Tile cutter

Tile cutter with cutting wheel

Tile adhesive

Fibreboard tiles
In addition to the basic cutting tools, you will need a hammer for nailing the battens to the ceiling and a staple gun for fixing the tiles to the battens.

Tile cutters
There are many types of tile cutter; some have a measuring gauge for marking an accurate cutting line. For fitting around pipes and other awkward areas, tile clippers, pincers or a tile saw should be used. A tile file is also available for smoothing rough edges. Finally, you will need a rubber grouter or sponge to fill the joints with grout and a sponge for wiping the tiles.

Polystyrene tiles and cove
Polystyrene tiles are available in 12in (30cm) and 24in (60cm) squares, and cove in 3¹/₄ft (1m) lengths, together with special corner pieces. You will need a sharp knife and a straight-edge for cutting, an old paintbrush for applying polystyrene adhesive and a filling knife for finishing joints and the edges of the cove.

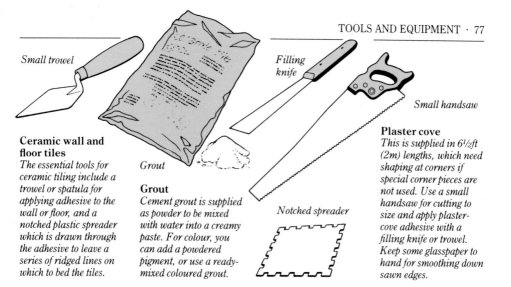

Small trowel

Filling knife

Small handsaw

Ceramic wall and floor tiles
The essential tools for ceramic tiling include a trowel or spatula for applying adhesive to the wall or floor, and a notched plastic spreader which is drawn through the adhesive to leave a series of ridged lines on which to bed the tiles.

Grout

Grout
Cement grout is supplied as powder to be mixed with water into a creamy paste. For colour, you can add a powdered pigment, or use a ready-mixed coloured grout.

Notched spreader

Plaster cove
This is supplied in 6½ft (2m) lengths, which need shaping at corners if special corner pieces are not used. Use a small handsaw for cutting to size and apply plaster-cove adhesive with a filling knife or trowel. Keep some glasspaper to hand for smoothing down sawn edges.

Choosing the right adhesive

As with wallpapers, it is crucial to choose the correct adhesive for the type of tile, the conditions and the area in which it is to be used. Ceramic tiles should be fixed with ceramic-tile adhesive, which is sold ready-mixed or in powder form.

Waterproof types are available for shower cubicles and sink splashbacks, frost-proof types for use on patios or balconies and heat-resistant ones for kitchens and fireplaces. There is also a flexible adhesive for tiling over a surface which is prone to movement, such as hardboard and chipboard: it often comes in two parts to be mixed before use. A thick-bed adhesive should be used on uneven surfaces. For even surfaces, thin-bed adhesive is preferable, as it is easier to use.

Cork tiles should be fixed with either non-flammable cork wall- or floor-tile adhesive, or a water-based contact adhesive, depending on the instructions supplied. A specific adhesive is also available for brick tiles. Mirror, plastic and metallic tiles are secured in place with sticky tabs. For each 10½ft^2 (1m^2) of tiling, you will need about 1¾ pints (1 litre) of adhesive.

OTHER USEFUL EQUIPMENT

- Mirror tiles are supplied with adhesive tabs. No equipment is needed beyond the basic measuring and cutting tools.
- For cork wall and floor tiles, marking and cutting tools are required, and a special cork wall-tile or floor-tile adhesive.
- Brick tiles are difficult to cut, so use an electric grinder, a circular power saw with a masonry disc, or a tungsten-carbide rod saw fitted in a hacksaw frame. Use brick-tile adhesive for fixing them and, for pointing, a dry mortar mix or a pointing compound and pointing trowel.
- Vinyl and plastic tiles require stringlines for marking out the floor, a sharp knife or scissors, and a straight-edge for cutting. Use vinyl flooring adhesive unless tiles are self-adhesive. As with cork, these kinds of tile do not need grouting.

TIPS ON BUYING TILES

- It is cheaper to buy tiles in boxes than singly.
- Count part tiles as whole tiles for estimating purposes, but remember that a large cork or vinyl tile can be cut into several border pieces.
- Always check tiles for chips and colour differences when you get them home.
- Allow a few extra tiles (about 5 per cent) for breakages and for future repairs.
- When cutting tiles, always exert even pressure and keep the tile supported, to make sure that the break is clean.
- Always make sure that you buy a sufficient amount of the right type of adhesive when purchasing your wall, floor or ceiling tiles. Running out of adhesive in the middle of a job is not only annoying; it could also delay completion, causing much domestic inconvenience.

Types of tile

Ceramic wall tiles come in a wide range of colours, patterns, textures and shapes. The range of ceramic floor tiles is less extensive. Plain tiles are often coloured to match standard bathroom fittings, and can be combined with complementary patterned tiles. You can also buy matching ceramic trim and tile accessories. Note that straight-edged ceramic tiles will need spacers, whereas those with angled edges will not. Some patterned tiles can be used as random cameos within plain tiling, while others are designed to be used in groups to complete a motif. Both smooth and textured finishes are available – also hand-painted tiles,

which are very expensive but can be used sparingly in strategic places. Heat-resistant and frost-proof tiles are also available. Other materials, such as cork, metal, glass and vinyl, offer an additional range of design effects.

Ceramic tiles are sold singly, by the square yard/metre or, more economically, in boxes of 25 and 50 or 16 and 36. Other types are sold in packs, but some suppliers will break open a pack to give you the exact number of tiles that you require. Take care to measure and estimate accurately (pages 84–5), and allow a few extra tiles – approximately 5 per cent – for breakages and for future repairs.

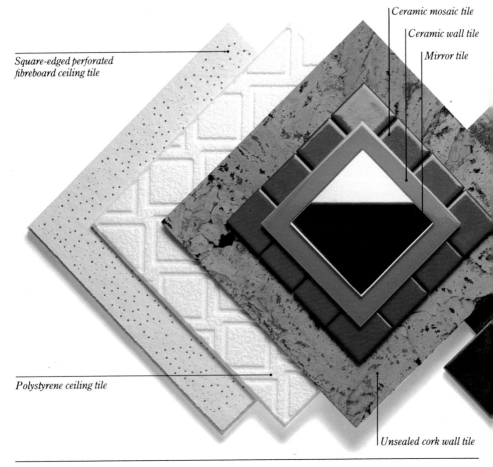

Ceramic mosaic tile

Ceramic wall tile

Mirror tile

Square-edged perforated fibreboard ceiling tile

Polystyrene ceiling tile

Unsealed cork wall tile

Ceiling tiles

Polystyrene tiles are the least expensive ceiling covering after paint. They are available plain for overpainting, or with a design embossed on to the surface. Avoid using polystyrene above cookers, since it may constitute a fire risk. Only use water-based emulsion paints for overpainting polystyrene tiles; oil-based paints can also be a fire hazard. Use the recommended adhesive.

Fibreboard tiles are made from compressed wood or mineral fibres and are thicker than polystyrene tiles. Some have tongue-and-groove edges which allow them to lock together and to be stapled invisibly to the ceiling joists. Others have straight edges and are fixed with adhesive. Both types come with either a plain or an embossed surface. Most fibreboard tiles are fire-resistant, and they can help to deaden noise.

POINTS TO REMEMBER
● Always take time to plan the job carefully before fixing tiles. The position of the first tile determines the end result. ● Remember to allow for grouting joints when mapping out the tiling area. ● Choose adhesives and grouting to suit both the tiles and the room conditions. ● Always buy a few extra tiles to cover both breakages and repairs, or you may have difficulty finding replacements later.

Sealed cork floor tile

Quarry tile

Self-adhesive vinyl tile

Marble tile

Ceramic floor tile

Wall tiles

Modern ceramic wall tiles consist of slabs of clay, decorated on one side with a coloured glaze. They are fired to produce a durable, stain- and water-resistant surface. Variants of the plain, coloured tile are single tiles with an individual pattern to break up an expanse of a single colour, and tile murals, which are used in groups to make up a complete pattern or motif. In addition to the range of design effects the different practical properties of each type of tile are listed on the opposite page.

Cork tiles are manufactured from pressed layers of tree bark. They are available either sealed or unsealed and come in a variety of natural colours, sometimes with a slight grain direction. Cork is warm to the touch and a good heat and sound insulator, but the surface must be sealed with a polyurethane varnish if it is to be cleaned easily. Some cork tiles are also treated with a washable and steam-proof finish.

Mosaic tiles consist of tiny ceramic tiles, about 1in (25mm) square. They can be square-shaped or interlocking, and are supplied mounted on a mesh or paper sheet. They are laid and grouted in the same way as ceramic tiles and have the same qualities, but are more expensive. Mirror tiles are square or rectangular pieces of clear or tinted mirrored glass. They are easier to work with than mirror sheets, but the wall surface must be perfectly smooth before the tiles are laid, or the reflection will be distorted.

Thin slices of real brick or man-made brick construction are available in several colours and cut to the same size as real bricks to give the wall an authentic appearance. Metallic tiles, usually coloured gold, silver or copper in a matt or shiny finish, provide a heat-proof surface. They are washable, but any splash marks must be cleaned off immediately. They have hollow backs, can be cut to shape with scissors, or bent around corners, and are fixed with self-adhesive pads. Since metal conducts electricity, these tiles should be trimmed around light switches.

Vinyl and plastic tiles are made from thin plastic or vinyl sheet. They are warm to the touch and help to reduce noise. Like metallic tiles, they have hollow backs, can be cut with scissors and are easily fixed to the wall with self-adhesive pads.

Floor tiles

Ceramic floor tiles are slightly thicker than ceramic wall tiles and fired at a higher temperature, so that the particles fuse, making the tile almost unbreakable when laid. They may be bought glazed or unglazed in a variety of earth colours. Glazed tiles may be cold and noisy underfoot, but the slip-resistant types are less dangerous when wet. Unglazed tiles should be sealed before use. Quarry tiles are unglazed and therefore rougher in finish and cheaper than ceramic tiles, but they have the same properties. They are laid on a cement bed, then sealed and polished. Colours are normally restricted to earth reds and browns.

Solid vinyl, latex-backed tiles are durable and comfortable, but can be slippery when wet. They are easier to lay than sheet flooring and less wasteful, especially in awkwardly shaped rooms. A choice of plain colours and patterns is available, some imitating other materials, such as stone and wood. Vinyl-coated tiles are smooth and easy to clean. They are much cheaper, but less comfortable and durable than vinyl tiles.

Rubber tiles are quiet and comfortable. Although expensive, they are hard-wearing. The colour range is limited, but studs and other embosses can create a "high tech" style. Marble tiles, durable and luxurious, come in slabs of the natural marble colours – pink, green, grey and black – and are laid on a bed of mortar.

Stone tiles, like marble, are enduring and expensive floor coverings. Slate is available in grey, green and blue squares or rectangles and is laid on a cement bed. Cork tiles are comfortable to walk on but not very durable. Some types are supplied with a polyurethane or thin vinyl finish; others have to be sanded and sealed after laying, to prevent water from penetrating between the tiles.

	SUITING THE WALL TILE TO THE ROOM		
Type	**Qualities**	**Room**	**Adhesive**
Ceramic	Hard-wearing, waterproof waterproof and stain-resistant	Kitchens and bathrooms	Ceramic wall-tile adhesive. Waterproof adhesive in areas likely to be splashed by water
Mosaic	Hard-wearing, waterproof and stain-resistant	Kitchens and bathrooms	As for ceramic tiles
Cork	Warm, reasonably hard-wearing and stain-resistant	Anywhere except excessively wet areas, e.g. showers	Cork wall-tile adhesive. Non-flammable emulsion types are safest. Contact adhesive is an alternative
Mirror	Hard-wearing and stain-resistant. Ideal for small feature areas. Gives a feeling of space	Anywhere except excessively wet areas	Adhesive tabs
Brick	Hard-wearing. Ideal for complete walls or feature areas such as fireplaces	Any room, but avoid areas where bricks could be affected by grease, excessive steam or water splashes	Brick wall-tile adhesive
Plastic and metallic	Fairly easy to clean, but some can be damaged by abrasive cleaners. Reasonably hard-wearing	Kitchens and bathrooms, but avoid using plastics near heat, and metallics near steam	Adhesive tabs or contact adhesive
	SUITING THE FLOOR TILE TO THE ROOM		
Ceramic	Hard-wearing, waterproof and stain-resistant, but cold and noisy	Kitchens, bathrooms and halls	Ceramic floor-tile adhesive
Quarry	As above	Kitchens, bathrooms and halls	Ceramic floor-tile adhesive or (for thicker types) mortar cement
Cork	Very comfortable, warm and quiet. Not very durable. Reasonably able to withstand water	Any room	Cork floor-tile adhesive as recommended by tile manufacturers
Vinyl	Very comfortable, warm and quiet. Durable on well-laid sub-floor. Reasonably able to withstand water	Any room but mostly kitchens and bathrooms	Some are self-adhesive. Others are laid with vinyl floor-tile adhesive
Marble	Hard-wearing and waterproof	Kitchens, bathrooms and halls	Mortar cement
Rubber	Comfortable and quiet. Hard-wearing, waterproof and non-slip	Any room, but mostly kitchens and bathrooms	As recommended by tile manufacturers

Decorative effects with tiling

Tiles offer countless opportunities for individual style and pattern, since they are laid individually and come in a vast array of colours, shapes, textures and patterns. They provide an interesting alternative to plain paint or wallpaper when a room needs something a little different, particularly in kitchens and bathrooms, where tiles have a practical as well as a decorative value. The best effects are usually created with the clever combination of plain or textured tiles in one or two colours. In most cases patterned tiles should be restricted to a single wall in an otherwise plain-tiled room, or interspersed individually or in rows among complementary plain tiles.

Murals can be effective if the style and scale are well chosen. In a small room, use a single background colour to avoid dividing the room into disparate blocks of colour.

Decorative tiling is as effective on floors as it is on walls. A shrewd choice of floor tiles can completely change the character of a room or hallway. Beware of overdoing the effect, however. For example, a bold, black-and-white floor needs to be offset by low-key walls, as in the picture on the right.

Reducing the space
Warm, advancing colours help to make a large, airy bathroom feel more cosy (above). The cherry floor colour taken a short way up the walls helps to reduce the height of the room, and blue tiles interspersed in the tiled area help to break up the spread of colour. Coloured grouting can also relieve the effect and complement or contrast with the basic colour.

Increasing the space
An all-over mosaic design (right) taken over the floor and the walls adds a touch of class to a simple bathroom and gives a feeling of space. Changeable accessories create a splash of colour.

A bold effect with patterned floor tiling

Black and white vinyl tiles can look striking, especially if laid diagonally (far left). Offset such a bold effect with low-key walls. A border of black tiles adds emphasis.

Soft and sophisticated hallways

Cool to the touch but warm to the eye, quarry tiles (left) set off the soft, neutral colours of an entrance hall and the natural pine finish of a kitchen, giving a warm continuity to the entire area.

The range of tile shapes

Most ceramic tiles are either square or oblong, but a range of interlocking circular, hexagonal and Provençale-shaped tiles are also to be found. The most common type of tile, known as a "field" tile, has square edges. Some manufacturers also produce "universal" tiles which have one or two glazed edges for finishing exposed edges. Quadrant tiles are round-edged slivers for use as border tiles on corners. Ceramic wall tiles usually come in 4in (100mm) or 6in (150mm) sizes, ceramic floor tiles come in 6in × 8in (15cm × 20cm) sizes, whereas most other tiles are 12in (30cm).

Estimating quantities

The same method of calculating the number of tiles required can be used for all types of standard tile. First make a plan of the area and measure the length of each edge, then work out how many tile widths will fit into each. For example, a 13ft × 10ft (4m × 3m) room using 12in (30cm) tiles will need 13 × 10 = 130 (13½ × 10 = 135) tiles. For large areas with no obstructions, divide the area into smaller squares, then add up a total. Since tiles are usually sold in boxes of a set amount, this may allow for wastage. If you are buying them loose, however, you should add an extra 5 per cent for accidental damage.

Remember that, depending on the area to be covered, you may also need quantities of trim tiles for internal and external corners, and also cap and base tiles. Measure for all these types separately. Most come in 6in (15cm) lengths. One pound (0.5kg) of grout (after mixing with water) will cover about 18ft^2 (1.7m^2).

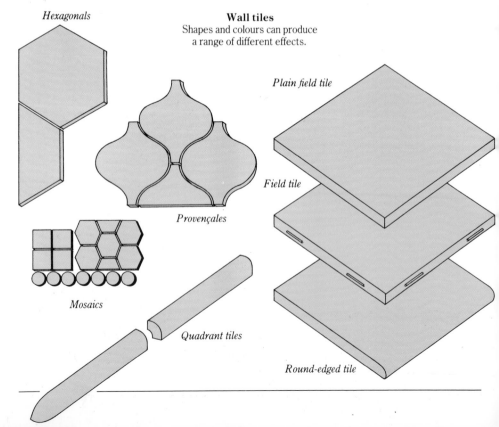

Hexagonals

Wall tiles
Shapes and colours can produce
a range of different effects.

Plain field tile

Field tile

Provençales

Mosaics

Quadrant tiles

Round-edged tile

Preparing the surface

Strip off any wall or floor covering material and flaking paint. Rub down sound gloss to take off the shine and key the surface for tile adhesive. If a layer of old ceramic tiles is flat, firmly fixed and well keyed, new ceramic tiles can be applied on top. If you choose to remove existing ceramic tiles, use a bolster chisel and club hammer or a small kango hammer with a chasing tool. If necessary, you should also reline the surface, using either plaster or plasterboard on walls and ceilings, and chipboard or plywood on floors.

It is difficult to align tiles unless the wall or floor is perfectly flat. Hold a long, flat piece of wood against the surface vertically, horizontally and diagonally to test for any "see-sawing" movement.

CALCULATING NO. OF TILES		
Size of tile	No/yd^2	No/m^2
6in × 6in	36	43
6in × 8in	27	33
10cm × 10cm	84	100
15cm × 15cm	36	44
20cm × 20cm	20.5	25
30cm × 30cm	9	11

ESTIMATING QUANTITIES OF SHAPED TILES

The method of estimating quantities of standard tiles will not apply to hexagonal and Provençale shapes. As a guide, for 6in × 6¾in (15cm × 17cm) hexagonal tiles, you will need 45 tiles per square yard (54 per square metre). For 6in × 8¼in (15cm × 21cm) Provençale tiles, you will need 36 tiles per square yard (44 per square metre). Again, buy extra tiles for repairs.

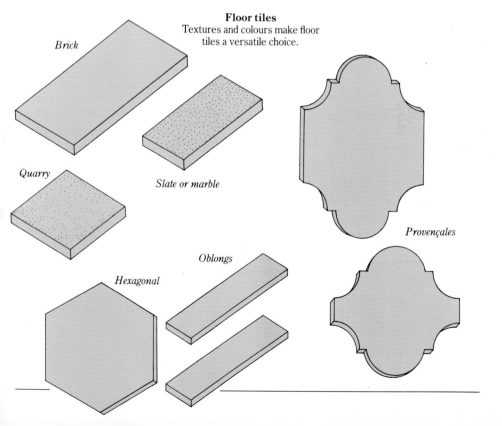

Floor tiles
Textures and colours make floor tiles a versatile choice.

Brick

Quarry

Slate or marble

Provençales

Hexagonal

Oblongs

Planning tiling

Planning is very important for any type of decorating, but is particularly so when you are using tiles. Not only does good planning result in a neater and more symmetrical finish, it also cuts costs and avoids wastage, which can prove expensive.

Marking out a centre point
A well-planned room will have equal-sized tiles at edges and corners, to give the area a symmetrical look. To achieve this effect, you should start in the centre of the area to be tiled. If you simply begin from a corner, you may end up with whole tiles on one side and narrow slivers on the other. So the first task is to find the centre of each side of the square or rectangle to be tiled, then snap a chalked stringline between both pairs of sides, to form a cross (page 64). Where the two lines intersect is the central starting point.

If the work area is of an irregular shape, it is usually better to line up the first row of tiles parallel with the wall opposite the main door. Snap a chalked stringline parallel with this wall, then, using a compass to scribe arcs, snap a second at right angles to the first. Finally, snap a third at right angles to the second, in the centre of the room. This cross gives the position of the first tile.

Working out the tiling sequence
It is best to tackle an area by dividing the job up into four segments sketched out by the chalklines. Fix the tiles diagonally across the square, to ensure that an equal number of cut

tiles of the same size will be needed at each of the borders around the edge of the area.

Work outwards in both directions from the first tile, to form a right angle and fill in the gaps as you go. If, however, the area is irregular, you may need to use a piece of wood to mark off the tile widths.

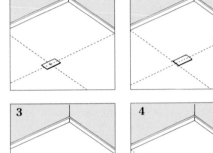

Where to place the first tile
The first tile may be laid in one of four positions:
1 *Centred on the cross,* **2** *Centred on a guide line,*
3 *In the right angle,* **4** *Centred on the other line.*
Before applying glue, plan out two rows of tiles at right angles to each other.

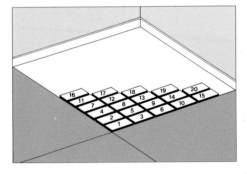

Tiling sequence
Work outwards in squares from the centre point, forming a right angle. Make sure that an equal number of cut tiles will be needed at each border.

FIXING FIBREBOARD CEILING TILES

If a ceiling is in poor condition, a new ceiling must be created before polystyrene tiles can be fixed. Tongued and grooved fibreboard tiles can be stapled directly on to 3in × 1in (75mm × 25mm) battens, nailed at right angles to the joists. Fix the battens at 12in or 24in (30cm or 60cm) intervals, so that the tile edges can be stapled through the flange of the groove into the batten. The tongue of the next tile then slides without difficulty into the groove of the first, and so on over the entire ceiling.

Fixing polystyrene tiles

These tiles can be fixed to any structurally sound ceiling, provided the surface is clean, dry and stripped of paper or flaking paint. They are suitable for any room, but are ideal in bathrooms, where condensation is likely. Since they provide good insulation, they also form a good lining to a ceiling without access from above. The normal starting point is in the centre of the ceiling, so find the mid-points of opposite walls and snap a chalked stringline in both directions. The position of a fluorescent light or the shape of the room, however, may mean that this point has to be shifted to even up the cut tiles at the edges.

Spread polystyrene adhesive all over the back of the first tile, then fix it so that its corner aligns with the crossing chalklines. Lay the remaining tiles by butting up their edges to adjacent tiles, and work progressively from the centre to the perimeter of the room. The tiles are lightweight and will stick firmly to the ceiling in seconds.

Polystyrene tiles can be painted with emulsion if you want a coloured ceiling. They

Securing tiles
Use a hardboard square, slightly larger than the tile, to press it into position. This will prevent your fingers from leaving small dents in the surface.

are awkward to paint, because of their texture and deep V-joints, so consider painting them a couple of days before fitting them to the ceiling. Remember, however, that you should never paint the tiles with gloss paint – it will constitute a fire risk. This problem does not arise with emulsion paint because it is water based.

Cutting polystyrene tiles

On most ceilings, a number of tiles will need to be cut to fit the edges. For straightforward edge tiles, place the tile to be cut exactly over the last full tile in the row. Then put a marker tile on top and jam it hard up against the wall. Using a pencil or ballpoint pen, trace its opposite edge on the tile to be cut; this will form the cutting line. Lay the tile to be cut on a piece of wood and score along the line with a sharp knife. The cut tile should then fit perfectly into the gap.

Extreme accuracy is less crucial where polystyrene cove is to be used to finish off the edges, since it should be wide enough to hide any marginal cutting faults (page 88). When cutting around an awkward shape, such as a ceiling rose, make a cardboard template and transfer its shape to the tile and cut with a sharp knife.

Cutting border tiles
Place the tile to be cut over the last full tile in the row. Holding a marker tile on top, pushed against the wall, trace a line along its opposite edge, then cut the tile with a sharp knife.

You should avoid using polystyrene tiles in the kitchen. Although they have good insulating properties and are lightweight and easy to use, they are also flammable.

Fixing polystyrene and cotton-fibre ceiling cove

Ceiling cove, fixed to the angle between the wall and the ceiling, will complement a tiled ceiling. It helps to take the squareness out of a room and hides cracks caused by the normal movement of a house.

There are three types of cove: plaster, polystyrene and cotton-fibre. Polystyrene cove is supplied in 3¼ft (1m) lengths, with special corner pieces for both external and internal corners.

Start by ensuring that the area to be covered is dry, clean and free from flaking paint and wallpaper. Then snap a chalked stringline on the wall as a horizontal guide line for the base of the cove. If you need to remove only a small strip of wallpaper from a papered wall, use a sharp knife and scrape off the paper dry. Do not use water, since it may loosen the remaining paper.

Brush a purpose-made adhesive on to the back of a corner piece and stick it in position. However, if either the wall or ceiling is uneven, use a thick, buttery ceramic-tile adhesive, to ensure that the cove grips firmly.

Continue fixing the straight pieces all along the wall, butting up the edges firmly. When cutting a length to fit, use a sharp knife against a steel straight-edge.

Working out from the corners

1 *Snap a horizontal chalked stringline on the wall for the lower guide line and trace the top line on the ceiling by holding the length in position. Then fix a glue-backed corner piece into place, following the guide lines. Leave to dry.*

2 *Apply adhesive to straight lengths and push the first carefully into position against the corner piece to form a neat butt joint. Continue fixing corners, then straight lengths, and use a sharp knife or fine-tooth saw to cut smaller lengths to fit.*

Fixing plaster ceiling cove

Prepare the wall and ceiling as for polystyrene cove. Go around the room, cutting lengths to fit, and tap nails above and below each piece for temporary support. Corner pieces are available, but if these are not used, the end of the cove must be mitred at internal and external corners. A paper template is usually supplied with the cove. This is placed on the cove and the angle of the cut line marked out for an internal or external corner. Use a fine-tooth saw to cut the cove and a saw or sharp knife when mitring corners. Any rough edges can be smoothed off with sandpaper.

Mix up plaster cove adhesive to a creamy consistency, and lay it thickly on to the back of the cove. Press the length into place. Use any emerging excess adhesive immediately to fill gaps at the edges or between the lengths and clean away the rest of the adhesive with a wet brush before it starts to dry. When the adhesive has set properly – usually after about 24 hours – the cove can be painted with emulsion paint.

Mitring corners

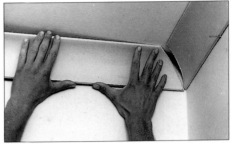

1 *Use the template supplied with the cove to mark off a corner mitre. Cut it with a sharp knife and smooth off the edge with sandpaper.*

2 *Spread a thick layer of adhesive on to the cove and push it into position. Tap in a support nail. Fill gaps with adhesive and wipe away the excess.*

Marking out a wall for tiling

It is unusual to be able to tile a wall without having to cut some tiles for the edges of the work. So, to ensure equal-sized border tiles, plan out the job carefully. The simplest way is to mark out your tile widths on a piece of wood, say 6½ft (2m) long. By holding the wood horizontally and vertically on a wall, you will quickly see how the tiles will end up. Since only a very few rooms can claim to have perfectly true corners, window and door frames, these cannot be used as a guide for the first row of vertical tiles. Likewise, skirtings cannot be used as a horizontal base. Instead you must establish a vertical pencil line, using a plumb line (page 64), and set up a true horizontal, using a spirit level, by nailing a wooden batten to the foot of the wall. This will form a base for the first course of whole tiles. Cut tiles should fall along the skirting. Try to avoid using cut tiles for the top row of tiles, unless the ceiling is crooked, because they are much more obvious in this position.

Fixing mirror tiles

Before applying these tiles, check that the surface is sound, dry and level. If it is of porous material, such as plaster or wood, seal it with a coat of oil-based paint, but do not use vinyl gloss. Leave it to dry for 72 hours. Remove any wallpaper from the area to be tiled, and if the walls are cold, heat the room first to ensure that the tabs adhere firmly; newly plastered walls must be allowed to dry out. The tiles must be perfectly aligned to achieve a good result, so mark guide lines. If the sticky tabs used to fix the tiles are not already attached, they will have to be bought separately. Avoid other adhesives: they may cause discoloration. Mirror tiles do not need grouting.

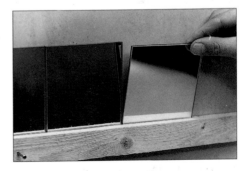

Applying the tiles to the wall
Use a sheet of chipboard or plywood to ensure that the wall is flat before starting: an uneven surface will distort the reflection. Place the tiles in horizontal rows from the bottom of the wall up. Leave a narrow gap between each one.

How to apply ceramic wall tiles

Having established vertical and horizontal guide lines, the outlined area can be filled with whole tiles. The tiles are applied in horizontal rows from the bottom up, working in areas of 10ft² (1m²). When the tiles have been in position for 24 hours, the horizontal batten can be removed and the borders filled with tiles cut to size. If plastic spacers have been used, remove them at this stage. After 24 hours the joins between the tiles are grouted. Finally, the tiles are sponged clean and, when dry, are polished with a clean cloth.

Laying the first block of tiles

1 *Begin at a lower corner. Smooth a layer of adhesive over about 10ft² (1m²) of wall with a trowel. Draw a notched spreader horizontally over the area.*

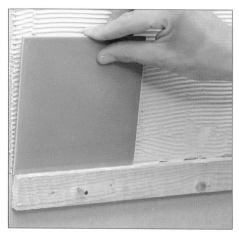

2 *Place the first tile on the batten, lined up against the vertical line, and press it firmly into the adhesive with a slight twist. Lay the tiles in horizontal strips.*

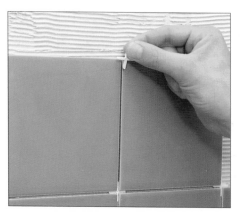

3 *If the tiles are self-spacing, butt them up closely so that the lugs are touching. If not, insert plastic spacers for uniform grouting lines.*

4 *Check that the tiles are straight, using a spirit level, and adjust as necessary. Spread adhesive over the adjacent 10ft² (1m²) area and repeat.*

Cutting ceramic tiles

You may need to cut tiles for the borders. There are various tile-cutting gadgets available, some incorporating a measuring and marking gauge. A regular tile cutter has a sharp tungsten-carbide tip, which scores through the glaze so that the tile can be snapped in half along the score line. Another type of tile cutter contains a small wheel to score the glaze, and jaws to hold and break the tile evenly.

When cutting tiles for borders, push the tile to be cut up against the wall and measure it against the gap, then mark it with a pencil. Score a line through the glazed side. If using a regular cutter, put two matchsticks beneath it and press down firmly on each side. With the clamp-like cutter, simply squeeze the tile between the jaws. Smooth down the rough edges with a tile file.

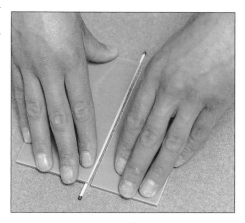

Breaking the tile
Having scored the glaze, place the tile on a flat surface and position two matchsticks under it, one at each end of the scored line. Press firmly down on each side. If you are using a clamp-like cutter, squeeze the tile between the jaws.

Shaping ceramic tiles

Where a specially shaped tile is needed, make a cardboard template of the shape you want and then transfer it to the tile. To cut out an L-shape around a switch, for example, a pattern of the shape is traced on to the tile. The tile is then scored deeply and evenly along the cutting line. To break up the glaze, criss-cross shapes are scored through the waste portion of the tile. These can then be chipped away with tile clippers or ordinary pincers. A tile saw will almost certainly be needed if slivers of the tile less than ½in (12mm) have to be cut. To cut around pipes, the tile is split in two and an arc is nibbled from each half. Alternatively, use a tile saw.

Cutting an L-shape

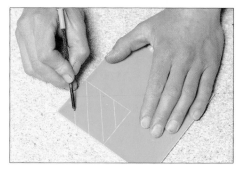

1 *Either use a tile saw or make a template of the shape and trace the lines on to the tile. Score deeply along the lines with a tile cutter, to pierce the glaze.*

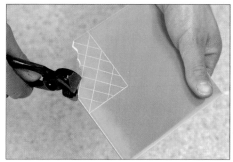

2 *Then score criss-cross lines through the segment to be cut and clip it off in small pieces. Trim to the deeply scored lines, then smooth the edges.*

Grouting ceramic tiles

When the tiles have been in place for about 48 hours, fill the joints with grouting cement. Grout is sold ready-mixed, but it is more economical to use powdered grout to which you add water and mix until it forms a creamy consistency. Coloured grout is also available – ready-mixed, as a dye to be added to the powder, or as a paint to be applied to the joints over old grouting. Use waterproof grout where appropriate and for tiled worktops, where dirt and germs will need to be washed off regularly. Prepare only a little at a time; it dries quickly.

Applying the grout

1 *Use a small piece of damp sponge and work the grout well down into the cracks between the tiles.*

2 *When the area is covered, draw a small, rounded stick into each joint to press the grouting tightly home.*

Fixing accessories

Tile accessories, such as towel rings, soap dishes and toothbrush holders, are either screw-fixed or glued to the wall. Those with a ceramic base the size of one or two tiles are fixed using standard tile adhesive.

Fix one or two tiles (the size of the accessory base) lightly in position. After 48 hours remove the tiles, butter adhesive on the back of the accessory and push it into place. Secure it in place for 48 hours, using adhesive tape. Finally, remove the tape and fill the joint around the edges with grout.

To fix a screw into ceramic tiles, use a masonry drill bit and a power drill. Do not attempt to drill straight into a tile, as the bit may slide around. Stick adhesive tape over the hole position, then drill.

Finishing off

To prevent water from seeping behind baths, basins and sinks, run a bead of silicone rubber sealant along the edges. This will remain flexible and so keep the gap permanently sealed despite any movement.

At external corners plastic beading forms a neat, rounded finish to the edge tiles. The beading is bedded well down into the adhesive with the larger lip resting on the sill edge. The last course of tiles on the sill then butts up against the rounded lip. Cut tiles on a window sill should lie at the back of the sill.

If a wall has been half-tiled over existing tiles, the top rim needs to be smoothed off. The gap between wall and tiles can be filled with hardwood beading – either plain or L-shaped – which will need varnishing.

 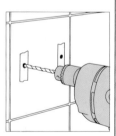  

Adhesive fixing
Glue the accessory to the tile and secure it with tape until set.

Screw fixing
Using a masonry bit, screw holes through the tape to avoid slipping.

Smooth edging
A sealant around baths and basins makes the joins waterproof.

Over-tiling
Add plastic beading to external corners for a neat finish.

Fixing mosaic tiles

Ceramic mosaic tiles are supplied as a sheet on a mesh backing and fixed to the wall with normal tile adhesive. Since the sheets may be as large as 13in × 20in (33cm × 50cm), the main area of wall should be completed quickly, leaving borders and awkward shapes until last. As with normal tiles, meticulous planning and preparation are essential, and horizontal and vertical guide lines should be marked (page 86). Having spread adhesive on the wall, press the sheets firmly into place, ensuring that any arrows on the back face the same way. To fit into corners and around obstacles, cut pieces to the required shape and fix them to the gap. If protective paper covers the face of the tiling sheets, leave it on until they are securely fixed, then finish the job by grouting neatly between the joints. Any small gaps may be filled with grout.

Fitting border pieces

1 *When the main area of the wall is covered by whole sheets, smaller pieces can be cut for the borders and to fit around obstacles. Measure the width and length of the area to be filled, then turn the sheet upside down and mark cutting lines on the back. Using a sharp knife, slice through the mesh backing.*

2 *Apply adhesive to the wall and fix the strip in place. Make sure that the border piece is perfectly aligned with the adjacent sheet. If any small gaps remain at the edge, break off individual tiles from the sheet with a tile cutter and slot them into the space. You should not need to break whole tiles.*

Fixing cork wall tiles

Check that the wall is flat, smooth and dry before applying cork tiles. You should unwrap the tiles 24 hours before use to allow them to acclimatize. Fix a horizontal batten to the wall as a guide for the first row of tiles, draw a vertical guide line and proceed as for ceramic tiles (page 90).

Using a special cork-tile adhesive, press the tiles firmly on to the wall and butt joint them closely. If you find that a tile has to be cut, make sure that you place it on a completely flat surface and use a very sharp knife held against a steel straight-edge.

If the tiles are not pre-finished, apply a couple of coats of varnish sealer with a clean brush to leave an easy-to-clean surface. Allow the first coat to dry before adding the second. Where cork tiling is taken up to external corners, such as fireplaces, the exposed edges can be protected from scuffing and chipping with wooden beading.

Fixing brick wall tiles

The secret of success with brick tiles lies in the careful planning of a realistic pattern. The easiest way to plan the first few courses of brick is to draw them on to the wall. Butter the adhesive on the back of each tile, using a trowel, and press the tile firmly on to the wall. As you lay each tile, insert spacers.

To achieve an authentic look, you will probably have to cut several bricks. Use either an electric grinder or circular power saw fitted with a masonry disc, or, though the method is slower, a tungsten-carbide rod saw fitted into a hacksaw frame.

When the tiles have been in place for 24 hours, remove the spacers and fill the joints with mortar or pointing compound. Use a small pointing trowel, taking care not to stain the bricks. If you prefer to avoid the labour of pointing, paint the wall with grey emulsion before fixing the brick tiles. Make sure that the paint is thoroughly dry before tiling.

Arranging the tiles

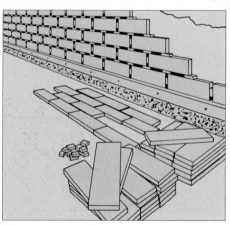

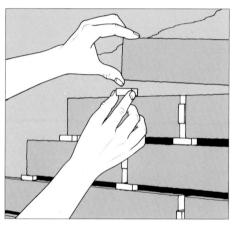

1 *Lay out several rows of tiles on the floor to work out the most realistic brick-bond pattern and pencil the pattern on the wall as a guide. Stagger the joins to imitate a brick wall, and, where available, use L-shaped corner tiles for authenticity.*

2 *To prevent the tiles from slipping, insert small pieces of wood, about ³⁄₈in (9mm) thick, between courses. Alternatively, saw up slabs of polystyrene packing material into small blocks. After 24 hours remove the spacers and fill the joints with pointing.*

How to lay ceramic floor tiles

The floor must be flat, dry, clean and stable before ceramic tiles are fitted. Timber floors should be well ventilated below and strong enough to support the tiling. The easiest way to provide a sound surface is to use either ½in (12mm) exterior-grade chipboard or ½in (12mm) plywood screwed to the floor at 12in (30cm) intervals. To ensure a good bond between the tiles and the floor, brush a primer over the whole floor and allow it to become "touch dry" before laying the tiles. For information on where to start, see page 86.

Always start in the middle of the room and work outwards. If you begin tiling against one skirting, the tiles running along the adjacent wall will not run square. So mark the centre point, adjusting it to leave at least half-tile widths at each skirting. Test the height of the tiles against the door. If thick tiles are to be used, the door may not open. Either remove the door and trim its lower edge, or fix rising butt hinges so that the door rises as it opens.

Ceramic floor-tile adhesive is supplied in large plastic buckets and should be prepared and applied according to the manufacturer's instructions. It is normal to stir the adhesive thoroughly and pour a thin layer over an area of about 10ft² (1m²) at a time.

Press and twist each tile into position so that it is well bedded down. When the first 10ft² (1m²) is complete, clean away any surplus adhesive from the face of the tiles and clean out the joints, ready for grouting later. Grout when the tiles have been in place for 24 hours.

GROUTING TILES

Grout the tiles after they have been laid about 24 hours. If you grout before the adhesive has set, you may dislodge the tiles.

Before you begin grouting, remove the spacers between the tiles. You can fill in any gaps, but wait at least another 24 hours before doing so. When the grout has set – it takes a couple of hours – wipe the new floor with a damp cloth or sponge. Do not walk on the freshly laid tiles for 48 hours or you may dislodge them. Rinse the floor when the grout is thoroughly dry, if necessary.

Fixing whole tiles

1 *First ensure that the floor is clean and level, and if it is wooden, apply a coat of primer. Spread waterproof adhesive on the floor and follow your planned order of working (page 86).*

2 *Bed each tile firmly into place with a pressing and twisting movement. Use chalked guide lines for positioning and work outward in both directions. Use spacer lugs if the tiles are not self-spacing.*

Cutting and fixing border tiles

 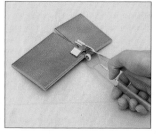 

1 *Lay the tile to be cut exactly over the last whole tile and half-cover them both with a marker tile butted up against a spacer at the wall. Trace the non-wall edge on the tile.*

2 *Using a steel straight-edge, score along the line with a cutting knife, then snap the tile with heavy-duty tile cutters. Smooth off rough edges with a tile file.*

3 *Comb adhesive on to the back of the cut tile and carefully slot it into the gap. Continue cutting and fitting until no gaps remain, then grout between the spaces.*

Laying vinyl and plastic floor tiles

Preparing vinyl and plastic floor tiles
When you are ready to lay the tile, peel off the protective backing.

Most vinyl tiles are self-adhesive. The protective paper covering the adhesive on the backing should not be removed until the tile is ready to lay. If the tile is not self-adhesive, spread vinyl-tile adhesive over about 10ft² (1m²) of the floor and cover it with tiles before applying adhesive to the next area. Always lay the tiles in the correct order (page 86) and butt up the edges closely, taking care to press down each tile firmly all over to ensure that it is well secured in the adhesive. Do not use the twisting movement as for ceramic tiles (page 95), or the adhesive will be squeezed up between the tiles.

At borders, mark and cut the tiles, taking care to match the design of any patterns. Cut edge tiles in the same way as border ceiling tiles (page 87). Place the tile to be cut over the last full tile in the row, then put a marking tile on top, with its edge hard up against the skirting. Using a marker, draw the opposite edge of the marking tile on the tile to be cut. Then cut along the line with scissors or a sharp knife held against a straight-edge.

For awkward shapes, such as around door architraves or pipes, make a cardboard template and transfer the shape on to the tile. When cutting a hole for a pipe, make a slit from

the cut-out hole to the tile edge; it will then run from the back of the pipe to the skirting and be barely visible. If the outline is curved, use wire solder to trace around the curve. Then transfer it to the tile to be shaped.

With marbled or grained vinyl or plastic tiles, lay them so that the pattern in adjacent tiles runs in opposite directions. This gives variation and emphasizes the tiling itself. Align the tiles correctly first time. If they are relaid, the adhesive weakens.

Cutting an L-shaped tile

1 *One side of the L-shape will need to be the same width as adjacent border tiles. Use a marker tile to trace the gap between the skirting and the last whole tile.*

2 *Then move the tile around the corner and, in the same way, scribe the outline of the gap to be filled on to the tile. This line represents the second "leg" of the "L".*

3 *Cut along the scribed lines, then apply adhesive to the floor and fit the tile into place, so that it aligns accurately with neighbouring tiles. Alternatively, use a template.*

Laying cork floor tiles

Ensure that the surface is free of dust and dirt. Cork tiles are laid in the same way as vinyl tiles (opposite) but they need a cork adhesive. Spread the adhesive over an area of about 10ft^2 (1m^2) at a time. If the tiles are to be taken up to exposed edges, they should be protected with wooden beading.

To cut cork tiles, use a straight-edge and a very sharp knife, otherwise the cork will crumble. Some cork tiles are supplied ready-sealed and waxed or coated with protective vinyl film and need no further treatment. Those sold without a protective finish need to be sealed with wax or polyurethane before the room is used. Several coats are needed. When applying the sealant, make sure that you keep the room well ventilated.

Shaping cork tiles
Use a template to trace the shape of architraves and other awkward areas.

Planning patterns with floor tiles

A patterned tiled floor is a versatile and easy way of adding colour and variety to a room (see also pages 82–3). Creating patterns with floor tiles is easy, and the resulting effects can be very striking. A simple arrangement of black and white tiles, for example, can make a bold statement. However, bear in mind that solid colours such as black and white can be more difficult to maintain, since they show stains and marks more clearly than tiles with an overall pattern or textured surface. With vinyl tiles, some colours – such as pale pastels – often have a tendency to fade if they are constantly exposed to strong sunlight.

To plan a simple, two-colour chess-board pattern, such as that shown at the top of page 83, first estimate the number of tiles as for a single colour (page 84). Divide the total by 2, and buy equal amounts of each colour.

For more complex patterns, use graph paper to plan the tile arrangement – each square on the paper being equivalent to one tile. Shade in the different colours, then count up the amount of each colour needed.

SOME FINAL TIPS FOR LAYING TILES

● Be careful not to apply too much adhesive when laying any sort of vinyl tiles.
● Do not leave any gaps between vinyl tiles; instead, make sure that you butt them up close together.
● Grouting material must be compatible with both the tile and the setting material.
● Use a suitable type of grout for areas which often get wet, such as kitchens and bathrooms.
● Allow new plaster to cure for at least a month before laying any tiles over it.
● Seal weak parts in a plaster wall with shellac.
● Support wallboards and sub-floors firmly, so that there are no loose or springy sections.
● Clean sound walls with a strong detergent and sand them to aid adhesion before tiling.
● If tiling directly over a sheet of plywood, use the exterior, waterproof grade, as the interior grade of plywood is thinner, and will not be strong enough to support a layer of tiles.
● When laying self-adhesive tiles, do not remove the protective backing from the tiles until you are ready to stick them down permanently.
● You need to be particularly careful not to take up self-adhesive tiles once you have laid them, since any relaying will weaken the adhesive, causing the tiles to loosen, so that they do not stick properly.

CHAPTER FOUR

FLOORING

New flooring is a major furnishing decision. The type of flooring you choose will depend upon the function of the room, the durability of the materials used, the look you want to achieve and the price you want to pay.

Wooden floors have a warmth, colour and subtlety of texture that cannot be matched by imitations. They look rich, are hardwearing, blend with both traditional and modern furnishings and are comparable in price with other floor coverings. A sanded floor is a cheap alternative to a new wooden floor. With a stained and sealed finish, it can add a touch of style to any room in the house. Wooden floors of all types are best for areas where there is little damp. Hardwood floors can be laid in kitchens and bathrooms, but they are not the most suitable types of flooring.

Sheet vinyl is a durable, easy-to-clean and attractive floor covering, particularly suited to kitchens and bathrooms. Once laid, it needs little attention, except sweeping and occasional washing and polishing. It makes an excellent waterproof barrier and is softer, quieter, cheaper and less slippery than tiles. Carpeting provides luxury underfoot – it is warm, comfortable, sound-proofing and comes in a wide range of colours, patterns and qualities to suit most rooms in the house. Matting is a budget-priced alternative to carpets – useful for rented flats and if you are planning to move house soon.

Wooden surfaces

Wood forms a warm, smooth and attractive surface. It is extremely durable, has acoustic and insulating properties and is easy to maintain. Most wooden flooring is solid hardwood laid over an ordinary sub-floor, such as chipboard, plywood or hardboard. Some types, however, consist of a hardwood layer bonded to a plywood backing. Flooring comes as either long strips of wood (woodstrip) or blocks arranged into patterns (woodblock or mosaic panels). Woodblocks can be arranged into a variety of patterns, and basketweave mosaic panels can be laid square or diagonally across the room.

Comparing types of wooden flooring

Wooden flooring receives a lot of wear and tear, and the timbers need to be durable. The availability of timbers for different floor types varies. Mahogany and oak, for example, are usually only available for mosaic panels, while ash and beech are generally only found as woodstrip flooring, but all are durable. Prices of timbers vary, and merbau, the most hard-wearing, costs a little more than oak and ash. Beech and maple are less expensive. In parquet flooring, all timbers cost the same, but ordinary parquet costs a third of the price of pre-finished parquet. In the mosaic panel range, merbau again is the most costly, followed by iroko and dark oak; eucalyptus is about three-quarters of the price of merbau. However, all reputable brands of flooring are hard-wearing, so do not hesitate to buy a cheaper kind if the colour and grain are right for your needs.

Protecting hardwoods

Everyone knows about the threat to the world's rainforests, but we do not always realize that our own consumption of hardwoods can make a difference. A large proportion of hardwood is imported from tropical countries. Much of this is valuable timber such as teak, mahogany, iroko and ramin. Only a very tiny proportion of these woods come from plantations which are managed in the proper way. At the present rate, less than one-third of the rainforests will be left by the year 2000.

Until there is an agreed policy about the production and use of hardwoods, it is better to avoid them altogether. A small but increasing number of importers and retailers are using hardwoods from ecologically sound sources. Look for the Good Wood seal of approval. A list of approved sources of hardwoods is available from Friends of the Earth.

TIPS ON BUYING TIMBER

• Many DIY shops and most supermarkets and hardware stores sell timber boards, pre-cut in packs, complete with a coverage guide. Always check that there is a good mixture of light and dark grains.
• Timber merchants sell wood planed and ready-cut to standard sizes, and most will cut hardwood to a special size if you give them a few days' notice.

• Timber merchants are often cheaper than DIY shops, especially for larger quantities, and will usually give good advice.
• Before buying, check timber for defects and avoid any that is bowed, cupped, twisted or heavily knotted. It will be impossible to straighten a distorted board. A few knots can look attractive, but always check that they are sound.

• Prices vary according to the outlet and the availability of timber, so shop around.
• Wherever possible, try to buy only timber from properly managed plantations. That way you will be encouraging the production of ecologically sound hardwoods. Timbers from these types of plantations are usually clearly labelled with the Good Wood seal of approval.

Tools and equipment

For most jobs you will need at least one hammer and one saw. A number of other items will be required, depending on the job you are doing. As well as the tools illustrated, a bolster chisel is invaluable for levering up floorboards. For sanding wooden floorboards, you need to hire equipment. If you are unfamiliar with any of the tools, you should practise first on spare pieces of wood, to avoid making expensive mistakes on the real thing.

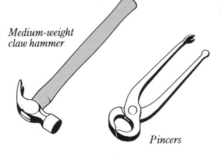

Chisel

Block plane

Mallet

Saws
For cutting along the tongue before lifting floorboards, you will need a circular power saw. A hand saw designed specifically for floorboards is also available. It has a blade with a curved end to make it easier to start the cut. A circular saw with a tungsten-carbide blade should be used for cutting chipboard, which blunts normal blades quickly. A power jigsaw is useful if you want to cut across floorboards, but you can use a pad saw. You will need a drill to make starting holes before using these saws. Most need a hole about $\frac{1}{2}$in (12mm) in diameter. For intricate cuts – for example, when you are laying flooring round obstructions – use a coping saw, while you can use a tenon saw for trimming by hand.

Medium-weight claw hammer

Pincers

Other equipment
A pair of pincers is useful for removing old carpet tacks and nails. You will need a medium-weight or a lighter claw hammer for most flooring work. For hammering down nails, use a nail punch. Some form of lever is needed for taking up floorboards. A bolster chisel is good for this, and you may also find a strong length of steel useful. Use a block plane when filling gaps between floorboards with thin strips of wood. A mallet and chisel can be used to chip away wood from the underside of a new floorboard, so that it matches older surrounding boards, and for jobs like taking out damaged blocks in a parquet floor.

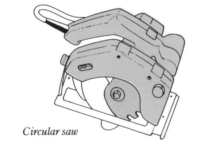

Circular saw

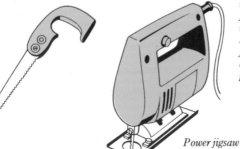

Pad saw

Power jigsaw

Wooden sub-floors

There are various materials which can be used as a basis for the flooring proper. One of the most common is chipboard, which consists of resin-coated woodchips compressed under heat and pressure into a board. Standard chipboard is usually used as a sub-floor, but an extra-strong type with tongue-and-groove edges can be used as a top floor covering.

Plywood is composed of thin sheets of wood glued together. There are two basic types of plywood: timber ply, which is made from a single type of timber and is used as a sub-floor; and veneered ply, which is made from a variety of woods and can be used as a substitute for timber flooring. Tongue-and-groove plywood is available for this purpose and the wood is graded according to the quality of the surface veneer and the glue. There are also special surface finishes, such as plastic, metal and varnish. For exterior use, choose boards made with moisture- and weather-proof glue.

Hardboard is made from pulped wood fibre, hot-pressed into thin sheets and, since it bends easily, it is generally used as a sub-floor over timber boards. There are a variety of types, but standard and water-resistant tempered hardboard are usual floor coverings. Standard hardboard has one smooth face and a textured back. Medium hardboard has a softer surface for lining walls and ceilings. Double-faced and plastic-coated hardboards are also available.

Fitting new floorboards

You may have to cut new boards along their length to make them fit a long, narrow gap in a floor. A bench-mounted circular saw is useful for making these long, straight cuts.

The new boards may not be exactly the same thickness as those that make up the rest of the floor. If they are slightly too thin, use pieces of wood as packing between the boards and joists. If the new boards are too thick, make them thinner at the joist positions. Make two parallel saw cuts in the joist and chisel out the wood between them.

You can fix most of the boards with 2½in (63mm) cut floor brads or lost-head nails. Screw down any boards that may have to be lifted in the future.

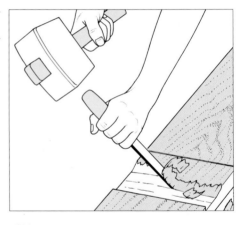

Chiselling away thick boards
Chisel away the wood between the two cuts until the boards lie at the same height as the original ones.

STAINING WOODEN FLOORS

There are three basic types of stain: water-based, oil-based and spirit-based.

Oil-based stains are applied with a rag or brush. Rub them in both with and across the grain. If the colour is too light, wait a little longer before wiping it off (but do not let it dry out). Apply a second coat after about 24 hours. If an oil-based stain does dry out, use turpentine and a clean rag to wipe it off.

Water-based stains are applied by spraying or with a sponge or rag. They dry quickly. Apply the first coat a shade lighter than you want the finished result. Then apply a second coat to darken it to the required shade. Mix enough to complete the whole job, since matching a second batch to the first will be difficult. Spirit-based stains are not as long-lasting as the other types. They can be diluted with solvent if required. Spray, brush or wipe them on. Wear gloves and do not smoke when using them.

When staining a floor, complete whole boards at a time. Work towards the door so that you can get out.

Woodstrip flooring

The most common varieties of woodstrip flooring are hardwood and plywood. Hardwood woodstrip consists of solid tongue-and-groove boards about ¾in (19mm) thick and in random lengths which slot together to form narrow floorboards. They are laid at right angles to the sub-floor and come in a range of solid timbers to form a luxurious floor. Some woodstrip floors are made from plywood strips overlaid with hardwood. The strips are either slotted together with tongues and grooves, allowing them to "float" on the sub-floor as one piece, or the plywood has interlocking "ears" which are pinned to the floor. The floor thickness can vary from ⅓in (8mm) to ½in (12mm) overall.

Bitumen-cork underlay is a coarse paper, impregnated with bitumen and coated with cork chips. It is used as an underlay for parquet panels.

Woodblock flooring

The most popular types of woodblock flooring are wood mosaic panels and parquet panels. Wood mosaic panels are made up of five or seven hardwood "fingers" in four parts (20 or 28 pieces overall), which are glued together on a bitumen-felt backing. The panels are usually either 12in (30cm) or 18½in (47cm) square and the individual "fingers" in each panel are arranged to build up a basketweave pattern. This type of floor usually requires sanding and sealing after laying. Some hardwood mosaic floors are supplied tongued-and-grooved, pre-sealed and finished in rigid panels, which are strengthened with soft aluminium pins or a plywood backing.

A parquet panel floor consists of shallow hardwood blocks which are interlocked with tongues and grooves into panels, to create a flat, solid surface. Traditional blocks can be laid in a variety of patterns – usually basketweave, but also traditional herringbone, brick-pattern and others. Unlike wood mosaic panels, parquet panels are pre-finished and simply float on an underlay of bitumen paper and cork granules. Traditional parquet blocks, however, are not tongue-and-groove and must be both sanded and sealed after laying.

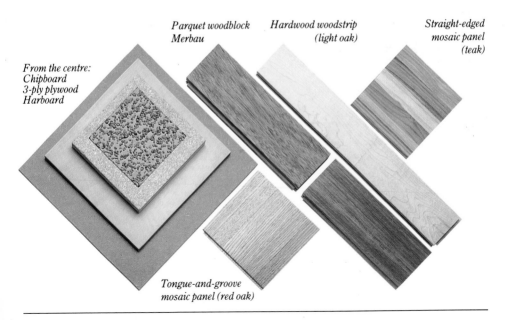

Parquet woodblock Merbau

Hardwood woodstrip (light oak)

Straight-edged mosaic panel (teak)

From the centre:
Chipboard
3-ply plywood
Harboard

Tongue-and-groove mosaic panel (red oak)

How to remove and re-lay floorboards

If a wooden floor is badly damaged or unsound, it is best to lift and re-lay the whole floor. Floorboards can have either square or tongue-and-groove edges, which are harder to lift up.

Before you begin to lift either type, look for screwed-down boards. These are easy to lift and will tell you what types of board make up your floor. Re-laying boards is straightforward. The main problem is getting them as close together as possible. Use a pair of wooden wedges to press together the floorboards before nailing them down.

Removing square-edged floorboards

1 *Insert a strong bolster chisel or a metal lever into the gaps between the boards. Prise up each one, starting close to a convenient board end. Providing it is strong, a long lever is easier to use.*

2 *Lift up the board until you can insert another chisel or lever on the opposite side. Then work both levers along the board until it is free. If the board is very stiff, enlist a helper at this stage.*

3 *To help loosen the board, place another lever under the floorboard, resting it on the adjacent boards. Press down on the free end and this will force it up. Move the lever along and repeat.*

Removing tongue-and-groove boards
Start by cutting through the tongue by sawing along the length of the board. Use a circular saw, set to cut about ¹/₂in (12mm) deep. This will leave a small gap which will need to be filled later. Alternatively, you can use a floorboard saw.

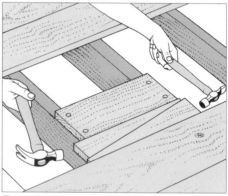

Re-laying floorboards
To ensure that you press the boards tightly together, use a pair of wedges made by cutting two pieces of board to a tapering shape. Lay four or five adjacent boards in position and nail a length of wood temporarily to the joists a short distance from the boards. Hammer the wedges into place between the boards and the fixed length of wood. This will tighten the boards. You can then nail them in place before removing the wedges and the temporary piece of wood. Use short nails to fix the temporary block, to save time and effort.

Removing boards by cutting

If you want to lift only a short length of floorboard, or release a long board that is trapped under the skirting, it may be necessary to cut across the boards before levering them up. This may also be a helpful method for taking up tongue-and-groove boards. First locate the joists which support the floorboards by inserting a knife blade between the boards. Avoid cutting through the joists – cut alongside one of them. They will extend 1in (25mm) to 1½in (40mm) on each side of the nails. Mark a cutting line to one side of a joist, cut through the board with a jigsaw and lift it out.

Cutting and lifting square-edged floorboards

 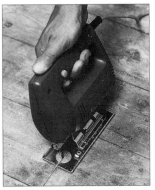 

1 *Find the joists, then drill a ½in (12mm) hole to take the saw at a position close to the joist edge. Draw a line along the joist edge.*

2 *Cut along the line with a power jigsaw or a hand pad saw, tilting the top of the blade slightly towards the centre of the joist.*

3 *This will create a chamfered edge, so that the board is supported when you replace it. Lift up the board, using a bolster chisel.*

Replacing skirting

If you need to replace skirting, you should use the method that was employed when the original boards were fitted. If the wall is made of solid bricks, the skirting boards may be attached directly to the wall with masonry pins or nailed to wooden blocks fixed to the wall. Pins should be long enough to penetrate the wall by ¾in (19mm). If the wall is a partition type, fix the skirting with nails that pass through the plasterboard to the uprights of the frame. In older buildings the boards are often nailed to wooden blocks. These may be set into the mortar joints between the bricks or simply nailed to the wall surface. With this type of construction you should attach new blocks to the wall using screws and wallplugs. You can then nail the skirting boards to the blocks.

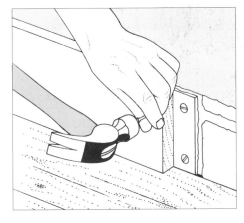

Fixing skirting to a masonry wall
Attach wooden blocks to masonry walls with screws and wallplugs and nail the new skirting board to these with masonry pins, avoiding the screws.

Sanded floors

A sanded floor is a cheap alternative to other types of wooden flooring. Stained and sealed, it can transform a room by giving it a rich, warm, yet polished look, which can complement a wide range of decorations and furnishings.

Make sure that all the boards are securely fixed. Look for split, damaged or badly patched boards and replace them. If the floor is badly damaged, or if there are a lot of gaps between the boards, it is better to take them up and re-lay them. Remove any nails or carpet tacks with pincers. If the nails that fix the boards to the joists protrude, hammer them well in, or they will tear the sanding belt. Use a nail punch to drive them well in.

Sanding equipment and abrasives

The main item that you will need for sanding floorboards is an industrial floor sander. This will enable you to sand the main part of the floor. You will also need a smaller sander for the edges. You can hire both from tool-hire shops, which will also supply abrasives. One day's hire should give you plenty of time to prepare a large room. You will also need a dust mask, a nail punch and hammer, pincers for pulling out protruding tacks and nails, and a hand scraper for corners. Use a dust mask even if the sander has a dust bag.

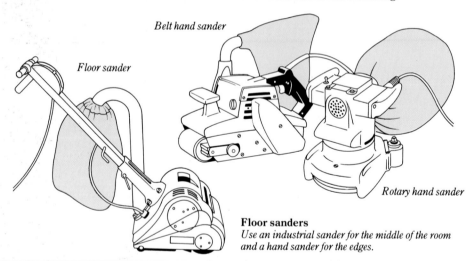

Belt hand sander

Floor sander

Rotary hand sander

Floor sanders
Use an industrial sander for the middle of the room and a hand sander for the edges.

Securing loose floorboards

It is worth lifting loose floorboards to see if the joists beneath are also moving. Sometimes, particularly in old houses, joist ends work loose where they are built into the walls. If this has happened, pack the hole with pieces of slate secured with mortar. Alternatively, support them on steel joist hangers. These are special galvanized steel supports, which must be firmly screwed to the wall. The joist ends then slot into them.

If the joist ends have rotted, either replace the affected joists or call in a flooring specialist to make the repairs. Secure loose boards by renailing them with 2½in (63mm) cut floor brads, or by screwing them down.

Decorative effects with sanded floorboards

Even the simplest of wooden floors can have a powerful influence on the character of a room. Floorboards that have been sanded, sealed and polished can give a room an atmosphere of luxury, especially when combined with other polished wood surfaces and matching rugs and carpets. A natural-coloured stain can bring out the richness of colour in the wood, bringing warmth and tone to the room.

But floorboards can also blend well with a simple decorative scheme, complementing a cottage interior. Because they wear well and are easy to clean and maintain, they are especially appropriate for living rooms, halls, passages and other areas of the home that have to stand up to heavy use. If you put rugs on the floorboards, make sure that they are non-slip, particularly in passages.

Rich, warm tones
In this children's room the natural wood colours of the door, window frame, cornice and floor harmonize to create a warm atmosphere. A wooden floor has other advantages – it is hard-wearing and easy to clean. Use only non-slip rugs in a children's room.

Sanding a floor

After you have prepared the floor, sand the main area with a large floor sander. Start with medium or coarse abrasive on the machine's drum, to strip away the surface, before changing to a finer grade to get a smoother finish. You will not be able to get right up to the edges of the room with the large sander, so use a hand sander for these areas. With both machines, work in a direction parallel to the boards, overlapping each pass by a few inches. Even a hand sander cannot get right into the corners of a room, so you will have to finish off these small areas, together with places where there are other obstructions to the sander, using a simple hand scraper.

Although sanders have dust-collecting bags, these are not capable of picking up all the dust. So when you have finished sanding, vacuum the floor thoroughly. Then clean it carefully with a damp cloth and leave the surface to dry completely before sealing it.

Using sanding machines

 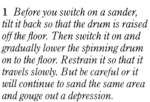

1 *Before you switch on a sander, tilt it back so that the drum is raised off the floor. Then switch it on and gradually lower the spinning drum on to the floor. Restrain it so that it travels slowly. But be careful or it will continue to sand the same area and gouge out a depression.*

2 *Work the machine forwards and backwards in the same direction as the floorboards. Overlap each pass by about 3in (75mm). Keep the cable out of the way by running it over your shoulder. If the floor is very uneven, make the first few passes at 45° to the boards.*

3 *Start working parallel to the boards when you switch to finer paper. Never run a sander at right angles to the boards – it will not even out the bumps. When you have sanded the main floor area, finish the edges with a hand sander and the corners with a hand scraper.*

SEALING FLOORBOARDS

When you have sanded a floor, you need to protect its surface so that it will resist wear. Make sure that the floor is perfectly clean and dry, then apply the first coat of seal. Use a pad made from lint-free cloth, rubbing it well into the floor. As soon as the surface has dried (which will take about 12 hours), apply another coat. Do not spread it too thickly, and brush it out well. After another 12 hours apply a third coat, and, within a further 24-hour period, perhaps a fourth. Applying the seal at these intervals will ensure that each coat bonds closely with the previous one. Once you have sealed the floor, you should not have to worry about it again. Cover it with rugs or matting.

TIPS FOR SANDING

• Hammer all nails well below the surface before you start, to avoid damaging the sander.
• Use only sanders designed for floors – an electric drill with a sanding attachment is not sufficient for the job.
• Let the drum sander move along the floor as soon as you lower it into position – if you do not let it move, it will make an indentation in the floor that is impossible to repair.
• For floors in poor condition, start by sanding at 45° to the floorboards before sanding parallel with the boards.
• Do not sand at right angles to the floorboards – the sander will not even out the surface and serious scratching will result.

Laying hardboard

Hardboard creates the ideal sub-floor for many floor coverings. Use standard hardboard, ⅛in (3.2mm) thick, or ³⁄₁₆in (4.8mm) hardboard for very uneven floors. In kitchens and bathrooms, use oil-tempered hardboard. Before laying, condition the boards. Separate them and stand them on edge for 72 hours in the room where you are going to put them down. In kitchens and bathrooms they should be sprinkled with water. Secure the boards with flat staples, hardboard pins or ring-shank nails.

Fixing hardboard sheets

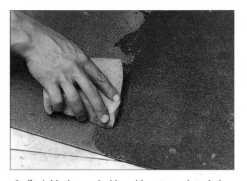

1 *Sprinkle the rough sides with water and stack the boards flat, back to back, for 48 hours (tempered board for 72 hours). Cut each sheet in half to provide for more expansion and cut some in half again.*

2 *Use these pieces at the start of alternate rows, to give staggered joins. Fix the boards smooth side down. The fixings should be 4in (100mm) apart at the edges and 6in (15cm) apart elsewhere.*

Laying chipboard

Chipboard comes with either straight or tongue-and-groove edges and in ¾in (19mm) and ⅞in (22mm) thicknesses. For most purposes, ¾in (19mm) chipboard is adequate, but use ⅞in (22mm) chipboard for joists spaced farther than 18in (45cm) apart. For a smooth, strong floor, tongue-and-groove-edged panels are best. These normally come in sheets measuring 8ft × 2ft (244cm × 60cm).

If you use square-edged boards, nail and glue 2in × 3in (50mm × 75mm) timber between the joists so that all the edges are supported. This will cut down flexing. With tongue-and-groove chipboard there is no need for cross timbers. The edges of each panel should come halfway across the supporting joists. Fix the panels with 2½in (63mm) lost-head wire nails. Leave screwed-down access panels over cables and pipes. Chipboard blunts saw blades, so if you are going to cut many panels, use a circular saw with a tungsten-carbide-tipped blade or a hard-point handsaw. A power jigsaw is best for intricate cuts. Make sure that the area is free from damp, as it will weaken the chipboard.

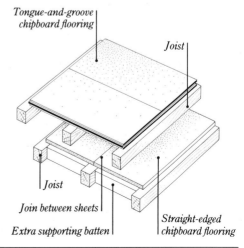

Tongue-and-groove chipboard flooring

Joist

Joist

Join between sheets

Extra supporting batten

Straight-edged chipboard flooring

Decorative effects with hardwood floors

Wooden floors can look effective in both traditional and modern homes. The most luxurious effects are usually obtained with hardwood floors, whether they are woodstrip or woodblock types. Narrow woodstrips can emphasize the length of a room, while woodblocks, laid in basketweave form, will provide an attractive yet unobtrusive pattern. Another effect of this type of flooring is that it gives a room unity. Wooden floors set off a wide range of furnishings, from antique to ultra-modern, and help them to look good together. An expanse of wooden flooring, for example, may echo the colour and grain in wooden furniture while it offsets brighter fabrics. A selection of ethnic or oriental rugs will add softness and comfort and can help to co-ordinate the colour scheme.

A patterned effect

Parquet flooring creates a subtle pattern that does not dominate a room (below).

Strongly patterned rugs can be placed on parquet without creating disharmony. The contents of this room encompass a wide variety of styles.

Antique chairs, a modern table, and rugs of widely differing patterns are all included. But none of these items seems to clash, because they all harmonize with the neutral wall colour and the rich wood of the basketweave pattern in the parquet floor.

A modern interior

The large windows and empty central area of this modern room (left) would look stark and cold if it were not for the polished woodstrip floor, which is easy to maintain, a bonus in modern life. Its colour adds warmth, the polished surface reflects a rich light, and its lines guide the eye from the furniture at one end to the rug and chair at the other, making it seem less empty. This type of floor is available in many different woods, so it is possible to get a good natural match, as here, between the colours of furniture and the floor.

Preparing a floor for woodstrips or blocks

If your existing floor is made of timber, make sure that any loose boards are secured (page 106). If necessary, lay hardboard panels rough-side-up to give an even surface (page 109).

For better insulation, and to give a sound-deadening effect, lay fibre insulation board under the hardboard. In kitchens and bathrooms, use boards impregnated with bitumen. Fix down the insulation board using the same method as for hardboard. Use ring-shank nails or screw-nails (with a gradual spiral at the point end) long enough to penetrate the floorboards by at least ½in (12mm). Stick the hardboard to the fibreboard with a bitumen flooring, contact, or PVA adhesive. Make sure that the joints in the hardboard do not align with those in the fibreboard: the floor will be less firm and the insulation less effective if the joints are directly in line.

If you are laying a hardboard floor on a solid floor, the original surface must be clean, dry and level before you start. If a solid floor is uneven, use a levelling compound, or smooth and insulate the surface using fibreboard and hardboard. Always use insulating boards impregnated with bitumen with solid floors, to protect against damp.

Laying woodstrip flooring

Woodstrip flooring consists of narrow pieces of tongue-and-groove-edged wood which come in random lengths. The grain colour can vary considerably, so it is a good idea to open the packs and check that the colours are consistent before you start to lay the floor.

Woodstrips often look best if laid in line with the doorway. But they can make long, narrow rooms seem wider if you lay them across the width of the room. Put a few boards in position before you start, to see what looks best.

It is best to condition woodstrip flooring for at least 48 hours before laying it. Open the packs in the room where you are going to install the flooring and let the timber get acclimatized to the temperature and humidity levels of the room.

Prepare the existing floor so that it is clean, level and dry. You can then lay insulating material to conserve heat and deaden noise. The woodstrips are then attached using pins.

Underfloor heating can make woodstrip flooring shrink. Consult the manufacturer before laying the strips.

If the room is square, lay the first strip parallel to the wall and ½in (12mm) away from it, to allow for expansion. If the room is not square, use a stringline to position the boards. If the strips are sealed, finish off the surface by polishing with an electric drill fitted with a lamb's-wool attachment.

Fixing woodstrips

1 *Fit the first strip, groove to the wall, at right angles to the floorboards. Fix it with pins through the tongues.*

2 *Butt joint the strips and nail them down. Add the next row, hammering it into place, protecting it with an off-cut.*

3 *Nail the strip through the shoulder. Stagger the joints between strips. Saw the last strip along its length to fit.*

Laying mosaic flooring

Mosaic panels consist of small pieces of hardwood shorter than those used in woodstrip flooring. They are glued to a flexible bitumen-felt backing. The blocks are usually grouped together to make up a larger panel of basketweave pattern, although they can be separated so that you can use individual blocks to fill small gaps and work around obstacles.

With mosaic flooring, the conditioning of the blocks before laying and the preparation of the floor itself are the same as for woodstrip flooring (page 111). Leave an expansion gap of ½in (12mm) around the edge of the floor area. Use a cork strip to help maintain the gap. Start by fitting the whole panels. Leave gaps where you have to trim and fit smaller pieces. Cut mosaic panels with a tenon saw, a power jigsaw, or a bench-mounted circular saw or handsaw. You can also use this method for cutting parquet panels. To go around pipes and similar obstacles, separate individual sections from panels and cut these into even smaller pieces if necessary.

Fixing mosaic panels

1 *Stick the panels down with flooring adhesive. Once you have laid the first row of panels, spread the adhesive in blocks of about 5ft² (0.5m²) and then lay the next row.*

2 *Cut some panels to fit the gap. To make them less obvious, put them at the side of the room farthest from the door, or where a large piece of furniture will stand, and away from the light of a window.*

3 *Tap the panels down firmly using a mallet, and make sure that the edges butt tightly together. For the small edge panels, it is usually best to split up the large panels into sections to fill the gaps.*

4 *To mark a panel for cutting, place it on top of the last complete panel in a row. Place another panel on top of this with its edge ½in (12mm) from the skirting. Draw a line along its edge on to the lower panel.*

Laying parquet flooring

Parquet blocks are assembled in a basketweave pattern and look rather like mosaic blocks. But unlike mosaic panels, they usually have tongue-and-groove edges so that they interlock and form a very flat, good-quality floor. Also unlike mosaic panels, parquet does not require sanding.

Parquet flooring needs a good underlay. You can lay it over either a hardboard sub-floor (page 102) or a special underlay. This consists of coarse paper impregnated with bitumen and covered with cork chips. It is laid cork-side-down over the original floor surface before the parquet panels are put down.

Parquet is usually loose laid. In other words, the panels simply "float" on the floor surface, and the interlocking tongues and grooves hold them all tightly together. When you are fitting the final edge pieces, knock them into place with either a proprietary knocking-up tool, which you may be able to hire for the purpose, or a hammer, protecting the edge from its blows with a scrap of flooring. Do not forget to leave an expansion gap. To fit the last corner block, you will have to cut off the tongue and the lower part of the grooves so that it simply drops into place. This will give you a good place to start if you ever have to dismantle the floor. Parquet flooring normally comes ready-finished, so there is no extra work to do once you have laid the blocks.

Fixing parquet blocks

1 *Make a basketweave pattern, using cork expansion strips to hold the blocks in place. Hammer the pieces together, protecting them with an offcut.*

2 *Measure the remaining gaps. Plane the tongues off edge blocks and drop them into the gap. Hammer them into place using an offcut to protect them.*

Finishing off a woodblock floor

To work around a door, saw horizontally through the base of the architrave at the height of the finished floor surface. Then push the flooring panels underneath. If you cannot do this, make a template and cut out the shape with a coping saw. Across the width of the doorway, finish off the edge with an aluminium binder bar or a hardwood strip that matches the wood of the floor to protect the exposed edge. Pre-sealed woodblock floors require no further treatment. Untreated types should be sanded smooth and sealed (page 108) to make the floor easy to clean and wear-resistant. A polyurethane-based seal forms a clear gloss or matt coat; an oleo-resinous seal soaks into the wood to give a scratch-resistant lustre surface. Both seals will darken the wood slightly. If there is a large area to sand, hire a floor-sanding machine and use it with fine-grade abrasive paper. But usually only a light sanding is needed, and an electric belt sander, or even a smaller finishing sander, will be suitable unless the floor is very large.

Floor coverings

Carpets are available in a variety of materials and are constructed in one of three ways. Woven carpets such as Axminster and Wilton are made from tufts woven in with the backing, tufted types have the tufts inserted into a pre-woven backing, and non-woven carpets are bonded, not woven, on to the backing.

Manufacturers produce carpet in roll form (broadloom), in strips (body), in large squares or rectangles (square), or as carpet tiles. Carpet squares, for example, may have unbound edges if they are remnants from rolls, and will be most suitable in a small room. Squares with bound edges are intended for

laying in the centre of a room with a large area of floor visible around the edge. Carpet tiles are easy to lay and trim, and, of course, to clean and replace. They can be moved around a room to ensure even wear, and are easier to transfer to a new home than carpet.

Unlike its predecessor, linoleum, sheet vinyl is relatively easy to lay. And although it takes longer to put down than vinyl tiles, it involves fewer joins and has the added advantage of offering a wider choice of patterns. The name vinyl derives from polyvinyl chloride (PVC), the flexible plastic from which it is made. Other materials are added, but the best-quality vinyls contain a high proportion of PVC.

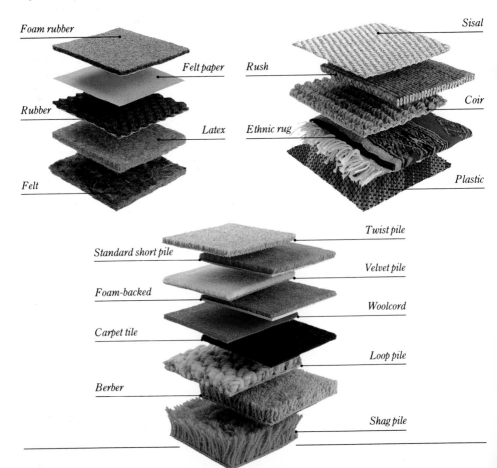

Foam rubber

Felt paper

Rubber

Latex

Felt

Sisal

Rush

Coir

Ethnic rug

Plastic

Standard short pile

Twist pile

Foam-backed

Velvet pile

Carpet tile

Woolcord

Berber

Loop pile

Shag pile

Carpets

Carpets can be divided into the following categories. There are tufted, woven and bonded types, which refers to the construction method; there are cut, looped cord and twisted types, which refers to the pile; and there are hessian-backed and foam-backed varieties, which refers to the backing material.

A standard pile carpet is available in either a woven form (such as Axminster and Wilton carpets, named after the looms on which they are woven) or in a cheaper, tufted form. The pile is cut short. Loop pile carpet has fine or coarse yarn woven into it, but this is left uncut to make a series of loops. Sculptured pile carpet is a woven or tufted variety that is a mixture of cut and looped pile. Some loops are cut and some left looped, to produce a three-dimensional result, which, though attractive, can be difficult to clean. Hair and woolcord carpet has the yarn woven into the backing, pulled tight and left uncut, to give a hard-wearing surface. The yarn in twist carpet is twisted before the carpet is woven, to give the carpet a textured, springy and very hard-wearing surface. Velvet pile is extremely dense, deep and smooth and is cut to produce a luxurious finish, with a definite right and wrong way. It will shade and track when walked on.

Shag is a luxurious carpet with a long-cut pile of 1in (25mm). The pile treads down easily and needs to be raked and cleaned regularly. Berber carpets have a dense, looped pile and are made from undyed sheep's wool.

Foam-backed carpet is usually a tufted carpet with a foam backing. It is easier to lay than hessian-backed types, but normally it does not wear as well.

Rugs and matting

Rugs and mats can be a relatively inexpensive way of covering floors, or of adding a touch of colour to an expanse of plain carpet.

Rugs
Ethnic rugs are available in cotton and wool. Ethnic Indian, African, European and American rugs are generally flat-weave. The price varies according to the fibre content and the intricacy of the design. Cotton rugs may "bleed" if laid over a pale carpet, so it is best to line them with fabric or paper and dry-clean.

Greek Flokati rugs, which have a luxurious, deep pile, are made from woven wool. They are machine washable.

Mats
Rush matting is usually woven in 12in (30cm) squares and can be sewn together to form larger pieces. It is available in a variety of designs, can be loose laid directly on to wood or concrete without an underlay and is easily rolled up to take with you when you move. However, it collects dirt and should be regularly lifted to sweep away the dust. It can be gently scrubbed with a soapless detergent.

Coconut matting is the coarse matting found at front and back doors and is available in a variety of sizes for use in areas of heavy and dirty traffic. Coir matting is a more refined form of coconut matting. Coir comes in a variety of thicknesses, colours, textures and weaves, from simple crossweave to a heavier, tighter loop with a non-slip backing. Split cane matting is similar to rush matting, but more rigid. It is inexpensive and hard-wearing, but attracts dust. Sisal matting is tough with a naturally white fibre that makes a good floor covering in halls and passageways.

Plastic matting is useful in kitchens and bathrooms. It is cheap, easy to clean and comes in a range of bright colours.

UNDERLAYS

The traditional type of felt underlay has been largely replaced by hessian-backed rubber underlay, although felt absorbs underfloor dust more efficiently. Hessian-backed or paper-backed rubber are the best quality underlays for most carpets and are essential for stairs. Foam rubber is only suitable for use in areas of light wear. It should have a layer of felt paper beneath. This prevents rubber-backed carpet and underlay from sticking to the floor. Other materials used as underlays include hard-wearing jute, waterproof PVC, and felt substitutes.

Suiting the floor covering to the room

Before choosing a floor covering, it is important to consider the demands that will be put on it – whether it will be subject to splashing, scratching, spillages or heavy traffic. The first decision is the type of floor covering – carpet, vinyl or matting; the next is the quality. Price will naturally be a controlling factor, but when selecting carpet, it is essential to choose a grade that will withstand the wear and not to make false economies. Once you have chosen the most appropriate type of flooring, it is worth buying the best quality you can afford: it will last longer.

Short-pile nylon or synthetic for easy cleaning, or loose-lay carpet tiles can be used in kitchens. However, sheet flooring is most suitable and can be set off with rugs or matting. For bathrooms, sheet vinyl is again the most suitable, being water-resistant. Carpet should only be selected if it is polyester and has a waterproof backing.

A hard-wearing grade of carpet is suitable for the living room; add rugs to brighten a large expanse or to hide worn areas. A light, cheap grade of carpet is a sensible choice for bedrooms, particularly for children's rooms. These may be too hard for adult taste, so strew rugs for comfort. For hallways, carpets need to be very hard-wearing to withstand heavy traffic, and sheet flooring may make more sense, particularly if you have pets or children. Mats and rugs can make bright, cheap coverings over sheet flooring, tiles, or plain carpet.

Types of carpet construction

There are three different ways of connecting the carpet fibre to its backing: by close interweaving, by stitching and gluing, and by simple glue bonding. Woven, tufted and bonded carpets are all available in a variety of fibres, pile lengths and roll widths. When you are looking at carpet samples, bend them back to see how dense the pile is and how it has been connected to the backing. Then tug at a few tufts to check that the fibre is securely fixed to the backing. If the pile seems to be uneven or the weaving method insecure, the carpet will probably not wear well.

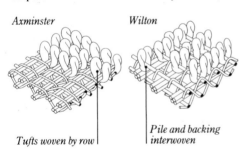

Axminster

Tufts woven by row

Wilton

Pile and backing interwoven

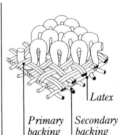

Primary backing | *Secondary backing*

Latex

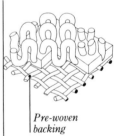

Pre-woven backing

Woven carpet
All woven carpets are made by either the Wilton or the Axminster method. These are two different weaving techniques, not brand names. Axminster carpets are woven one row of tufts at a time, so that the loom anchors the U-shaped tufts into the

backing material as it weaves each row. Wilton carpets are woven in one continuous length, and the pile and backing are closely interwoven for extra strength and thickness. Wilton backings are usually flatter and more dense than Axminster.

Tufted carpet
The yarn is stitched into a "primary" backing to give a looped or cut pile. The primary backing is then coated with latex to secure the tufts and a second backing is added in order to make it stronger and easier to handle.

Bonded carpet
This is a newer manufacturing process in which the pile fibre is bonded on to a pre-woven backing. Bonded carpets will not fray when cut. They are available in plain colours only, but in a number of different types of fibre.

Suiting the underlay to the carpet

Underlay plays an important part in the life of your carpet. It increases its heat- and sound-insulating properties and gives it a softer tread, so be sure to choose the right one. Carpets with a woven backing need to be laid over a good-quality rubber underlay with a paper or hessian backing or over felt underlay. Foam rubber underlays are also available, but are only advisable in areas of light wear. They need a layer of paper underneath to prevent them from sticking to the floor. Most cheaper carpets have a built-in foam backing and should be laid over felt paper underlay. Use felt underlay where there are gaps between floorboards to improve insulation.

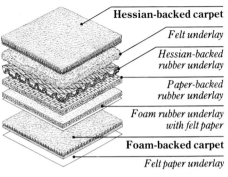

Hessian-backed carpet
Felt underlay
Hessian-backed rubber underlay
Paper-backed rubber underlay
Foam rubber underlay with felt paper
Foam-backed carpet
Felt paper underlay

Hessian-backed carpet
Use paper-backed or hessian-backed rubber underlay for most rooms. Use felt in rooms with underfloor heating.

Foam-backed carpet
The only underlay appropriate to a foam-backed carpet is a felt paper one. The choice of underlay is as important as the choice of carpet.

TYPES OF CARPET FIBRE

Wool, the traditional carpet fibre, is expensive but warm, hard-wearing, dirt-resistant, naturally fire-resistant and easy to clean. Any carpet which bears the "Woolmark" will have passed stringent tests for fading, wear and shrink-resistance.

Synthetics include the following materials: acrylic, which is closest to wool in feel and appearance; nylon, which is cheap and hard-wearing, but attracts dirt and dust; and polyester, which is soft and reasonably water-resistant for

bathrooms, but less hard-wearing. Mixtures are a blend of two fibres to combine the best properties of each. The most popular combination is 80 per cent wool, 20 per cent synthetic, since it reduces the price of the carpet but looks like wool.

Types of sheet flooring construction

The quality of sheet flooring is determined by its construction. Sheet vinyl consists of an outer "wear" layer, a filling and a backing. The most comfortable vinyl has a "cushioned" filling

layer, the cheaper types have a pattern layer instead of foam cushion, while in the more durable solid vinyl the design is integrated in the material. Rubber flooring consists of layers of natural and synthetic rubber, compressed under high pressure and temperatures into a strong sheet. "Lay flat" vinyl is easier to lay and transport than other types.

Rubber

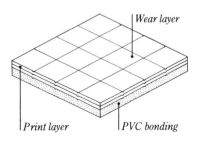

Wear layer
Print layer
PVC bonding

Sheet vinyl

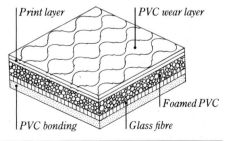

Print layer
PVC wear layer
PVC bonding
Foamed PVC
Glass fibre

Carpets

Choosing a carpet is an expensive decision, so it is tempting to "play safe" and settle for a plain carpet that will not "date" and will not need replacing with every redecoration. Nevertheless, a carpet can help to unify and bring life to a room, it can play visual tricks, it can suggest and reflect style, and it can bring interest to the flat expanse of the floor. But a carpet must be made to "work" with the decorating scheme. Its most important role is to co-ordinate with the walls, the furniture, furnishings and accessories. For good colour balance, a room should be divided into three: 60 per cent covered in a basic colour (usually the walls and floor), 30 per cent in a second colour (often furnishings) and 10 per cent in a third, accenting colour (accessories). A fourth, neutral colour can form a useful link. When choosing a carpet, remember that the carpet colour intensifies wall and ceiling colours.

Traditional designs
The rich colours of oriental carpets create an appropriate, dignified backcloth for a traditional setting (left). Warm reds and golds breathe life into a subdued room and bring a luxurious, cosy feel to a study. Smaller oriental carpets and rugs laid in simple rooms often reflect Islamic or Far Eastern culture and lend an ethnic touch.

A winding stair
A diagonal stripe on a winding stair (left) creates an intriguing network of angles with the lines of the banisters and harmonizes with the conflicting shapes. If the wallpaper is patterned, make sure that the carpet is of a suitable design to go with it; do not overdo the effect. A plain background colour will set off the strong design to the best advantage.

Modern design
Geometrics are cool, clean and allow you to play games with shapes. A carpet with parallel stripes, for example (above), draws the eye from wall to wall and appears to elongate the room. If you have stripes or geometrical designs elsewhere in the same room or area, ensure that they harmonize with the carpet pattern: use a sample to test it out.

An integrated effect
The carpet in this room acts as a neutral base, blending subtly with the paintwork. The same colour is picked out in the patterned wallpaper, and is set off by the cool greys and warm oranges of the accessories and furnishings.

Tools and equipment

The number of tools required depends on the type of carpet being laid. Foam-backed carpet simply demands cutting and fixing equipment – a trimming knife, adhesive tape, gripper strips and binder bars. Hessian-backed carpet, however, needs tools to ensure that it is stretched and securely attached – a knee kicker (which can be hired), angled grippers or carpet tacks, a bolster chisel and carpet adhesive. Upholsterers' tacks, which have a bright, domed head, are not suitable for use when laying carpets.

Other essential tools are a hammer and nail punch for fixing grippers, a straight-edge and a cutting board. If necessary, use a wedge of wood to help you push the carpet securely behind the grippers.

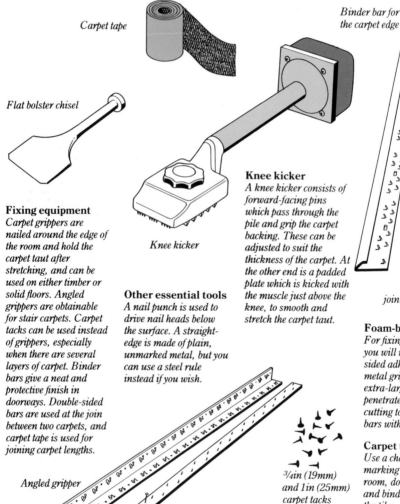

Carpet tape

Flat bolster chisel

Binder bar for the carpet edge

Knee kicker
A knee kicker consists of forward-facing pins which pass through the pile and grip the carpet backing. These can be adjusted to suit the thickness of the carpet. At the other end is a padded plate which is kicked with the muscle just above the knee, to smooth and stretch the carpet taut.

Knee kicker

Fixing equipment
Carpet grippers are nailed around the edge of the room and hold the carpet taut after stretching, and can be used on either timber or solid floors. Angled grippers are obtainable for stair carpets. Carpet tacks can be used instead of grippers, especially when there are several layers of carpet. Binder bars give a neat and protective finish in doorways. Double-sided bars are used at the join between two carpets, and carpet tape is used for joining carpet lengths.

Other essential tools
A nail punch is used to drive nail heads below the surface. A straight-edge is made of plain, unmarked metal, but you can use a steel rule instead if you wish.

Binder bar for joining two carpets

Foam-backed carpet
For fixing down the edges you will need double-sided adhesive tape or metal gripper strips with extra-large pins to penetrate the foam; also cutting tools and binder bars without pins.

Carpet tiles
Use a chalkline for marking the centre of the room, double-sided tape and binder bars for fixing the tiles.

Angled gripper

³/₄in (19mm) and 1in (25mm) carpet tacks

Standard gripper

Dealing with damp

If damp is not detected and cured at an early stage, it will spread rapidly and ruin any newly laid carpet. If you have noticed "tide marks", or if you suspect that the room is damp, test the area to see if the problem is caused by superficial condensation or rising damp. You *must* cure rising damp. Before treatment for damp, ensure that the surface is clean and dust-free. When painting the floor and wall with damp-proof membrane, take it up the wall to link with the damp course.

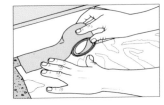

Testing for rising damp (left)
Tape a square of polythene over the affected area. Droplets on the underside indicate rising damp.

Curing rising damp (right)
Remove the skirtings and paint the floor and wall with membrane.

Estimating quantities for floors

Some retailers will measure and estimate free. If this service is not available, or if you wish to forecast and check the supplier's estimate, mark the measurements on a plan of the room.

Then choose a suitable carpet width for the minimum of waste and calculate the length required. If your room is 15¾ft × 12½ft (4.8m × 3.8m) and if a 13ft (4m) roll is not available, you would need a 12ft (3.6m) width with a 1ft (0.3m) strip. Or you will have to use a 15ft (4.57m) width and waste a strip.

Drawing up a plan
Sketch an outline of the room, including doors and windows. Measure the length and the width of the room, allowing for alcoves and doorways, then mark the maximum measurements on your plan. You can then calculate the most economic arrangement of carpet lengths.

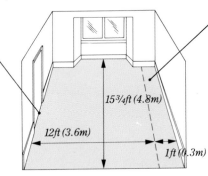

15¾ft (4.8m)

12ft (3.6m)

1ft (0.3m)

Positioning joins
If a standard carpet roll width will not fit very conveniently into your room, or if you are using carpet squares, you will have to make at least one join. Run the pile to face away from the light and position seams by a wall at right angles to the main window. Do not lay strips in a doorway.

Estimating quantities for stairs

Either make an accurate plan for the supplier, or if you do an estimate yourself, follow these instructions. Assume that the landing carpet will overlap the top riser. Then measure from the top tread over each tread and riser to the foot of the stairs. Add 1½in (40mm) to the total length of each tread to allow for the underlay and for tucking into the grippers. Add a further 1½ft (50cm) to allow the carpet to be moved up or down occasionally to even out the wear. To establish the width of your carpet, measure the width of the treads, and if the treads have one open side, allow ½in (12mm) for turning under at the edge.

On winding staircases measure along the outer edge for the longest length. Then allow 1½in (40mm) extra for tucking in the underlay and an extra 1½ft (50cm) for moving the carpet, as with straight stair carpets. The pile should always run down the stairs.

Preparing the floor

Before laying carpet you should check that the floor is smooth, dry, clean and firm. Repairs undertaken at this stage will save taking up the carpet later. For repairs to timber floors, see pages 104–5. Cement screed and concrete floors may be concealed beneath other surfaces, so ensure that the floor is dry and level. Undertake minor repairs where possible, but if the floor is uneven, apply screed. This is mixed with water until creamy, then poured on the floor.

Applying screed
Spread it roughly with a trowel, working towards the door. Screed can be covered by carpet after 24 hours.

Minor repairs
Scrape away flaking or crumbling sections. Vacuum the floor to remove dust, and fill indentations with cement mortar or filler.

Fixing carpet grippers

Before fitting underlay, secure grippers around the edges of the room with the pins angled towards the wall. Leave a gap of about ¼in (6mm) between the grippers and the wall to allow the edge of the carpet to be tucked down neatly against the skirting. The strips should form a continuous line and shorter lengths can be butted together.

On timber floors, grippers can be nailed into position, but on concrete, use either hardened pins or an adhesive recommended by the manufacturer. The alternative to fitting grippers is to use tacks.

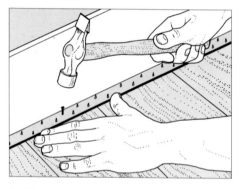

Nailing grippers
On timber floors, nail grippers around the edges of the room, using a hammer and nail punch. Position them ¼in (6mm) from the skirting and angled to the wall.

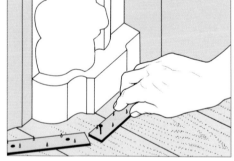

Fitting grippers around awkward areas
Around curving places, such as door architraves, fireplaces and recesses, saw a gripper into several short lengths and nail the pieces at each end.

CARPET GRIPPERS

Carpet grippers hold the carpet taut and are invisible after fixing. They consist of plywood strips through which a series of angled nails protrude towards the skirting. The strips, about 1in (25mm) wide and ¼in (6mm) thick, are usually available in 30in (76cm), 47in (120cm) and 6ft (183cm) lengths and can be cut to length with a saw. They come with ordinary nails for fixing to timber floors, or with masonry nails to solid floors. Be very careful when handling and cutting the carpet grippers, as the protruding nails are extremely sharp and can catch on clothing and furnishings. If you are not used to handling them, wear protective gloves.

Laying underlay

A good-quality underlay will improve a carpet's heat- and sound-insulating properties and will increase its life-expectancy. The two chief types of underlay are rubber and felt (page 117). They are fitted in different ways because of their differing consistencies, and the method is determined by the type of floor.

In most cases it is best to move the carpet into the room before fitting the underlay. In this way, the underlay is not disturbed when the carpet is dragged into the room. The carpet is then rolled back to allow the underlay to be fitted.

If you are laying carpet over thermoplastic tiles, or if you are laying foam-backed carpet, always use felt instead of a rubber or plastic foam underlay.

Securing rubber underlay

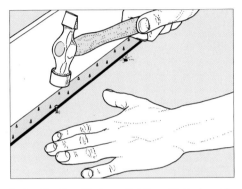

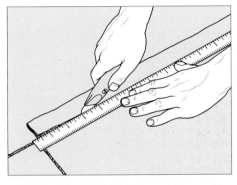

1 *Lay it rubber side down. Cut it roughly to size and fix it first in one corner of the room, with the carpet half rolled back. Fasten it just inside the gripper strip running along an adjacent wall. On a timber floor, secure it with rustproof tacks.*

2 *Fold back the other half of the carpet, then unroll the rest of the underlay and fix it down at the far wall. If two pieces of underlay need to be joined, overlap the edges and cut both layers, then fix down the edges with adhesive, staples or tacks.*

Securing felt paper underlay

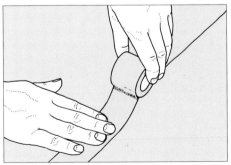

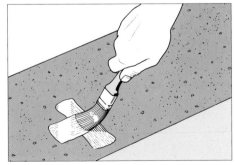

1 *To form the underlay, first join strips of felt paper with heavy-duty adhesive tape. Then secure it to the floor. On a timber floor, fix down the paper with staples or tacks, which should be inserted into the underlay at 12in (30cm) intervals.*

2 *Use adhesive on a solid floor. The underlay should stop 2in (50mm) from the skirting so that double-sided adhesive tape can be used to secure the carpet edges. There is no need to allow for extra layers of underlay in areas of heavy wear.*

How to lay and stretch hessian-backed carpet

When the underlay is down, the carpet can be rolled out on to the floor. It should be placed so that the pile leans away from the light, to prevent uneven shading. It will save trimming the carpet along all four walls, if it is positioned so that only about ½in (12mm) of material turns up against two adjoining walls. The carpet is then fixed to the grippers or tacked on one side, stretched across the room and hooked on to the rest of the grippers or tacked before trimming and finishing. The correct method is described in detail below.

Fixing the carpet on to grippers

1 *Bring the carpet to a corner and line it up so that it overlaps the grippers by ½in (12mm) on each wall. Push down the edge to hook the backing on to the gripper pins, for about 12in (30cm) on each wall.*

2 *Then rub along the gripper strip covered by carpet with the side of a hammer or mallet, to ensure that the pins of the grippers engage with the carpet backing for a firm grip.*

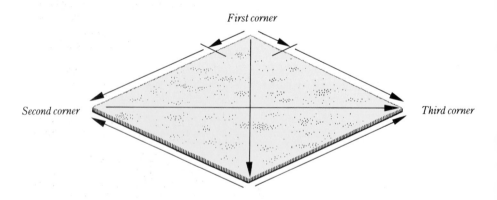

First corner

Second corner

Third corner

Fourth corner

Stretching hessian-backed carpet
First hook the carpet on to the grippers in one corner for 12in (30cm) on each wall. Next, stretch the carpet across the room to an adjacent corner, using the knee kicker, and hook it on. Then complete the wall between the two corners. Stretch the carpet along the other wall from the first corner and secure it on the gripper in the corner diagonally opposite to the second corner.

Finally, stretch and smooth the carpet right across the room to the last corner. Hook it into the corner and complete the last two walls.

If using carpet tacks, insert temporary tacks about ½in (12mm) from the skirting. When the carpet has been stretched, fold the edge under and drive tacks through the double thickness well down into the pile, at 6in (15cm) intervals. Remove temporary tacks.

Stretching the carpet
Place the head of the knee kicker on the carpet and adjust the pins so that they engage in the backing without tearing the pile. Then kick the pad with the muscle just above your kneecap (not the kneecap itself), while smoothing the carpet with your hands.

Trimming off excess carpet
Crease back the carpet at the skirting board and mark a cutting line along the back. Then fold the carpet right back and cut along the line, with a cutting board protecting the carpet beneath. Roll back the carpet to try the fit, and retrim the edges if necessary.

Finishing off edges
Once you have cut off excess carpet at the borders, trim it carefully against a straight-edge so that only ½in (12mm) rests against the wall. Press a paint scraper into the gully between the gripper and the wall, until the carpet is neatly tucked against the skirting.

Laying carpet tiles

The technique for planning out carpet tiles and the working sequence are the same as for floor tiles (page 86). The first tile should be secured in place with double-sided adhesive tape, while subsequent tiles can be loose laid. If, however, the tile manufacturer recommends securing the tiles at random intervals to prevent them from moving and creating gaps, use a flooring adhesive or double-sided sticky tape. Working from the centre, butt up the tiles tightly against each other and ensure that the arrows on the tile backs point in the same direction, unless you prefer to lay them in alternate directions for a chequerboard effect.

Always cut border tiles on a cutting board to avoid accidents, and secure them in doorways with a carpet-tile binder bar.

Fitting around problem areas

To allow the carpet to fit snugly in alcoves or around projections such as fireplaces, you must make vertical release cuts from the carpet edge to the floor. If the carpet has a tendency to fray, first coat the back with latex adhesive. To fit around pipes, cut a slit in the carpet from the front of the pipe to the edge of the carpet behind it. Ease the carpet around the pipe, making small release cuts where necessary, then trim to fit the wall.

Door architraves
Make cuts in the carpet until it lies flat. Trim until ½in (12mm) rests against the architrave. Push behind grippers.

Fireplaces
Allow an overlap of 1in (25mm) and cut. Press down and trim, allowing ½in (12mm) to ride up against the fireplace. Secure edges.

LAYING FOAM-BACKED CARPET

Foam-backed carpet needs no stretching. You simply lay it on the floor, butt up two adjacent edges against the skirting and trim the other two edges to fit.

Trim the carpet in position, or as for hessian-backed carpet (page 124). Gripper strips with extra large pins are available for foam-backed carpet, but it may prove easier to fix down the edges with double-sided adhesive tape or tacks. If you are using underlay, remember to use a felt paper one (pages 114–15).

Joining carpet pieces

However carefully you plan, joins may be necessary. If seams are unavoidable, the options are to seal the edges with 2in (50mm)-wide carpet tape and latex carpet adhesive, or, if the join falls in a doorway, to use a binder bar with twin grooves (page 120). These narrow aluminium strips have angled grippers to hold the carpet taut and a protective edge to prevent the carpet from fraying. Trim the edge of the carpet, tuck it into the binder bar and press it down flat. Then, using a piece of softwood to protect the bar, hammer down the lip to meet the carpet surface.

Using carpet tape

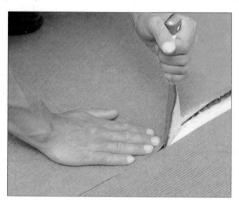

1 *Brush a 1in (25mm) band of adhesive along a half-width of the tape, and along the back of one edge of one of the pieces to be joined. When the adhesive is dry, press the glued tape on to the glued carpet, leaving the other half of the tape free.*

2 *Coat the remaining half-width of tape and the back of the other carpet. When the adhesive is nearly dry, join the glued surfaces, taking care to ensure a close joint without marks. When laying carpet squares, tape the entire border.*

Preparing the stairs

Before laying carpet, it is wise to examine the stair surface and make any minor repairs. Loose nails should be pulled out or punched below the surface, and any suspect holes treated with woodworm fluid. Any rotten treads or risers can be replaced by knocking out the glued wedges, removing the old board and sliding in a new one.

A creaking stair will be silenced by gluing and screwing a wooden block into the angle between the front of the tread and the riser below, working from below the stairs. If the stairs are boarded in, screws driven through the front of the tread into the riser below should cure the squeak. Finally, the stairs should be vacuumed and, to avoid taking up the carpet later when you wish to redecorate, the entire staircase should be given a fresh coat of hard-wearing gloss paint.

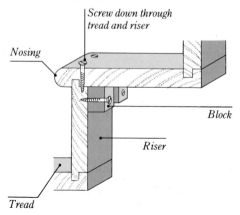

Screw down through tread and riser

Nosing

Block

Riser

Tread

Fitting underlay on stairs

There are two ways of fixing stair carpet: with grippers or with tacks. The method used will determine how the underlay is to be fixed. If the carpet is to be tacked, the underlay must also be tacked.

If angled stair grippers are to be used to secure the carpet, a pad of underlay is placed over each tread and half-way down the next riser, then tacked into place. Angled grippers are then fixed on top of the underlay. If normal grippers are to be used, these are nailed directly on to the stairs in pairs, with the pins pointing into the stair angle. The underlay butts up to the edges of the grippers, leaving a gap between each pair for tucking in the carpet. Whichever method is used, guide lines must be marked for the position of both carpet and underlay. However, if the carpet is to be fitted to the full width of the stairs, fit the grippers ¾in (19mm) from the banister edge and ¼in (6mm) from the wall.

Marking guide lines

1 *On the first tread, mark with a pencil where the edges of the carpet will fall, taking care to ensure that the borders on either side of the carpet width are equal. Then make a second pencil line ¾in (19mm) inside each mark as a guide line for the underlay. Repeat this procedure on the bottom tread.*

2 *Suspend two stringlines from the two inner points on the top tread, pull them taut, so that they form a straight line, and secure them to the two inner points on the bottom tread. You can then use the stringlines to make pencil guide lines for the position of the carpet and the underlay on each tread.*

Carpeting a winding staircase

The treads of corner stairs in a winding staircase are triangular, so it is best to use a separate piece of carpet for each individual tread with its riser.

To ensure a good fit, it is a good idea to make a paper template of the stair shape. If grippers are to be used, two strips are fitted as for straight treads, to allow the carpet to be tucked down firmly. But, in addition, a third is nailed along the wide, wall edge. Leave a small gap between the gripper and the skirting board. Always cut the carpet slightly larger than you think will be necessary, to allow for mistakes when cutting.

Ensuring a good fit
Use a third gripper along the wall edge of the tread, and two at a corner.

Carpeting a straight staircase

Once the underlay is in position, the stair carpet can be fixed on top. The carpet *must* be securely held, or accidents may occur. The carpet can be fixed using either tacks or grippers, and this decision must be taken *before* fitting the underlay.

If the underlay is tacked, the carpet must also be tacked. If you have chosen to use plain grippers, the carpet is inserted into the gap between the grippers; the "teeth" or pins hold the carpet backing. If angled grippers have been fixed, the carpet is inserted between the two rows of teeth on each gripper. If the carpet is to be fitted to the full stair width, the grippers are fixed ¾in (19mm) from the banister edge, to allow the cut edge to be turned and tacked. Although foam-backed carpet is not generally recommended for stairs, some types of foam-backed carpet are hard-wearing enough. Special gripper strips, without pins to tear the backing, are available, but tacks provide a firmer fixing.

If you are also carpeting the landing it should be fitted in the same way as a floor carpet (pages 124–5). On an open landing, the edge bordering the stairwell should be turned under and held with tacks or a binder bar.

Using carpet grippers

1 *Arrange the carpet with the pile running down the stairs and align the edges with the guide lines on the top tread. Push it firmly on to the gripper teeth and tuck the edge into the stair angle. A tack at each side will ensure that the edge does not move while you fit the carpet in place.*

2 *Draw the carpet tightly across the tread, down over the riser below and on to the next tread. Push the carpet securely on to the gripper pins by hammering a wooden wedge or a thin, flat bolster chisel into the gaps between gripper strips. The gripper strips will hold the carpet securely in place.*

3 *Continue drawing the carpet over the stairs, fixing it firmly on to the grippers. Make sure that you check the alignment, ensuring that a row of tufts in the pile runs across the nosing in a straight line, and that uncarpeted borders are of equal width, so that the carpet covers the centre of the stairs.*

4 *At the bottom of the staircase, turn under a 3–4in (75–100mm) hem of carpet and neatly tack or staple it to the bottom riser. Working from the centre outwards, attach it at 2¾in (70mm) intervals. This surplus will allow you to move the carpet up later when it becomes worn, should this be necessary.*

Using carpet tacks

 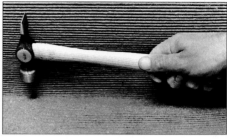

1 *With the top edge turned under by about 3in (75mm), align the carpet and tack it down on the top tread at 4in (100mm) intervals. Check that the carpet is correctly aligned straight down the stairs and that the pile runs downwards, then begin fitting. Pull the carpet tightly over the first tread and down to the base of the riser below.*

2 *Tack down one corner into the base of the next tread down, stretch the carpet across the tread and tack the other corner. Insert tacks at the back of the tread at 4in (100mm) intervals between the two holding tacks, close in to the corner between tread and riser. Repeat this process of securing, stretching and tacking down the carpet, until you reach the bottom stair.*

3 *Pull the carpet taut over the last tread. Fold under a 3–4in (75–100mm) hem of surplus carpet, so that the crease in the carpet lies in the angle between the bottom riser and the floor, making sure that you align the fold along a row of tufts.*

4 *Then fold the inner vertical edges under to give a neat single thickness of carpet. Finally, tack or staple through both thicknesses on the bottom riser to encourage the hem to lie flat against the floor and form a neat finish.*

Carpeting an open-tread staircase

Since these stairs have no risers, each tread should be individually wrapped in carpet. When measuring, allow 1½in (40mm) for hemming. The underlay is flapped over the tread and tacked or stapled to the underside, 2in (50mm) from the edge of the stair. The carpet is then laid on top so that the tufts line up with the nosing. The edges are then folded under by ¾in (19mm) and tacked at the centre of the tread on the underside.

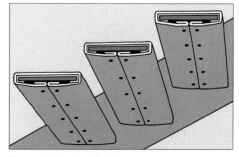

Securing the underside
Lay the carpet over the tread and tack down the folded edges under the tread, at the mid-point.

Vinyl

The latest vinyls come in roll widths of up to 13ft (4m) and in virtually unlimited lengths. This means that all but the largest rooms can be covered in one sheet, thus avoiding having to make joins. Most vinyls are available in an easy-to-match pattern, so that if smaller widths are used, and they are laid carefully, the seams will not be obvious.

Tools and equipment

For laying sheet vinyl, you simply need cutting, measuring and adhesive equipment and a ballpoint pen. Other useful items include a small block of wood for making trimming lines and some thick paper if you are going to make templates. Remember to clean any dirty equipment after use and store rolls of vinyl on their sides. Never stand unsupported rolls on end, as the vinyl may distort and crack.

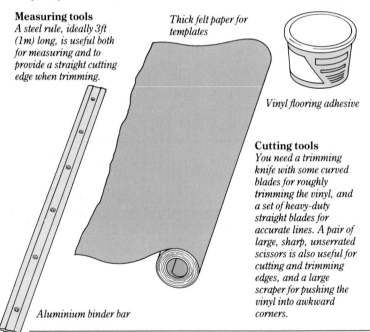

Measuring tools
A steel rule, ideally 3ft (1m) long, is useful both for measuring and to provide a straight cutting edge when trimming.

Thick felt paper for templates

Aluminium binder bar

Vinyl flooring adhesive

Cutting tools
You need a trimming knife with some curved blades for roughly trimming the vinyl, and a set of heavy-duty straight blades for accurate lines. A pair of large, sharp, unserrated scissors is also useful for cutting and trimming edges, and a large scraper for pushing the vinyl into awkward corners.

Strong adhesive tape

Adhesive equipment
Use either vinyl flooring adhesive or double-sided adhesive tape for sticking down at doorways and along seams. Only use tape approved by a flooring manufacturer, since some types damage the vinyl with time. A plastic adhesive spreader may come with the can, but durable metal spreaders are available from tool shops for large flooring jobs.

Extra equipment
A binder bar will make a neat finish in doorways.

Preparing the floor and vinyl

Clear the room of all movable furniture and remove the doors. If you are fitting out a new bathroom, lay the vinyl before fitting skirtings or bathroom equipment. First screw down any loose floorboards (page 106), and sand uneven areas (page 106). If the floor is still distinctly coloured by wood preservative or perhaps woodworm fluid and smells strongly, cover it with foil-backed building paper and tempered hardboard (page 109).

Leaving the vinyl to adjust to normal room temperature makes it more supple and easier to lay. Lay the vinyl on its side, loosely rolled with the pattern facing outward, and leave it for 24 hours in the room where it is to be fitted. In cold weather, heat the room to a comfortable working temperature.

Sheet vinyl

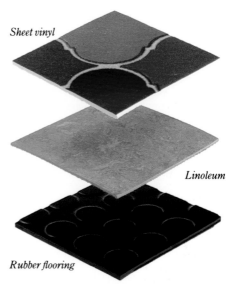

Sheet vinyl

Linoleum

Rubber flooring

Sheet vinyl is a durable, easy-to-clean and attractive floor covering, particularly suited to kitchens and bathrooms. It needs little attention except for sweeping and occasional washing and polishing. If a glossy vinyl fades, it can be recoated. Vinyl comes in a range of qualities, textures, patterns and colours. Most have a cushioned backing which makes them comfortable and quiet. The easiest type to lay is the "lay flat" variety. It needs no adhesive except at doorways and seams. Any large areas of damage can be patched with an offcut. The new patch will need to be cut larger than the tear and adjusted to match the pattern. Having chosen a suitable line of pattern for the edge of the patch, you cut through both pieces of vinyl, using a sharp knife. The old piece is removed and the new patch coated with adhesive and pressed into place.

Rubber is a hard-wearing type of flooring which is quiet and waterproof. It is more difficult to lay than vinyl, and marks more easily. Linoleum is hard-wearing, but rots if water gets underneath.

Making a room template

The best material for making a template is thick paper felt sold as carpet underlay, which can be taped together to form the room shape. If replacement vinyl is being fitted, the old sheet can serve as the template. Outline the walls on the template, mark the position of any doorways and cut out holes to allow for awkward fittings. Lay out the template on the vinyl in a larger room or outdoors and centralize the pattern, then stick the template to the vinyl with adhesive tape. Transfer the outline of any obstacles from the template to the vinyl and cut a hole within the outline to allow for trimming. Then cut the vinyl about 2in (50mm) larger than the template.

Tracing obstacles on to the template

1 *Cut a line from the edge of the template to the back of the pedestal and cut a rough hole around it. Then, using a 1in (25mm) wooden block to trace the contour, pencil a line, 1in (25mm) larger than the object.*

2 *When transferring the shape to the vinyl, use the block to make the hole 1in (25mm) smaller than on the template, so that the cutting line falls within the template outline, allowing a generous margin.*

How to lay and trim sheet vinyl

If you have used the template method (page 131), lay the cut-out vinyl sheet on the floor, taking care to align the pattern with the walls and allowing the surplus to rest against them. Smooth out the main area, eliminating any bubbles. Fit the vinyl around any obstructions by making release cuts at the edges. If possible, follow the natural lines in the pattern to disguise the cut marks. When the sheeting is in position, trim and fit the internal corners first, then the external corners and finally the borders. Pull the vinyl back at doorways and seams, spread a band of adhesive on the floor and smooth down the vinyl over it. If the room is too large to be completed with a single sheet, cut several lengths and join them. For joining sheets, see opposite. Never remove old vinyl by sanding or grinding; harmful asbestos fibres may be released into the air – they can be dangerous to health.

Fitting internal corners

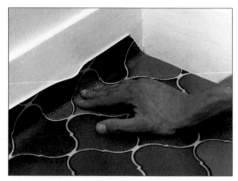

1 *Gently push the vinyl into the corner, allowing a 2in (50mm) surplus. Fold it back and mark the position of the corner on the back. Make a release cut down to the point of the corner.*

2 *Then cut away small pieces to remove the surplus until the vinyl lies flat along one wall, but work carefully to avoid overcutting. The vinyl will then need to be trimmed against the other wall.*

Trimming with scissors

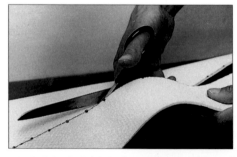

1 *Having fitted the corners, the remaining edges need to be trimmed around the skirting boards. The easiest way is to use scissors. Press the vinyl into the skirting with a large scraper, fold back the surplus material and mark dots along the fold line.*

2 *Pull the vinyl right back until it lies flat, join up the dots with a rule and cut along the line with scissors. If the vinyl buckles slightly at the wall when it is replaced, retrim the edges until it lies flat. Always cut off too little, or you may be left with a gap at the skirting.*

Trimming with a knife
The fastest way to trim the edges is to cut freehand, but this may need some practice to ensure a good fit. Press the vinyl firmly into the angle between the floor and the skirting with a broad paint scraper and cut to fit with a sharp trimming knife, held at an angle. Continue working all the way around the room and cut off the remnant strips.

Marking trimming lines with a scriber
Another method of trimming vinyl is to use a block of wood and pencil to mark a cutting line. Pull the vinyl slightly away from the wall, keeping the line of the material straight. Lodge the block firmly against the wall and trace the contours of the room on to the vinyl. Cut and fit, then repeat the sequence along the remaining walls.

Joining sheets of vinyl

Where more than one sheet is to be used, and joins are inevitable, add 3in (75mm) to each sheet for trimming on the overlap. You should mark a chalked guide line across the floor for the first length and try not to position seams in heavy-traffic areas.

Fit the sheets to the edges of the room, ensuring that the pattern matches at the overlap. Trim the edges, and secure the vinyl to the floor with adhesive. At this stage, if the vinyl is not the "lay flat" variety, it can be secured to the floor with an overall coating of adhesive. Where the two sheets meet in the main area of the room, make a cut through both sheets at the join along a suitable pattern line. Remove the offcuts and press the edges down on to a band of adhesive to form a neat seam. Subsequent sheets are joined in the same way, and when the last sheet is in place, any loose edges can be secured with adhesive. Wipe any surplus adhesive off the surface with a clean, damp cloth or rag.

To protect the material from scuffing, or to hide a bad join, fix binder bars in doorways or at joins. These aluminium bars have pre-drilled holes and are fixed down with screws.

Making the first join

1 *Overlap two sheets and, using a knife held vertically, cut through both layers.*

2 *Remove the top offcut strip, then fold back the edges of both sheets and remove the other.*

3 *Spread an 8in (20cm) band of vinyl adhesive on the floor along the join line. Replace the edges and press down firmly.*

4 *If necessary, use a wallpaper seam roller to ensure a firm bond. Finally, wipe off any surplus adhesive.*

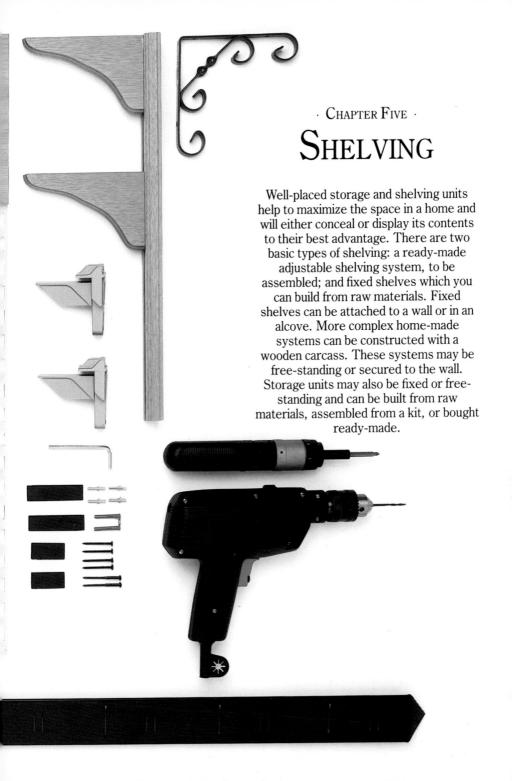

· CHAPTER FIVE ·

SHELVING

Well-placed storage and shelving units
help to maximize the space in a home and
will either conceal or display its contents
to their best advantage. There are two
basic types of shelving: a ready-made
adjustable shelving system, to be
assembled; and fixed shelves which you
can build from raw materials. Fixed
shelves can be attached to a wall or in an
alcove. More complex home-made
systems can be constructed with a
wooden carcass. These systems may be
free-standing or secured to the wall.
Storage units may also be fixed or free-
standing and can be built from raw
materials, assembled from a kit, or bought
ready-made.

Tools and equipment

If you are buying an adjustable shelving system, you may find that you need a hack-saw to cut the metal strips to the right length. If you have not bought your shelves ready-cut, or if you are building a timber framework, you will need a small hand- or power saw. For boring holes, use a hand-brace and drill bit, or a power drill with a masonry bit for solid walls, and a twist drill bit for wood. Use 2in (50mm), 2½in (63mm) or 3in (75mm) countersunk screws of the correct gauge and wallplugs for solid walls, and cavity dowels or toggles for hollow walls. You will also need a measuring tape, rule and spirit level.

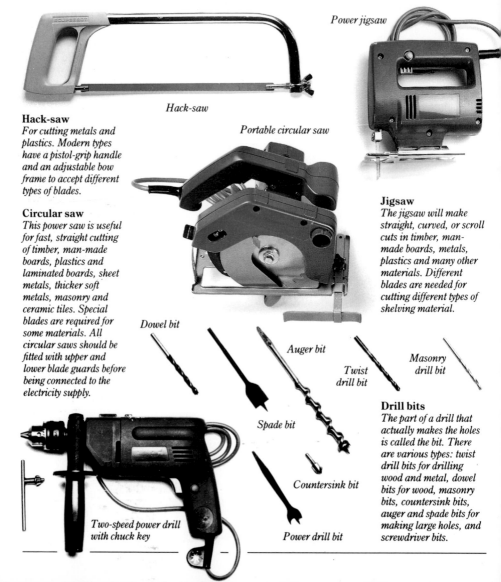

Power jigsaw

Hack-saw

Hack-saw
For cutting metals and plastics. Modern types have a pistol-grip handle and an adjustable bow frame to accept different types of blades.

Portable circular saw

Circular saw
This power saw is useful for fast, straight cutting of timber, man-made boards, plastics and laminated boards, sheet metals, thicker soft metals, masonry and ceramic tiles. Special blades are required for some materials. All circular saws should be fitted with upper and lower blade guards before being connected to the electricity supply.

Jigsaw
The jigsaw will make straight, curved, or scroll cuts in timber, man-made boards, metals, plastics and many other materials. Different blades are needed for cutting different types of shelving material.

Dowel bit

Auger bit

Twist drill bit

Masonry drill bit

Spade bit

Drill bits
The part of a drill that actually makes the holes is called the bit. There are various types: twist drill bits for drilling wood and metal, dowel bits for wood, masonry bits, countersink bits, auger and spade bits for making large holes, and screwdriver bits.

Countersink bit

Two-speed power drill with chuck key

Power drill bit

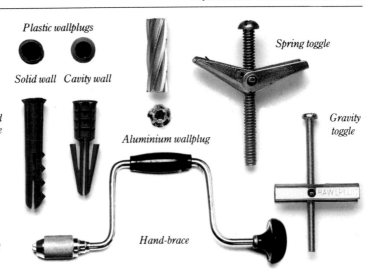

Wallplugs
Used in brick, concrete and masonry. There are different types for solid and cavity walls.

Plastic wallplugs

Solid wall   Cavity wall

Aluminium wallplug

Spring toggle

Gravity toggle

Toggles
Spring toggles are pushed through a pre-drilled hole and spring apart in the cavity. Use gravity toggles for vertical surfaces only.

Hand-brace
To drill large-diameter holes in wood. Fitted with the appropriate bit it can also drive and withdraw screws.

Hand-brace

Fixed shelf supports

For wall-mounted, fixed shelving, brackets or wooden battens can be fitted. L-shaped brackets fit standard shelf widths and are fixed to a flush wall if there is a suitable width of shelf. Wooden battens are only suitable in a recess, since there is no supporting arm. For a long shelf, fit an extra batten on the back wall. Triangular brackets and angled metal strips are also used in alcoves. Cantilever brackets are inserted into the back edge of the shelf at each end, to provide an invisible support.

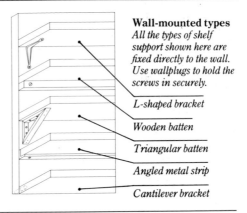

Wall-mounted types
All the types of shelf support shown here are fixed directly to the wall. Use wallplugs to hold the screws in securely.

L-shaped bracket

Wooden batten

Triangular batten

Angled metal strip

Cantilever bracket

Adjustable shelf supports

For lightweight, adjustable shelving, pegs, dowels, plastic studs, clips and wire can be inserted into holes in wooden uprights. Metal or plastic studs come in various shapes and sizes. They slot into holes in wooden uprights at each corner of the shelf. There are special ones designed for glass shelving. Wooden dowels can be cut to length and tapped into holes at the corners. Invisible wire supports and metal clips are neat and unobtrusive types of equipment.

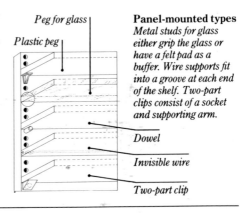

Peg for glass

Plastic peg

Panel-mounted types
Metal studs for glass either grip the glass or have a felt pad as a buffer. Wire supports fit into a groove at each end of the shelf. Two-part clips consist of a socket and supporting arm.

Dowel

Invisible wire

Two-part clip

Choosing and fixing storage systems

Storage space is at a premium in most homes, and whether you choose storage units or shelving will depend both on the space available and the use to which it will be put. Fixed storage systems include fitted cupboards, modular units, and some types of shelving. More flexible varieties are free-standing units and adjustable shelving.

Storage units and shelving kits can be bought ready-cut to be assembled at home. This is the quickest way to create storage space. Instructions are included, but you should check that all the necessary parts are there. You may not find kits that meet your needs, however, and you will have to create your own units. Some types of shelving material can easily be cut to fit awkward corners, but make sure that the material is strong enough for the purpose, otherwise it will bend and look unsightly.

Loft space
The existing room shape will often suggest storage space. Alcoves, corners, or the space created by the slope of an attic roof (below) can be transformed into attractive features, while housing books, ornaments or household items. Cellars and attics need to be warm and dry for storage, so insulate them first.

Grids and hooks
Hanging racks and hooks provide convenient storage in a kitchen (above) and make an attractive frame for herbs and utensils.

Window space
Objects displayed on window shelves and sills make an attractive arrangement (right) but the window must be sealed first.

Using storage space

Every room offers more storage space than meets the eye. Under beds, sofas and window seats, over doors, beds and staircases, in corners, lofts and cellars, and behind doors, there is usually space to be used. Storage units can be built around washbasin pedestals, to span alcoves and overhang beds; wardrobes can be fitted to the full height of the wall, and extra shelves can be added to cupboards.

Fold-away and pull-out tables and beds help to keep the living area of a room clear. Practical storage ideas can also be decorative, and it is worth improvising for individual effects. Everyday items such as shoes can be openly displayed on hooks, for example; and old tins, paint cans, barrels and chimney pots make useful and attractive containers. Keep an eye open for the decorative possibilities of storage systems. Ideally, all storage and shelving systems should be moveable and adjustable, to take account of changing needs.

Modular and built-in units
Units built up from shelves, drawers and cupboards offer flexibility and choice. Two modules can be spaced apart to allow a shelf or desk top to rest on top. Free-standing units can be used as room dividers but must be weighed down at the bottom to prevent toppling. Built-in cupboards may be designed to fit into chimney-breast alcoves or perhaps to bridge a gap between various kitchen fittings, for example.

Free-standing drawer units
Drawer units can be bought ready-made, as a kit, or built from raw materials. Moulded drawers, made from high-impact polystyrene, are also available.

How to make a screw fixing

Most shelf supports need to be secured to a wall or panel by means of screws. The weight of the load will determine the size and strength of the screw, and the type of wall will determine the style of the fixing. For most shelves you will need 2in (50mm), 2½in (63mm) or 3in (75mm)-long screws, according to the size of shelf. Likewise, you should choose a screw gauge suitable for the maximum shelf weight. No. 6 screws are adequate only for light weights, while No. 10 screws will support a heavily laden shelf. Use these two extremes as a guide for choosing a suitable gauge. Screws will not grip on their own in masonry or plasterboard, so in most cases you will have to use some sort of wallplug (page 137).

Fixing screws in solid walls

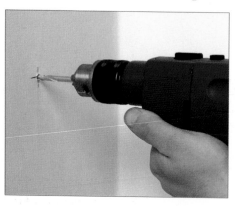

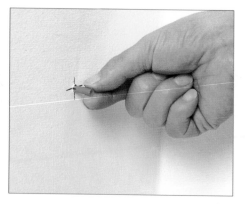

1 *Drill a hole into the wall to the depth of the wallplug. To prevent the drill bit from slipping before you begin, make a small indentation in the wall by turning the drill manually. Plaster is not strong, so be sure to penetrate deeper into the masonry. To avoid drilling too far, however, wrap some adhesive tape around the drill bit, the length of the wallplug away from the tip.*

2 *Insert the wallplug into the hole and drive in the screw. The plug will then expand and the screw will be held securely in the wall. Take care, however, not to tighten the screw so hard that it breaks through the end of the plug. Do not drill holes near electrical switches or sockets or if you think pipes may run behind the wall; it could prove dangerous.*

Fixing screws in cavity walls

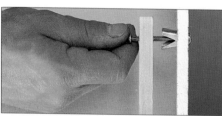

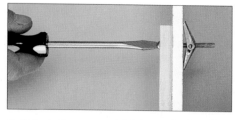

1 *A partition wall is too thin to allow a screw to grip sufficiently. Drill a hole and insert the toggle into the wall. When it no longer meets the resistance of the wall its "wings" open and anchor the fixing in position. Only drill a small hole, just wide and deep enough to take the plug or toggle.*

2 *Drive in the screw, maintaining tension by pulling back the fitting. This will cause the plug or toggle to open. If you have a partition wall with a timber framework, drill and screw directly into the supports. To locate the timber uprights, tap the wall and where it makes a dull sound, make your drill holes.*

Fixing screws in wooden surfaces

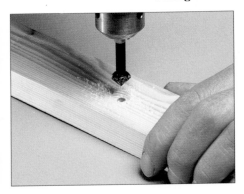

1 *To ensure straight fixing holes when you are putting up a wooden batten, try drilling right through the wood and into the wall in one go. Use a twist drill bit to drill a hole slightly smaller than the screw. This will ensure that it grips well. Alternatively, drill a pilot hole, then countersink the hole.*

2 *Insert a wallplug, tap it flush, then tap the screw into the end of the plug. When the end of the plug lies flush with the wall, drive in the screw with a screwdriver until it lies just below the surface of the wood. For larger holes, use a hand-brace and bit or a power drill and flat bit.*

Putting up a fixed shelf

When you have decided how much weight the shelf is to bear, choose a suitable thickness and width of shelving and sufficiently sturdy brackets and screws. L-shaped brackets are the best for fixed shelves. For small shelves or if your wall is even, it is worth fixing the bracket to the shelf before screwing it to the wall. If your wall is uneven, or if the shelf is very long, it may prove easier to put the brackets on the wall first, then fix the shelf to the brackets. If the shelf is to bear a heavy load, use cantilever brackets.

Use a spirit level to mark the position of both brackets. Drill two holes in the wall for the first bracket, and when it is in position, insert

Fixing brackets to the wall
Hold the shelf up to the wall with a spirit level on top, and when you have it at the correct height and level, mark the position of both brackets on the wall with a pencil.

and tighten the screws. Then repeat for the second bracket. With the two brackets in position on the wall, put the shelf on top, centre it over the brackets and push it firmly against the wall. When it is in position, screw the first bracket to the underside of the shelf. Check that the shelf is straight, then screw the second bracket to the shelf.

FITTING ALCOVE SHELVING

Recessed shelving can be supported by wooden battens, angled metal strips or triangular brackets, which are fitted to the wall in the same way as L-shaped brackets. If, however, the walls are very uneven, it may be best to make two

wooden side uprights to fit against the walls and fix the shelves to them.

Cut three battens to length, one to span the back wall and two for the side walls, each slightly shorter than the width of the shelf. Drill holes in the

battens every 18in (45cm), then drill corresponding holes in the wall, along the horizontal line. Insert wallplugs and screw the battens into position. Rest the shelf in the alcove on the battens. No further fixing is required after this point.

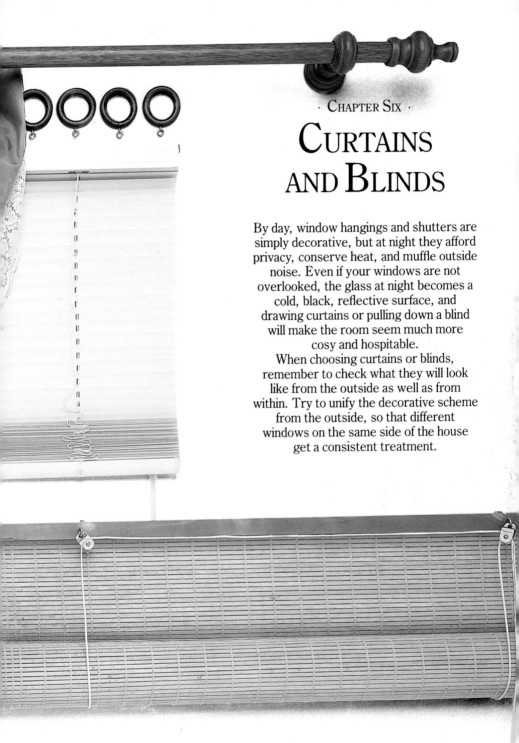

CHAPTER SIX

CURTAINS AND BLINDS

By day, window hangings and shutters are simply decorative, but at night they afford privacy, conserve heat, and muffle outside noise. Even if your windows are not overlooked, the glass at night becomes a cold, black, reflective surface, and drawing curtains or pulling down a blind will make the room seem much more cosy and hospitable.

When choosing curtains or blinds, remember to check what they will look like from the outside as well as from within. Try to unify the decorative scheme from the outside, so that different windows on the same side of the house get a consistent treatment.

Sewing equipment

If you do a great deal of sewing, it is a good idea to convert part of a room, or even a whole room, to suit this purpose. In this way, items of equipment are less likely to go missing, and you will not feel that the work is taking over. Shelving and cupboards are useful for storing equipment and fabrics; otherwise, you should keep all your equipment together near where you work.

You need a space which has good lighting, either natural or artificial, with lights and lamps arranged so that they cast as little shadow as possible. If you use adaptor plugs for sewing equipment and lighting, be careful not to overload them. Also, keep an eye on stocks of pins, needles and markers, so that you do not run out of these essential sewing supplies in the middle of a job.

Sewing machines

An electric machine with straight-stitch and zigzag settings is efficient and adequate for work on home furnishings. A machine with these relatively limited functions is called a zigzag or swing-needle model.

A semi-automatic machine is rather more sophisticated, including facilities for blind-hemming, buttonholing and a few simple embroidery stitches. A fully automatic model has all the above and a stretch-stitch capacity that is ideal for knit fabrics. This offers additional embroidery stitches and a more efficient method of working buttonholes.

Electronic machines have exceptionally easy, push-button or touch-control selection for a wide range of stitches, often with a "mirror" facility that allows any pattern to be worked in reverse, so that the pattern direction can be alternated. Other functions include an automatic technical adjustment that allows equal needle penetration at all speeds on all types of fabric. There may also be stitch-by-stitch control for accuracy in areas of intricate work, and a memory that stores a selection of stitches and repeats them as required at the touch of a switch. It is also possible to work lettering and border motif repeats.

Threading the machine

Machine stitching is formed by the interlocking of an upper and lower thread; the upper thread comes from a bought reel slotted on to the machine, the lower from a bobbin loaded with thread and positioned under the needle plate.

Most machines are threaded in a similar way – the upper thread is taken across from the reel, down into the tension discs, up through the take-up lever, down again and through the needle. Thread the machine with the take-up lever and presser foot raised: the instruction booklet will explain this and how to wind thread on to the bobbin and insert it below the needle.

In straight stitch the needle creates a single line of stitching. In zigzag and decorative stitching the needle swings from side to side as well as moving forward. Stretch stitches include a backward movement which allows "give", so that stitches do not break as the fabric itself – jersey or knit fabric – gives with use. Some of the stretch stitches provide useful extra strength in stitching heavy fabrics. A wide range of machines also have the facility for twin-needle work, which creates a double line of stitching.

The presser foot of a machine controls the feed-through of the fabric. There are usually several types supplied with the machine and one of the most useful is the zipper foot. This allows you to stitch very close to the teeth of an inserted zip and works equally well for seaming alongside a bulky piping cord.

Sewing-machine needles are available in all points, as for hand-sewing needles – *sharp* for woven fabrics, *ballpoint* for knits, *wedge-shaped* for leather, suede and vinyl. Correct size is important; the wrong needle puts a strain on the thread, and if it is too thick it can leave ugly holes in the fabric, or split the seams of fine fabrics such as voile and organdie. Be guided by the instructions supplied by the sewing-machine manufacturer.

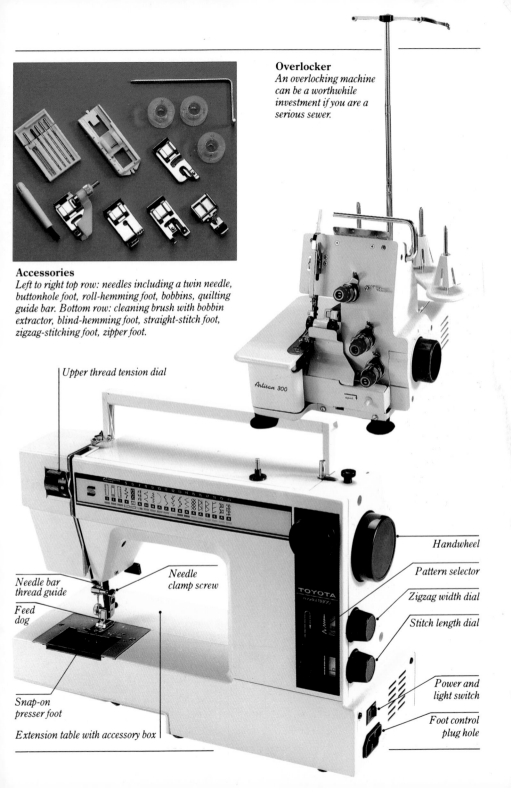

Overlocker
An overlocking machine can be a worthwhile investment if you are a serious sewer.

Accessories
Left to right top row: needles including a twin needle, buttonhole foot, roll-hemming foot, bobbins, quilting guide bar. Bottom row: cleaning brush with bobbin extractor, blind-hemming foot, straight-stitch foot, zigzag-stitching foot, zipper foot.

Upper thread tension dial

Handwheel

Pattern selector

Zigzag width dial

Stitch length dial

Needle clamp screw

Needle bar thread guide

Feed dog

Power and light switch

Foot control plug hole

Snap-on presser foot

Extension table with accessory box

Cutting equipment

Cutting out fabric with poor scissors is hard work and leads to inaccuracies which will ultimately show up in the hang or fit of the finished item. Have two pairs of good scissors – one used only for cutting out fabric and the other for close cutting when making up. Keep these separate from household scissors so that the blades are not blunted by general use.

When choosing scissors, take along fabric pieces of different weights and ask if it is possible to test before buying. If the scissors are sold in sealed packaging, a sample pair may be available for testing. Check that they not only perform the task of cutting efficiently, but also are well-contoured and feel comfortable in your hand, for straight cutting and curves.

Dressmaker's (sidebent) scissors are large and suitably weighted for cutting out fabric. Eight to 10in (20 to 25cm) is a suitable length. Left-handed and "ambidextrous" models are now available.

Needlework (embroidery) scissors are small, about 5 to 5½in (12 to 14cm) long. They are sharp at the point and cut with a clean, quick action for trimming or clipping threads and seams, for cutting into confined areas or for following intricate shaping. Electric scissors are either mains or battery operated. Test them before buying, as some types are not useful for fine or bulky fabrics, although they deal efficiently with medium-weight materials.

Pinking shears are more useful for dressmaking than for soft furnishings but can be used on small items, to trim seam allowances on non-fraying fabric as an alternative to overcasting. The shears should be used for neatening seams after sewing, not for initial cutting out. A seam ripper is indispensible for quick unpicking of seams. It has a small, sharply curved blade with a long and short point fixed in a narrow plastic handle, and a protective plastic cover.

Sewing aids

There is a wide range of modern, well-made and attractively designed equipment available which is suitable for both the amateur and the professional. Most of the items are inexpensive.

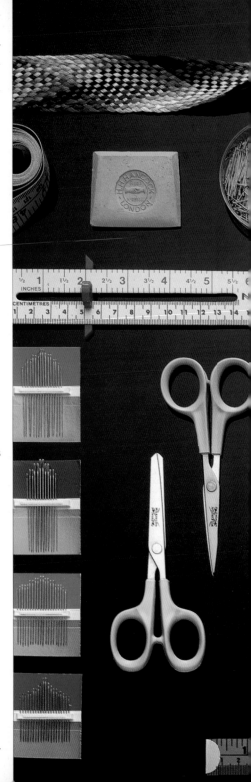

Types of needle

Although sewing machines have taken away much of the slow and tedious work of hand sewing, some stages of any job will involve hand sewing nevertheless. You will need a range of needles, therefore, for fine and heavy fabrics. Tacking, finishing and embroidering decorative details also need different types and sizes of needle.

Sharps are used for general domestic sewing. They are long and have oval eyes, which make them suitable for a wide range of fabrics. Milliner's needles are similar to sharps, but are longer. They are used for jobs such as tacking, where their extra length is an advantage. Betweens are also similar to sharps, but are shorter and used for medium and heavyweight fabrics.

The bodkin is used to thread cord, elastic or ribbon through a casing. It is blunt and thick since it does not go through the fabrics. Ballpoint needles are used with knit fabrics. They push the fibres aside, thus leaving the texture itself undamaged. Tapestry needles, used for embroidery and tapestry work, can also be used for threading ribbon or elastic.

Marking and measuring equipment

Curtains and blinds rely for their effect to a great extent on both accurate cutting and measuring. Curtains in particular should have hems and heads of equal length, or they will have a distinctly amateurish look. Inaccurate measuring can lead to a great waste of expensive material, so take care at this stage. Tailor's chalk is sold in various colours. Ideally you should have at least two, to mark light- and dark-coloured materials. It comes in pencil form and in flat pieces. An alternative is to use a water-soluble marker. The colouring can be rinsed out with water.

There are various types of measure, the most common of which is the tape measure. Use a fibreglass or linen one if possible, since these hardly stretch at all and thus give greater accuracy. The metre stick is useful for measuring curtains. It will not stretch and is easier to handle than a tape measure.

Sewing aids

If you find it difficult to thread fine needles, a threader is a useful, inexpensive investment. A fine metal, looped filament passes through the needle eye; the thread is slotted into the loop and drawn back through the needle. The thimble is a useful but often ignored sewing aid, invaluable when you are dealing with a tough fabric or with several heavy layers.

Pins

You can choose the plain stainless steel type, or the larger glass-headed pins which come in several colours. These are more easily seen when they are embedded in the fabric. Ballpoint pins are available for use with knit fabrics. Do not use pins on leather or suede; keep the edges together with small pieces of adhesive tape on the wrong side.

Pins
The smaller types are available in plain stainless steel, while the larger ones have glass heads in various colours, making them easy to see against the fabric.

Make sure that you have sufficient pins when starting a big project. Keep them together in a box and do not use any that are rusted or bent. Do not leave them too long in the fabric, as they may cause marking. A pincushion makes them more accessible while you are working; a magnet is a handy device for picking up spilled pins.

Special fabric adhesive, which is usually sold in stick form, is quick and easy to use when turning up a hem on lightweight fabrics before you finally stitch it in place.

Pressing equipment

Pressing is an important part of home-sewing projects – to flatten and smooth out seams and hems as you go along and to give a crisp, professional look to the finished item. Equip yourself with a steam or steam-and-spray iron; it is not the weight of the iron but the heat and moisture which take out the creases. Ask for pressing instructions as well as washing and cleaning advice when you purchase fabric. Match any symbol markings on the fabric label to the settings on your iron. A non-stick coating on the soleplate of the iron gives easy movement over the fabric; take care not to press any pinned areas, as the pins could damage the coating.

Choose an ironing board or table of suitable height and width – a pull-out sheet rail, available on some models, is very handy for pressing large items, keeping them flat and clear of the floor.

A muslin or soft cotton cloth, slightly dampened, protects the surface of the fabric while it is pressed, although some steam irons can be used without a pressing cloth. A piece of light, firm woollen cloth, again made lightly damp, prevents the flattening of woollen fabric. Wash out the cloth before use to remove any dressing. It can be kept damp during pressing by sprinkling with water – a plant-mister spray

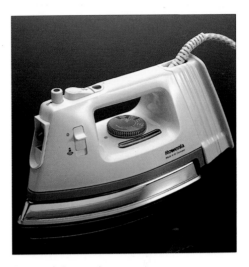

Steam-and-spray iron
The heat and moisture, rather than the weight of the iron, take the creases out of fabrics.

is an inexpensive but invaluable accessory for this purpose. When pressing pleats, use brown paper under the folds to prevent depressions from pressing into the fabric underneath.

If the soleplate of the iron picks up a deposit from dressing in fabric, periodic use of a proprietary brand cleaner, usually sold in stick form, helps to restore "slide" to an iron that has developed a tendency to drag on the fabric.

Choosing the right thread

Thread should be chosen individually for each project to suit the weight and type of fabric. Use cotton thread for natural fabrics, such as cotton, linen and wool. Synthetic threads are made for use with man-made and synthetic fabrics, for example acrylic, polyester and nylon. Silks and fine fabrics should be stitched with silk thread or a fine cotton filament. Special tacking threads are available, or you can use up left-over reels for tacking, but do not make do with what you have for finished stitching: an unsuitable thread is likely to break or cause puckering. If you use the same thread

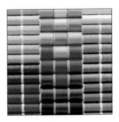

Shades of thread
Try to match thread and fabric as closely as possible. If the match is not precise, a darker rather than a lighter shade will blend better with the material.

as you will be using for finished stitching, you risk running out of thread later on. When buying thread, if you cannot get a precise colour match between thread and fabric, choose a slightly darker shade, which will blend in more evenly than a lighter colour. Secure the loose ends on the reels after sewing, and keep them together in a box.

Curtains

When choosing fabrics for curtains it is important to select colour, pattern and texture to suit the style of the room. The price, of course, will also be a significant consideration, and it is always better to buy a slightly cheaper fabric and use it lavishly than to skimp on a more expensive material. Curtains need to be about two to two and a half times the width of the window, and they will never look good if they are not full enough. Also, you should allow for wastage and for pattern repeats where necessary.

Hanging curtains

The method you choose for hanging curtains may affect the way they should be made, so you must consider the type of track, pole or rod that can be used at the same time as deciding on a suitable heading tape for the styling you have in mind.

Poles and tracks

A basic track supports the curtains directly; the hooks attaching the heading tape function as both hook and runner and are threaded over the track.

A traditional track is designed to have runners or gliders hanging from the track. Hooks are inserted in the curtain heading and then attached to the runners. Any standard or decorative heading tape can be used.

A decorative metal or wooden pole can be of any thickness you wish, providing it will support the curtains adequately and you can find rings large enough to thread over the pole. Large curtain rings are fitted with a smaller ring at the base to which the curtain hooks are attached. The pole is fixed on brackets screwed into the wall or the ceiling.

Expandable or sprung-tension rods are ideal for nets or sheer curtains. They are fitted between flat facing walls, in a narrow bay or across the window inset. Fine rods and curtain wire can support a lightweight curtain directly through a cased heading on the curtain which threads over the rod or wire. Narrow metal and plastic rods are available. Curtain wire is a coiled length in a plastic sheath, slightly expandable and fixed by means of eyelets screwed into the wire at either end, which can be attached to simple cup-hooks.

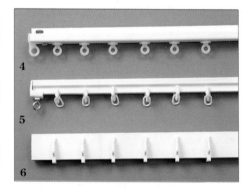

Poles and tracks
Curtain tracks were traditionally hidden by a pelmet or curtain valance, but the modern streamlined tracks are unobtrusive when curtains are drawn back, and poles are a decorative feature. Some are flexible, making them suitable for bay windows.

1 *Light wooden pole with concealed runners*
2 *Metallic-finished pole with rings*
3 *Polished wooden pole with rings*
4 *Track with concealed runners*
5 *Track with exposed runners*
6 *Basic track with combined hooks and runners*

Choosing the hanging method

Whichever type of track or pole you choose, make sure that it is available in long enough lengths for your windows; joins are impractical. It must also be strong enough for the type of curtain you want. If you have curved or bay windows, choose a track that can be bent around corners. Check also whether a cording set can be fitted to the track. Most types of straight track accept pull cords, so that you can close and open the curtains from one side. But some types of curved track will not take pull cords. The traditional brass curtain track has been largely superseded by nylon, plastic and aluminium track, and wooden poles. As well as the traditional brass tracks, those used with a pelmet include aluminium and plastic types with nylon runners.

Fixing curtain tracks to a wall

Most curtain tracks are sold with the brackets you need to put them up, and sometimes with the screws and wallplugs as well. Putting up poles involves the same technique as putting up curtain rails. True poles only require brackets at either end, so they may not be the best choice for long windows, unless they are strong enough to take the weight of the curtains without sagging. Imitation poles can be fitted with brackets at intervals.

Curtain tracks can be fitted to the window frame itself, but it is unlikely that there will be enough space in the reveal for anything except lightweight net curtains. So the best solution is to fit the rail to the wall above the window. Drilling the wall and inserting wallplugs should be simple with a hammer drill and a masonry bit unless there is a concrete lintel above the window. In this case, the best solution is to fit a batten above the window.

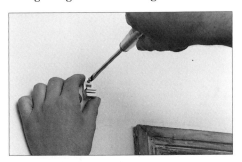

Fitting brackets to the wall
Drill holes in the wall at regular intervals to take the screws and wallplugs. When you mark the positions for the holes, always use a spirit level to make sure that they are level.

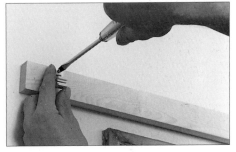

Fitting brackets to a batten
Remove any paper from the wall. Then attach the batten at either end with screws and wallplugs and secure the central part with contact adhesive. Paint or paper over it.

FIXING CURTAIN TRACKS TO A CEILING

If the top of the window is very close to the ceiling, it may be easier to fix the brackets to the ceiling. Hollow wallplugs in the ceiling itself will not be strong enough. Find the positions of the joists above the ceiling and screw into these. They are usually about 16in (40cm) apart. On lower floors, the easiest way to pinpoint joists is to lift a floorboard in the room above and make a tiny marking hole through the ceiling next to the joists. On top floors, find the joists by going into the loft. If the joists run at right angles to the wall, fix a bracket to each one. Use screws that are long enough to go through the full thickness of the ceiling plaster and into the joists themselves. If the ceiling is in poor condition, fix a batten first, and the track to it.

Visual effects

It is possible to use fabric to alter the appearance of less-than-perfect windows, to make them seem larger or smaller, of better proportions, or simply to make them look more interesting or unusual. To block a dreary view, hang full-length pretty nets or sheers that will admit enough light into a room that is in permanent daytime use.

To preserve your privacy without cutting out all the light, place café curtains over the lower half of the window. This also draws attention away from ageing or unpleasantly designed window frames.

To make a large window look smaller
Fix curtains to meet at the top of the window, but loop them up at the sides with tie-backs.

To avoid covering a radiator
Hang long "dress" curtains, but keep them drawn back, and use a blind to cover the window.

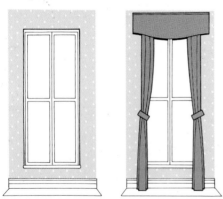

To lower the height of a tall window
Fixing a deep pelmet or valance across the top of a window will make it seem lower. A pelmet fixed above a window will make it seem taller.

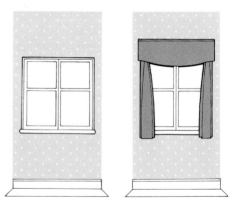

An illusion of width
Extending the curtain rail at either side of the window improves the proportions of a narrow window, making it appear wider than it is.

Other effects with curtains

For a dramatic effect, or if paired curtains would overpower a narrow window, a single, asymmetrical curtain can be very effective. A flat curtain suspended from hooks through eyelet holes in the fabric can be attractive, and tie-backs can create interesting shapes. Other interesting effects can be created with net curtains. While their main purpose is to prevent people seeing in, you can use them more imaginatively, by draping them elaborately, using them to diffuse light, or gathering them on the type of headings used on conventional window curtains.

Matching fittings
Curtains, tie-backs, pelmets and cushions made of the same fabric create a harmonious effect in this spacious bay window.

Curtains and blinds
The combination of curtains and blinds gives great flexibility – the translucent blind lets in some light, while the curtains either side act not only as light shields but also as decorative features.

Net curtains can diffuse light
You can diffuse bright sunlight with full-length net curtains. In this room the striped and textured effect of the full net curtains is picked up by the reflective glass surface of the coffee table.

Curtain fabrics

Curtain fabrics are available in an almost endless variety of colours, textures and patterns, ranging from lightweight sheers to heavyweight velvets and figured weaves. There is no particular restriction on the type of fabric you could use – as long as it suits your purpose and is reasonably practical from the point of view of cleaning and rehanging. Loose-weave and open-textured fabrics can be a problem, tending to sag dismally soon after hanging, but you can get around this by supporting them with a firm, medium-weight lining. Of course, as the fabric must hang permanently in the window, choose a type that does not fade or discolour in the sun.

Lightweights, such as sheers, voiles, laces and nets, are primarily used to provide some privacy while allowing light to come into the room, so they are often hung under heavier curtains. These fabrics are usually sold in light colours – white, cream, beige and pale pastels – although some stores stock deep-coloured laces which create an unusually dramatic effect. If you are given to browsing around second-hand shops and markets, you may be lucky enough to come upon an undamaged length of old lace which will enhance a period décor or disguise a stained table.

Medium-weights are available in a variety of fibres and in a wide range of patterns and finishes. These are the most popular and versatile curtaining fabrics. Medium-weights can be used almost anywhere and are particularly useful if you want the loose covers and cushions in the room to be made to match.

Heavyweights include brocade, linen union and velvet, suitable for traditional and formal styles of curtaining. It is usual to line heavy fabrics, and they have excellent draping qualities for floor-length curtains, hanging evenly by their own weight. They also have good insulating properties, although medium-weights can be given insulating linings which can be just as effective.

Choosing fabrics

Fabrics are made from different fibres, come in a range of weights and textures, and are found in hundreds of different colours and patterns. The fabric you choose should be appropriate in its use as much as in its appearance. Many shops now helpfully indicate suitable uses for the various materials, and sales staff should be able to give sound advice. Always read the label on a roll of fabric, to check its fibre content and any special properties. Be sure of instructions for care and cleaning; whether or not a fabric is washable may be the most important thing you need to know about it.

Check that fabrics are fade-resistant; this, obviously, is very important for curtains, blinds and curtain linings.

Do not try to save on the amount of fabric you buy in order to afford your most expensive choice; it is a false economy and you will get a better effect from being generous with a less expensive material. But do go for good quality, whatever the price range: it is not worth spending time and effort on making up an item which soon appears worn and lifeless. If your budget, or the effect you want, seems to dictate a choice of inexpensive light- or medium-weight fabric, rub it between your hands to see if any dressing comes out, leaving the cloth itself rather limp. Check for flaws in the weave or pattern; these should be indicated by a contrast thread marker at the selvedge. Be sure to buy sufficient length to complete what you intend to make; it may be difficult to colour-match fabric from a different roll later on.

Some fabrics have a shrink-resistant finish. If not, shrinkage must be generously allowed for, as it can make a considerable difference to the calculation of the amount needed: there may be 6 per cent or more shrinkage on untreated cottons. Certain synthetics require this allowance, too, particularly loose-weave types. When thinking about trimmings, such as frills, ribbons or tassels, make sure that they are compatible with the fabric and the lining.

Colour and pattern

The design on a fabric goes a long way towards setting the style of a room. It is a message about your personality and way of life, so your instincts and natural preferences are important when it comes to choosing colours and patterns. Colour creates impact, and many people find it difficult to visualize colour effects on a relatively large scale. This often leads to a choice of "safe" or neutral colours for basic décor, with small areas of contrast or bold focus. Although colour may be the strongest feature of a design, it is never an independent factor. Two colours always affect each other.

If you intend to use patterned fabrics, your thoughts on colour become further complicated by the style and scale of the pattern design. Co-ordinated fabrics may solve the problem, but it can be more exciting, and a far more personal choice, to mix and match from the full range available. Think about mixing large and small patterns, using the same fabric in reversed colourways, opting for a monochromatic or harmonious scheme, or a riot of paintbox colours.

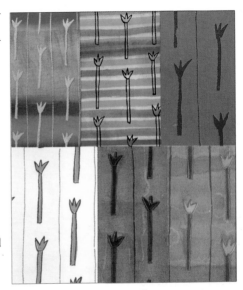

The effects of colours on each other
The variations of colour in this basic pattern show how colours affect each other, producing warm, cool, exotic or simple effects. If you are mixing patterns, take a key element such as shape, colour, scale or direction to make a link between them.

PATTERN AND TEXTURE CHECKLIST

- Patterned fabrics are more practical than plain, as they do not show soiling as readily.
- Texture affects the "seen" value of colour, and this varies with change of light.
- Viewed from a distance, subtle colouring can merge and pattern detail may disappear.
- Light colours suggest an expansive effect, whereas dark shades tend towards intimacy.
- Fabric patterns should be printed on the straight grain of the fabric, to give the correct effect at seams and hems.
- A large pattern repeat will mean that more fabric is required overall.
- When different patterns are combined to make up a single article, the fabrics should have equal weight and "give".
- The mutual enhancement or contrast of colours may be visible between schemes in adjoining rooms, as well as within a single room.
- A plain, textured fabric can create a focus without the need of patterns. Such a fabric is useful if a room will become visually cluttered by the use of another pattern.

FABRICS CHECKLIST

- Always use washable, easy-care fabrics for articles which need regular cleaning.
- When budgeting for fabric, choose to buy a generous quantity of inexpensive material rather than risk a skimped effect with a more expensive type of fabric.
- If using two or more fabrics to make up a single item, select similar weights and check that they are compatible for washing or cleaning.
- Allow for shrinkage if the fabric has no shrink-resistant finish and is not pre-shrunk.
- Check fabrics for flaws before purchasing.
- Try to get the full length you need taken from one fabric roll. If two rolls are used, check that the colours match perfectly.
- Test inexpensive fabrics for large amounts of dressing which will wash out at the first laundering, leaving the fabric limp and lifeless.
- Make sure that your fabric choice has the finishes – easy-care, shrink-, stain-, fade- and flame-resistance – required for its purpose.
- Do not use dress fabrics for main furnishing items, except as trimming or decoration.

Fabric construction

The majority of fabrics used in home furnishings are plain weaves, with the pattern, if there is one, printed on the surface. However, many types of fabrics are also woven to produce textured surface effects, self-coloured pattern motifs and pattern weaves of two or more colours.

Weave

Most furnishing fabrics feature weaves that it is possible to construct on a basic loom with no special attachments. These provide a surprising range of textures. Plain weave is the simplest woven structure; it may be made in one or more colours and with various types and thicknesses of yarn. When different colours are used for warp and weft, the result is described as "shot" fabric. With satin weave, more warp thread is exposed on the surface of the fabric than in plain weave, resulting in a smooth, unbroken and luxuriously shiny surface appearance. Twill weave is a diagonal, ridged pattern of varying effects according to yarn weight and direction of ridging. Traditional herring-bone is a variation on twill weave; diagonal ridging is reversed at regular intervals to create a zigzag pattern.

Leno weave is a lacy, open weave which may be combined with other weaves. It is made by twisting warp yarns around each other in figures-of-eight as the weft passes between them. Dobby weave has a more intricate texture, such as small geometric motifs woven in at regular intervals. Pile fabrics, such as corduroy and velvet, are produced by the use of two warp threads, one of which forms the base, the other being pulled upwards and cut to form the pile.

Texture

The texture of a fabric derives from the fibres and the method of construction. Textural variations are applied to the complete range of fabrics, from the finest sheers to the heaviest of natural-fibre materials. Their visual and tactile surface qualities create the atmosphere of a room design scheme.

Smooth, shiny surfaces give a cool look appropriate to sophisticated schemes. Depending upon the weight of the fabric, this can be designed to complement sleek hi-tech styling, or a formal, traditional style of décor. Rough or soft textures – matt, fluffy, slubbed, loosely woven – create a warmer atmosphere which may be formal or luxurious, with a rich pile fabric such as velvet, for example, or casual and informal, as with a coarsely woven material such as hessian, or a heavily slubbed weave. Fine ribs and inlaid pattern motifs can be used in any type of décor as a balancing factor. The introduction of textural interest is important where plain colours are favoured rather than a patterned fabric scheme.

Jacquard fabrics
These are produced on a special type of loom invented in 1801 by Joseph Jacquard for the weaving of figured fabrics. Self-coloured designs or designs of two or more colours can be woven. In damask, flat figuring is created by a contrast of satin and matt finishes; in brocade, on the other hand, the pattern is raised from a differently coloured background area.

Types of curtain heading

The important thing about your curtains is how they look to you. They can set the style of the whole room, and although they must have the necessary practical qualities, easy-care properties will not compensate for a mistake in styling that you will have to live with day in and day out.

Once you have an idea of the type of fabric you may choose, the next important decision is the heading tape, which can dictate informal or formal styling, the fullness, width and overall effect of this focal point in the room.

There is a remarkable range of heading tapes now available, in different materials to suit different fabrics – special tapes for nets and sheers, for example – and with a good variety of interesting design effects. The tape gathers or pleats the top of the curtain by means of cords threaded along the length, which draw up the fabric to a specific style – simple gathers, smocked gathers, narrow pencil pleats, clustered triple pleats. The tape also has lines of pockets where the curtain hooks are inserted and can be narrow or deep, with one row of pockets or three. Deep tapes allow you to position the curtain hooks to bring the top of the heading level with the track or standing slightly above it. If you are using a decorative pole to hang the curtains, the hooks can be placed on a line which leaves the curtain heading clear of the pole while concealing the hooks and base rings.

Pencil pleating
Classic pencil pleat heading tape forms crisp, even, upright pleats. The type shown has a special monofilament thread woven in, which keeps the heading upright. This tape requires 2¼ to 2½ times curtain fullness. It has two alternative rows of suspension pockets, so it can be used with any type of curtain track or with a decorative curtain pole.

Triple pinch pleating
An elegant heading tape with groups of three pleats spaced apart. The pleats are pinched in close together at the lower edge of the tape and fan out at the top. This tape requires 2 times curtain fullness. The tape has two alternative rows of suspension pockets, making it suitable for any type of curtain track or pole. Special curtain hooks are needed.

Lightweight pencil pleating
This type of heading tape is specially designed for use on lightweight fabrics, sheer fabrics and nets. It normally takes 2¼ to 2½ times curtain fullness, but on static nets, which will not be drawn back, 3 times fullness looks more attractive. This type of tape also has two rows of suspension pockets, making it suitable for any type of track or pole.

Standard heading tape
This is a narrow heading tape, about 1in (25mm) wide, which forms gathers. It is used mainly on small informal curtains and valances, and where the curtain heading will be hidden behind a valance or pelmet. It requires 1½ to 2 times curtain fullness. Standard tape has only one row of hook suspension pockets, so the tape should be positioned so that it will hide the track.

Estimating quantities

When measuring for curtains, use a wooden rule or a steel tape measure and hold it at eye level. It is essential that you calculate the fabric amounts accurately – guesswork inevitably results in too much or too little, either way an expensive mistake.

When you have decided on the full width, fix the track or pole. Measure with a wooden rule or steel tape to arrive at the width of the finished curtains after the heading is drawn up.

The measured width of the track is the basis of your calculation. Remember to allow a little extra if you are having an overlap at the centre. Multiply this measurement by 1½, 2 or 2½, depending on the heading tape (page 157). It may be necessary to join widths of fabric to make up this full measurement.

As well as deciding on the finished drop of the curtains, allow for the heading to cover or stand slightly above the curtain track. If you are hanging the curtains from a decorative pole, they will hang just clear of the pole, so that it is visible. Measure from the point where you estimate the top of the curtain should be to the point representing the finished length.

To this measurement you need to add allowances for the top turning and lower hem. The top turning allowance is generally 1½in (40mm) when a heading tape or facing is to be attached, but allow more if you are making a gathered heading with a frill standing above the tape. The lower hem is usually 6in (15cm) for unlined curtains – more if shrinkage is likely – and 4–6in (10–15cm) for lined curtains.

To work out how many drops are needed, divide the total width of both curtains by the width of your chosen fabric. Round up the final amount to the next whole number, which will create an allowance for seams and side hems. Divide the figure in two to find out the number of full-length fabric pieces in each curtain. This will also tell you whether a half-width is needed on either side.

The number of drops multiplied by the cut length is the total amount of fabric you need to buy. Remember to add a little extra material for pattern matching if necessary.

Measuring cross-over drapes

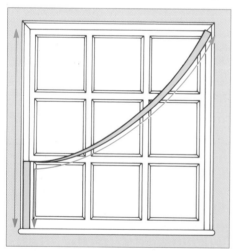 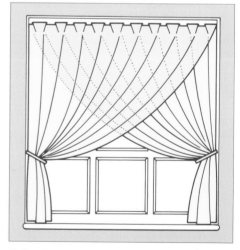

1 *The outer edge of each curtain should equal the window drop. To find the length of the inner edge, drape a tape measure across the window and down to the sill. Cut both curtains to the longer length. Mark off the shorter length down one side.*

2 *Lay the curtains with right sides together and cut diagonally across the bottom from the marked shorter length. Lay one curtain on top of the other, right sides upwards. Tack the top edges together. Hang the curtains, catching them back with tie-backs.*

Patterned fabrics

When selecting a patterned fabric for curtains, consider first how large an area they will cover when closed. A large pattern on a large area may be either exciting or overwhelming, according to your personal taste.

If you use patterned fabric, an allowance must be made for matching the pattern at seams and across both curtains. One extra pattern repeat should be allowed for each drop of fabric after the first (so add two pattern repeats if your curtain has three drops, and so on). In a pair of curtains, the pattern repeats should occur in the same place on each length for both curtains.

An easy method for matching the pattern in different lengths is to place a cut length over the next section of the fabric, aligning pattern details and marking them with pins. There will probably be some excess material to cut away between the end of one curtain length and the start of the next; these offcuts come in handy for tie-backs, a valance or pelmet, or cushions to match the curtains.

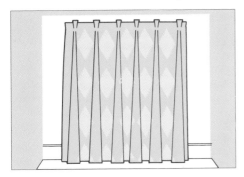

Partial repeats for long curtains
If you cut through a horizontal motif, position the partial repeat at the bottom of a floor-length curtain, where it will not be noticed.

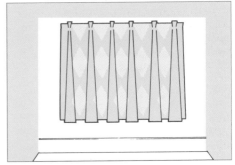

Partial repeats for short curtains
Place the cut-off repeat at the top and a full motif at the bottom, where it will be in the direct line of vision of those seated in the room.

QUANTITIES FOR DIFFERENT CURTAINS

- If you are having heavy, luxurious, floor-length curtains, you may wish to allow the full width to be drawn back clear of the window glass. This will take up quite a bit of space, since the heading will not bunch up tightly due to the thickness of the fabric. This means that the curtains will have to extend beyond the window area.
- If you choose lightweight, cotton fabric, on the other hand – for gathered kitchen curtains, for instance – these will not need much extra width beyond the window frame.
- The type of heading tape will also have a bearing on the width of the curtain.
- You may want to make an extra allowance for a generously draped effect with full-length curtains, with some of the fabric actually lying on the floor once the curtains are hung.
- Ask your fabric supplier to check your measurements if you do not feel confident when you are ordering the material.

POINTS TO REMEMBER

- Measure the width of the track or pole. Multiply by 1½ or 2½ (according to your choice of heading tape, page 157) for the finished width of curtains. Round up to the nearest whole figure for the number of drops required.
- Multiply the total number of drops by the cut length to find the total amount of fabric that you will need to buy.
- When measuring for curtains, always allow extra material for hems, headings and pattern repeats. If you find this difficult to calculate, an experienced assistant in a furnishing fabrics department will be able to help you if you provide the basic measurements.
- Make sure that any curtain rails or poles you want to use are available in sufficient lengths – joins are not usually possible.
- If you are using a batten to support curtain rail brackets, fix it securely to the wall using screws and, if necessary, adhesive.

Unlined curtains

Quick and simple to make, inexpensive but attractive and practical, unlined curtains are ideal for the kitchen or bathroom, or other working areas where they may be exposed to dirt and need frequent washing. Printed cottons are definitely the best choice and offer a range of lovely colours and patterns, from quaintly traditional florals to bright, bold abstracts and geometricals.

You will probably need to join several fabric widths in order to make up the total width required for each curtain. If you have to cut a half width as well as full widths, place the half width at the outer edge of the curtain. You can join the panels with a simple flat seam, but a flat fell seam conceals the raw edges.

To make a flat fell seam, place the fabric right sides together and pin and stitch a flat seam. Turn the fabric over and press the seam open. Trim one seam allowance to ⅛in (3mm) and turn under ¼in (6mm) on the other seam allowance and press. Fold the larger seam allowance over the trimmed one to enclose the raw edge. Press to the main fabric. Stitch through all the fabric layers close to the edge of the fold. Only one line of stitching will show.

A gathered heading suits the simple styling of unlined curtains, but you can use a more elaborate pleated or smocked effect; look at the range of available heading tapes and decide on the style when you choose the fabric, so that you know how much to buy. With a gathered heading, you can allow for a small frill standing above the heading tape, turning over 1½in (40mm) at the top edge of the curtain and stitching the tape 1in (25mm) below.

Calculating fabric amounts

Width: Multiply the width of the track by the fullness required for the heading. Add 1½in (40mm) for each side hem. Divide the total by the width of the fabric, rounding up to the next full width. Allow 1¼in (30mm) for each join.
Length: Measure the length of the area you are curtaining; add 1½in (40mm) for the top heading hem and 6in (15cm) for the bottom hem. Multiply the length by the number of widths needed to give the fabric amount.

Making up unlined curtains

1 *Along each side of the curtain, turn a ½in (12mm) hem to the wrong side. Press in place. At the bottom of the fabric, turn 3in (75mm) of the hem allowance to the wrong side. Pin and press. Remove the pins.*

2 *To make neat corners at the bottom, measure a further 3in (75mm) from the raw edge of the turned-under hem towards the top of the fabric. Fold over the side hems from this point and press in place.*

3 *From the point of the raw edge of the bottom hem, turn the remainder of the side hem allowance to the wrong side. Pin and press it firmly in place to provide a steep diagonal edge at the bottom. This forms half a mitred corner. Repeat the same procedure at the other side. Although mitring is not absolutely necessary, it results in a neater finish.*

4 *Fold over the other half of the bottom hem, aligning the two diagonal edges of each mitred corner. Pin down and press in place. Slip-stitch down the diagonal joins to secure the corners. Then neatly slip-hem the side hems and bottom hem in place. This completes the bottom hem. (Note that mitring also reduces the bulk of the material.)*

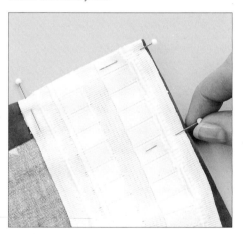

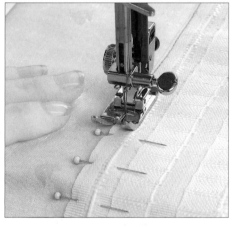

5 *Turn a 1½in (40mm) hem to the wrong side at the top of the curtain fabric and press it firmly in place. Cut a length of the correct type of heading tape to the finished width of the curtain plus an extra allowance of ¾in (19mm). Place the heading tape on the wrong side of the top of the curtain, just below the top edge. Tuck under the raw ends of the tape level with the side edges of the curtain. Then pin and tack the tape in place, ready for stitching. There is no need for any special sewing-machine attachment.*

6 *Machine-stitch the heading tape to the curtain. Stitch one short edge first, then one long edge and the other short edge. Repeat stitching the other long edge, so that the short ends are stitched twice to secure the ends of tape cord. It is a good idea to stitch the long edges in the same direction to make sure that the tape does not pucker. Gently gather up the fabric by pulling the tape cords from the centre. Hold the cords together with one hand and ease the tape into pleats with the other. Finally, loosely knot the cords at the centre.*

Lined curtains

A wide variety of fabrics can be used for curtain linings. They protect the face fabric, add body and improve drape, and should be chosen to suit the weight and type of the main fabric and the use – for example, both fabrics should be either washable or for dry-cleaning only. Cotton sateen is widely used as a lining for curtains. Insulated fabric treated with aluminium is available for curtain lining; the metallized side is placed to the wrong side of the curtain fabric. Linings can either match or contrast with curtain fabrics.

Tube-lined curtains

It is often assumed that because curtains are large items and tend to be dominant in a room scheme, they are difficult to make, especially if lined. Tube-lining requires no more sewing skill than making unlined curtains; the lining is simply machine-stitched to the main fabric at the side seams only – forming a "tube" of fabric, hence the name. The proper finish is achieved by cutting the lining slightly narrower than the full curtain, so that when the tube is turned out to the right side and pressed flat, the main fabric laps around on to the back of the curtain, forming a neatly finished edge at both sides, with the seams and lining completely invisible from the right side of the curtain. With this construction, the raw edges of any seams joining fabric widths on curtain or lining are concealed within the tube. However, as the lining is not attached to the curtain at any point within the width, it can move independently of the main fabric, and tends to separate as the curtains are pulled back, effectively forming two draped layers. This is not necessarily a disadvantage, depending on the curtain width and type of fabric, but if you want absolutely smooth draping, use the locked-in lining method shown on page 164.

Calculating fabric amounts
Curtain fabric: Calculate the width and length as for an unlined curtain (page 160).
Lining: The width should be 2in (50mm) less than the finished width of the curtain; the length should be the same as the finished curtain minus the hem allowance at the top.

Making up tube-lined curtains

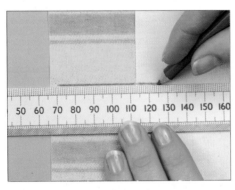

1 *With the right sides together, place the lining on the curtain fabric, carefully aligning the bottom edges. Then, with tailor's chalk, clearly mark the centre point of the curtain width on both the curtain and lining fabric pieces.*

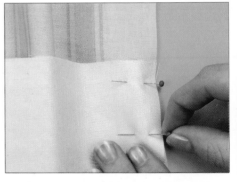

2 *Pin and tack the side edges of the lining and the curtain fabric together. As the curtain fabric is slightly wider than the lining, allow the curtain fabric to form undulating folds beneath the lining while you tack it firmly in place.*

3 Mark the finished length of the curtain together with the hem sewing line on the lining with tailor's chalk; allow for a 6in (15cm) hem. Turn, pin and machine-stitch ³/₈in (10mm) side seams from the top of the lining to within 4in (100mm) of the hem sewing line at the bottom of the curtain.

4 Turn right side out. The curtain fabric should pull over to the lining side at the side edges by 1in (25mm). Press the curtain and lining. Match the centre-marked points on the lining and curtain fabric at the top. Fold over the curtain fabric at the top edge of the lining and press in place.

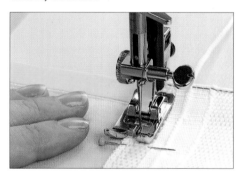

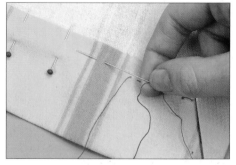

5 Position the heading tape just below the top of the curtain fabric, tucking under the raw ends to neaten. Pin and tack in place. Machine-stitch one short side first. Then stitch each long side in the same direction to avoid puckering.

6 Do not pull the cords up yet. At the bottom of the curtain fabric, turn under a double 3in (75mm) hem and press in place. Mitre the corners to minimize the bulk in same way as with an unlined curtain. Tack the hem in place to secure it.

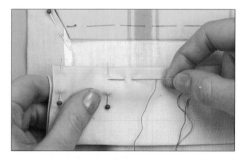

7 Turn up a double hem to the wrong side of the lining fabric. The lining should hang about ³/₄in (19mm) above the hem level of the curtain fabric. Trim any surplus lining. Tack the hem of the lining in place.

8 Pull up the curtain heading tape. Hang the curtain for several days to allow the fabric to drop. Only then slip-hem the hems and the lining to the curtain down the rest of the sides.

Locked-in curtain linings

A locked-in lining is the most professional finish for lined curtains, especially good for wide and deep curtain styles where fabric widths are joined to make up the full finished width of the curtain. The lock-stitching must be done by hand, but this should not deter you because the stitching method is surprisingly quick.

The lining is lightly sewn to the curtain fabric at regular intervals vertically across the width and right down the length, so that the fabric layers move as one and the lining cannot bunch up behind the drawn curtain, to spoil the smoothness of the drape. If you are using a dense, heavy fabric, the lining adds thickness and improves insulation, as well as making the curtains look well finished from the reverse side; with a looser weave or textured curtaining material, the locked-in construction prevents the main fabric from sagging in an unsightly way when hung.

For the main fabric, choose the traditional formality of velvet, brocade or heavy chintz and team it with a richly coloured sateen lining, or a slightly slubbed and sheeny synthetic. For less formal styling, consider a roughly textured, heavyweight fabric such as hessian or a tweedy weave.

As the main fabric and lining are locked across the whole construction of the curtain, it is vital that you check the care instructions for both to ensure that they can be cleaned in the same way and, if washable, do not shrink at different rates.

Calculating fabric amounts

Curtain fabric: Calculate the width and length as for an unlined curtain (page 160), but allowing only 4in (100mm) for the bottom hem of the curtain.

Lining fabric: The width should be the same as the unmade curtain width; and the length should be the same as that of the required finished curtain length.

Making up locked-in curtain linings

1 *Stitch the curtain fabric widths together with flat seams to make up the full curtain width. Press the seams open. Pin and stitch the lining widths together and press the seams open. Trim 1½in (40mm) from the side edges of the lining, and turn and press a ¾in (19mm) hem down the sides, and a ½in (12mm) hem along the bottom of the fabric. Then turn another 1½in (40mm) under along the bottom. Pin and stitch the lower hem firmly in place.*

2 *Next, press a generous 1½in (40mm) turning down each side of the curtain fabric to the wrong side of the fabric. Then turn up a 4in (100mm) hem at the bottom of the curtain and mitre the corners neatly. Slip-stitch the mitred corner seams. Then, using a large herring-bone stitch, sew the side and bottom hems. When stitching, make sure that you pick up just a thread of the flat fabric with each stitch, so that the stitching will not show on the right side of the fabric.*

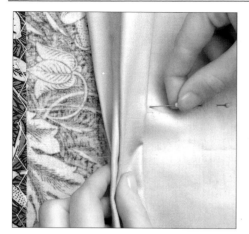

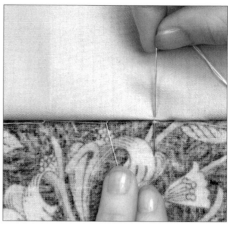

3 At 12in (30cm) intervals, mark vertical lines on the wrong side of the curtain material with tailor's chalk. Place the lining on the fabric with the wrong sides together so that the side edges of the lining are ³⁄₄in (19mm) in, and the lower edge is 2in (50mm) up from the curtain edge. Then trim the top of the lining level. Tack the lining and curtain together, following the first vertical line and beginning 6in (15cm) down from the top of the curtain fabric.

4 Fold back the lining material along the tacked line. Lock-stitch the curtain fabric to the lining fabric, beginning 6in (15cm) from the top of the curtain fabric. Make sure that you pick up only a thread of the curtain fabric at a time so that the stitching will not show on the right side of the curtain fabric. To avoid puckering the fabric, do not pull the stitches tight and make sure that you space them wide apart. Then remove the tacking stitches.

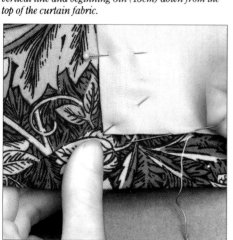

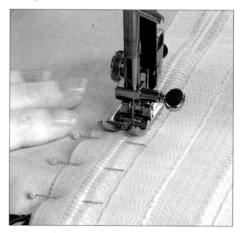

5 Tack and lock-stitch the fabrics together along the next vertical line, and so on until the lining is lock-stitched in place across the full width of the curtain. Next, pin and tack the sides and bottom edge of the lining in place, and slip-hem the folded-in sides of the lining to the folded-in edges of the curtain fabric. Then slip-hem the bottom hem of the lining to the bottom hem of the curtain fabric, and remove all the tacking stitches.

6 Turn the hem to the wrong side at the top of the curtain and lining and press it. Cut the heading tape to fit the top edge, allowing an extra allowance to turn under at each end of the curtain. Position the length of the heading tape just below the top edge of the curtain, turning the raw ends of the tape under neatly. Pin and tack the tape in place. Stitch along the short end and then along both long sides in the same direction to prevent the stitching from puckering.

Detachable curtain linings

A detachable lining does not follow the folds of the curtain fabric in the same way as a sewn-in lining, so it does not affect the hang of the main curtaining. It does, however, protect the fabric as much as any other type of lining, and there are various advantages in its construction. Because it is separate, the lining does not have to be as fully gathered as the curtain, so you save on the amount of fabric – one and a half times the track width should usually be ample for the lining width.

The lining can be taken off for washing separately if the main fabric is dry-clean only. This is a further advantage of detachable linings – you do not have to ensure compatibility of washing and care instructions because the curtain fabric and the lining can be treated as separate articles. Detachable linings are also an economical way of lining curtains intended for a short life – if you are putting up temporary furnishings until you are fully settled in a new home, or if the room needs a facelift but you are planning to move in the near future. A final advantage is that you can add a detachable lining to an existing curtain without fully remaking it, or you can transfer the lining to a new curtain when you are revising a scheme of decoration to give a room a new look with different patterns and colours.

Calculating fabric amounts

Make up the curtain in the same way as an unlined curtain (page 160). Attach the heading tape to the curtain in the usual way.

Hem the sides and bottom of the lining fabric in the same way as the curtain fabric, but leave the top edge unhemmed. Trim the top edge so that the lining is a little shorter than the finished curtain. Lining tape has two skirts and is fitted so that one skirt falls to each side of the lining fabric.

Curtain fabric: Calculate the width and length of the curtain material in the same way as for unlined curtains (page 160).

Lining fabric: Calculate the width and length of the lining fabric in the same way as for the curtain fabric.

Making up detachable linings

1 *Cut the lining tape the width of the curtain plus another 4in (100mm). Then knot the two cords together at the end that will be over the inner edge of the curtain. With the lining tape the right side up and the lining fabric the right side up, ease the lining fabric between the skirts as shown. The knotted end of the lining tape should overhang the centre edge of the lining fabric by about ⅜in (10mm).*

2 *Turn a ¼in (6mm) hem on the knotted end of the lining tape. Turn a further ¼in (6mm) hem to the wrong side of the lining fabric, so that the tape is flush with the edge of the lining. Pin the lining tape in place. Make quite sure that the top raw edge of the fabric is slotted right into the tape. This will prevent the fabric from pulling out if the raw edge frays when the curtains are being cleaned.*

3 *At the other end of the lining tape, pull the cords free, so that about 1½in (40mm) of each cord hangs down. Trim the surplus lining tape, so that only ⅜in (10mm) overhangs the outer edge. Turn a double ¼in (6mm) hem to the wrong side of the lining fabric, as for the end of the lining tape at the inner edge. Leave the tape cords free for gathering the lining, and tack the tape firmly in place.*

4 *Take care to stitch right through the two sandwiching layers of tape. Close to the bottom and side edges, stitch the lining tape in place. Next, remove the tacking and gently pull the two loose cord ends, easing the lining fabric along at the same time with your other hand. Even out the gathers until the width of the lining exactly matches the width of the curtain itself, then firmly knot the cords.*

Hemming curtains

Hems are used to finish the edge of fabric. The depth of the hem can vary between ¼in (6mm) and 6in (15cm) and should relate to the size of the item; a narrow hem on a large item will give an oddly unfinished look, while too deep a hem on a small item will look very clumsy.

Hems can be stitched by hand or machine. Hand stitches include blind hem stitch, hemming and slip-hemming, and the choice between these stitches is really a matter of personal preference. Herring-bone stitch is worked over the raw edge of a single hem on lined curtains, and is especially useful on thick fabrics. Straight stitch machined hems are quick to make, especially on large areas. Machine blind hem stitch is suitable for thick-pile fabric where the stitches do not show. Zigzag machine stitch gives a strong hem stitch used for its decorative effect.

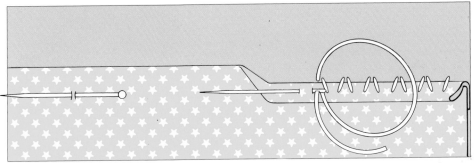

Blind hem stitch
Work from right to left if you are right-handed. Fold back the hem edge and fasten the thread inside it. Sew a small stitch in the fabric about ¼in (6mm) to the left.

Then sew a small stitch in the hem, ¼in (6mm) to the left again. Repeat the stitches, alternating between fabric and hem, all the way along. You can also work blind hem stitch with a sewing-machine.

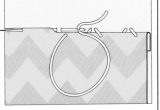

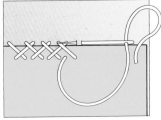

Hemming stitch
This is the most basic and simple stitch. Work from right to left if you are right-handed, with the turned-under edge facing you. Make two stitches on top of each other on the folded fabric to secure the thread. Just above the folded edge pick up a couple of threads of flat fabric. Insert the needle slightly to the left into the two layers of fabric close to the fold and draw the thread gently through. Repeat the stitch to complete the hem.

Slip-hemming
Beginning at the right (if you are right-handed), make a couple of stitches in the folded fabric to secure the thread. Do not put the needle through to the side where it will show. Catch the flat fabric and then insert the needle inside the folded edge, sliding it along for about ¼in (6mm). Then bring the needle out of the fold and catch a couple of threads from the flat fabric immediately opposite the point where the needle emerged.

Herring-bone stitch
With herring-bone stitch, you work from left to right if you are right-handed. Secure the thread in the folded fabric as described before. Carefully pick up a couple of threads from the flat fabric with the needle pointing from right to left. Then pull the thread gently but firmly through. Position the needle further along the fabric to the right, but still pointing it to the left, and take a horizontal stitch through the folded fabric.

Sheer curtains

Fine, translucent fabrics create a light, sunny effect perfect for summer. They mask the window subtly and cut down strong sunlight, but admit enough light during the day. Sheers can be hung as the only form of curtaining, or combined with heavier curtains which can be drawn to block out the light.

Nets serve the same purpose as sheers: they protect privacy while also letting in some light. Some are closely constructed to give a sheer, translucent effect; others have a relatively complex pattern repeated regularly throughout, which may give a very open style with a loose, stringy texture.

Sheer fabrics

Some of the more commonly used sheer fabrics are lace, loose-weave fabrics, net and cheesecloth. Lace used to be entirely handmade, but is now almost exclusively made by machine. Available in nylon, cotton or viscose in a range of elaborate designs, lace is expensive and its crisp texture is best suited to gently gathered curtains. Lace should be given a lining – a net backing will accentuate the design. Lace and other sheer fabrics can be difficult to sew and may slip on a sewing machine, so put tissue paper under them.

Loose weaves will add texture to lined curtains and filter harsh sunlight through a window. They are made from most natural fibres and come plain or with a simple design woven in. Cheesecloth is a soft cotton or cotton/polyester blend. This gauzy fabric is loosely woven to give a sheer texture. Naturally cream-coloured, it can be dyed and is cheap enough to be used generously.

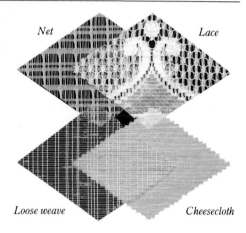

Net

Lace

Loose weave

Cheesecloth

The fine fibres in net curtains are knotted, instead of woven or knitted together like other fabrics, to form a mesh. Usually made from synthetic materials, such as nylon or polyester, net will diffuse the light coming through the window, and coloured net curtains will soften the effect, adding tone and colour to the room.

CALCULATING FABRIC AMOUNTS

The following calculation applies to all sheer fabrics except net fabrics, which are dealt with separately below.
Width: Multiply the width of your track or pole by 2 to 3, depending on the fullness required. Add ¾in (19mm) for each side hem. Divide the total by the width of the fabric, rounding up to the next full width and allowing for seam allowances for each width join. Divide the

total obtained by the number of curtains needed.
Length: Measure the length of the window area. Add 1½in (40mm) for the top heading and 2in (50mm) for the bottom hem.
For net fabrics:
Width: Measure the width of the window area and multiply by 2 to 3, depending on the fullness required. Add 1in (25mm) for each side hem.
Length: Measure the height of

the window area. Add 2½in (65mm) for the top hem and the same amount, 2½in (65mm), for the bottom hem.

These calculations are particularly important if you are using an old piece of lace or other unique fabric obtained in a second-hand shop. It is extremely unlikely that you will ever be able to replace it or match it if you make a mistake when cutting.

Making up sheer curtains

A finely woven heading tape is available, specially designed for use with sheers and netted fabrics, and if two types of curtain are combined, you can hang them on a double curtain track which automatically holds them at the same level and leaves sufficient space between the layers for both curtains to draw easily and separately.

If necessary join fabric widths with French seams: wrong sides together, stitch a flat seam of ¼in (6mm) and trim to ⅛in (3mm). Turn so that the right sides are facing. Pin and tack two layers together. Machine-stitch ⅜in (10mm) in from the first seam. The raw edges are completely enclosed in the seam and to the back of the fabric; in addition, no stitching line is showing.

Double hems are essential when using sheer fabrics, so that raw edges are concealed in the fold of the hem edge. Turn a ⅜in (10mm) hem to the wrong side along the side edges and press. Turn over again by the same amount. Press and pin the hem in place, then stitch firmly through all the layers.

Next, turn a 1in (25mm) hem to the wrong side at the bottom of the sheer curtain fabric. Turn over again by the same amount to make a double bottom hem. Press the hem, then pin and stitch it in place. When the curtain is

Heading tape
This allows you to draw the sheer fabric into neat pencil pleats. You can then either thread the bars fixed to it on to a narrow rod or elasticated wire, like net curtains, or hang it like an ordinary curtain by fixing curtain hooks at regular intervals to the pockets, which are also provided.

hanging, you will find that no raw or uneven edge will be visible through the fabric. Finally, turn 1½in (40mm) to the wrong side at the top of the curtain and press in place. Position translucent lightweight net tape wrong side down just below the top of the curtain. Pin in place. Turn under the ends to align with the curtain edges and stitch the tape in place.

Making up net curtains

Cut the fabric to the required size. Avoid joining the fabric; rather make separate curtains. If the side edges of the fabric are raw cut edges, turn a double ⅜in (10mm) hem to the wrong side along both edges. Pin and stitch.

Along the top raw edge of the fabric, turn under ⅜in (10mm) to the wrong side and press. Turn under a further 2¼in (55mm) and pin and tack in place.

Next, turn under ⅜in (10mm) and a further 2¼in (55mm) hem along the bottom raw edge. Pin and tack in place.

Measure 1¼in (30mm) in from the outer fold at the top of the net fabric. Machine-stitch parallel to the top folded edge at this point keeping the stitching level. Then machine-stitch 1¼in (30mm) from the bottom folded edge of the net curtain fabric in the same way.

Machine-stitch parallel to the tacking stitches ¼in (6mm) from the inner fold at the top hem. Machine-stitch ¼in (6mm) from the inner fold along the bottom hem. This completes the top and bottom casings. The curtain wire will thread between the two rows of stitching so that a self frill is formed at the top and the bottom of the net.

Thread a piece of curtain wire through the top casing and another piece through the bottom casing. The hooks at either end hook on to screw eyes, which are inserted at either side of the window.

Café curtains

Café curtains can be made with a faced, scalloped heading and hung from decorative rings which are threaded on to a curtain pole. Café curtains of this type do not need to be lined, but a lining can protect the main fabric from dirt and exposure to light and helps the curtain to hang elegantly.

Calculating fabric amounts

Curtain fabric: Measure the width of the window. Add 4in (100mm) so that the curtain is not absolutely taut. Add 1¼in (30mm) seam allowances. Measure the length of the area to be curtained. Add 2⅜in (60mm) for the hems. Facing: The width of the curtain multiplied by 8in (20cm) deep.

Making up café curtains

Decide on the size of the scallops at the top of the curtain. Add ⅜in (10mm) to the inner curve for the seam turnings. Using a pair of compasses or a suitably sized plate or bowl, make a semicircular template.

Cut a strip of paper the width of the finished curtain and draw a line to represent the top of the curtain, adding on ⅜in (10mm) for the seam turnings. Fold the paper in half widthways; crease and unfold. Place the template on the centre of the strip with the straight edge of the semicircle, aligning with the top line. Draw around the template.

Continue along the paper strip. Work outwards from the centre, leaving regular gaps between each semicircle of no less than 1½in (40mm) and finish about 1½in (40mm) from each edge.

Cut the semicircles from the paper pattern. Cut out the curtain fabric to the required size. Pin the paper pattern along the top of the curtain fabric on the wrong side. Cut out the scallops and remove the paper pattern. Next, cut out the facing. Pin the paper pattern to the top edge of the facing and cut out the scallops, making sure that they match those at the top of the curtain. Turn a double ⅜in (10mm) hem along the unscalloped long edge of the facing. Pin and stitch in place.

Turn a double ⅜in (10mm) hem along the side edges of the curtain fabric. Pin and stitch in place. Turn a double 1in (25mm) hem along the lower edge of the curtain. Pin and stitch the hem in place.

With the right sides together and raw edges matching, pin the scalloped edge of the curtain fabric to the scalloped edge of the facing. Tack along the scalloped edge. Machine-stitch the scallops together, ⅜in (10mm) from the raw edges. Remove the tacking. The raw edges of the facing at the sides will overlap the hemmed edges of the curtain fabric at the sides.

Turn under the raw side edges of the facing and press. Slip-stitch the turned-under edges to the hemmed edges of the curtain. Press.

Oversew a curtain ring at the centre of the space between two scallops to the wrong side of the curtain. Finish the ends securely.

Cutting out the scallops
Pin the paper pattern along the top of the curtain fabric on the wrong side. Cut out the scallops to match the top edge, and then remove the paper pattern.

Neatening the scallops
To reduce the bulk of the material, clip around each curve and across the corners of the scallops. Turn the corners right side out and press them carefully.

Fixing the curtain rings
Oversew each ring firmly to the centre of the space between the scallops, on the wrong side of the curtain. Finish the ends securely and neatly.

Binding curtain edges

Binding is a simple but effective finish which not only secures curtain edges more firmly, but also gives them a professional look. The bias binding purchased in milliners' shops is made from a fairly lightweight material, and is more suitable for edging smaller items – table mats, napkins and table-cloths – than for use with larger items and heavier materials. For curtains and other large items, it is best to make bias strips out of a fabric which is of a similar weight to the item to be bound, as this will give it a much better finish. If the material is striped or checked, the bias strips, being cut diagonally on the fabric, will create a special effect. A simple method of making these bias strips is given below.

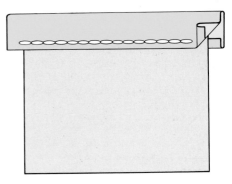

Applying binding with a sewing machine
Fold the bias binding, wrong side down, over the raw edge of the fabric to be bound, and press. Tack in place and then machine-stitch through the fabric and the two folds of binding, close to the edge of the binding. Remove the tacking.

Applying binding by hand

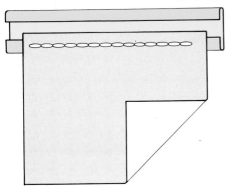

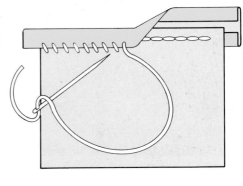

1 *Open one folded edge of the bias binding and match this edge to the raw edge of the fabric to be bound, right sides together. Pin and stitch them together down the fold line of the binding.*

2 *Refold the binding and turn it over to the wrong side of the fabric, enclosing the raw edge. Pin in place and slip-hem the second folded edge of the binding to the fabric along the first line of stitching.*

FINDING THE BIAS OF A PIECE OF FABRIC

Bias binding is used both to strengthen raw edges and to add a decorative finishing touch. Because it is cut on the bias, it has more give than binding cut on the straight grain.

To find the bias of a piece of fabric, fold a straight raw edge diagonally so that it is parallel to the selvedge of the fabric. This fold line is the bias line.

Mark out 1½in (40mm) strips parallel to the bias line, and cut them out. To join the strips, place two with right sides together and at right angles to each other. The raw edges will be parallel and there will be two triangular corners. Pin and stitch the seam ¼in (6mm) from the raw edges. Open the seam out flat and press with a hot iron. Finally, trim the corners.

You can use bias binding to make a false hem if you find that you do not have enough fabric for the hem.

Types of pelmet

A pelmet is a stiff, panelled heading to curtains, unlike the valance, which is draped. It must be based on a rigid support for the fabric covering, which may be a sturdy wooden "box" mounted above the windows or a specially made stiffening designed as an interlining to fabric for this type of effect. Self-adhesive backing is available, which makes the work of stiffening the fabric quite simple, or you can use traditional buckram, a woven cloth that is treated to maintain rigidity, in combination with a heavy interlining.

Because the pelmet is rigid you can cut the lower edge to any shape – regular scallops or zigzags, or a broad arc at the centre of the window, sweeping down to flat panels at either side over the drawn-back curtains. The simplest way to apply trimmings is to stick on braid or fancy edging with a fabric adhesive after the pelmet has been made up.

There is a variety of fabric pelmet designs. They can either take the form of a gathered valance, or be treated with a stiffener. Valance pelmets can be hung from a shelf above the window or suspended from a second curtain track in front of the main one. Another type of pelmet, sometimes known as a draped pelmet, is made up of swags draped across the top of the window and tails decorating the edge. This type of pelmet looks very effective on large windows, but takes up a lot of fabric. So before you commit yourself by buying material, it is best to experiment with a sheet to find out approximately how much you will need to get the effect you require.

It is also possible to combine the strength of a wooden or hardboard pelmet construction with the elegance of a fabric design to produce a fabric-covered wooden pelmet. This can either have a simple rectangular shape or have curved edges to give an effect similar to a valanced pelmet. The fabric can either match or contrast with the curtain material.

Pelmets
To hide the heading and give interest to the top of the curtain, you can use a pelmet. Pelmets allow you to fit the curtain track in two pieces with an overlap at the centre. They are also useful to give two adjacent windows a unified look.

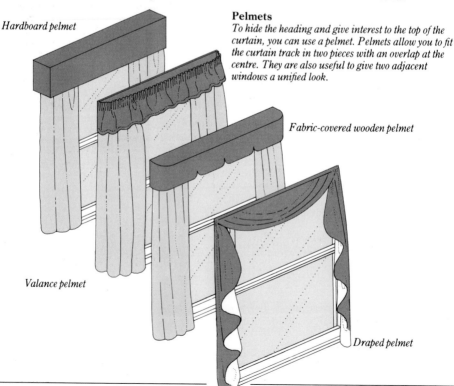

Hardboard pelmet

Fabric-covered wooden pelmet

Valance pelmet

Draped pelmet

Pelmet trimmings
The simplest way to apply trimmings is to stick on braid or fancy edging with a fabric adhesive after the pelmet has been made up.

Fixing the pelmet to the window (below)
The fabric pelmet is mounted on to a wooden pelmet board which has small side boards (known as returns) attached at each end. The pelmet board is fixed above the window with angle irons and is positioned so that the top of the board will be level with the top of the pelmet. Attach the pelmet with touch-and-close fastening or with tacks along the top of the pelmet and front and side edges of the board.

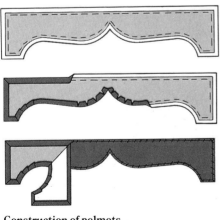

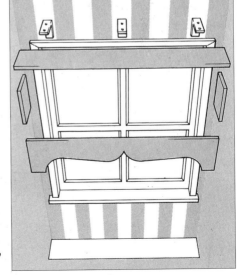

Construction of pelmets
Cut all the materials to shape, plus ½in (12mm) for turnings. Stitch the interlining to the fabric. Tack the stiffening to the fabric and interlining. Turn the fabric over the stiffening and glue in place. Stitch the lining to the back of the pelmet.

Curtain valances

A deep frill of fabric gives a finished look to the top of a window, framing the proportions of the window and curtaining and providing the final disguise for the curtain track. As with the main curtains, the valance can be hung on a track, rod or pole, depending on the weight of the fabric, and the fixings can be mounted on a narrow, shelf-like projection fitted above the window frame to fall cleanly and loosely over the curtain heading. Decide on the depth and decorative treatment of the valance after the main curtains are hung. To create a stylish effect the valance should be of the same fabric as the curtains. A contrast or co-ordinate will look odd unless well linked to other furnishings.

Calculating fabric amounts
Width: Measure the width of the window area and multiply by 1½ to 3 times, depending on the fullness required. Add 1in (25mm) for each side hem allowance.
Depth: Divide the curtain drop by 6; add 1in (25mm) for the lower hem allowance and 1½in (40mm) for the top hem allowance.

A co-ordinated finish
A deep frill of fabric gives a finished look to the top of a window and disguises the curtain track.

Making up a curtain valance

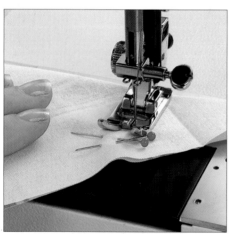

1 *Press 1in (25mm) hems at the sides and lower edge. Unfold the hems and fold the corners diagonally, right sides together. Stitch at right angles to the fold from the corner crease to ³⁄₈in (10mm) from the edge.*

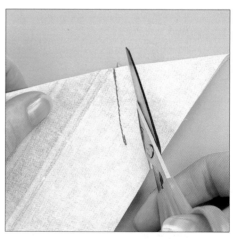

2 *Cut off the corner ³⁄₈in (10mm) away from the stitching, using a pair of very sharp scissors. Then turn the fabric right side out and carefully poke out the new corner.*

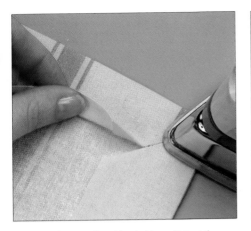

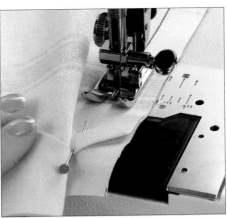

3 Press the seam flat with a hot iron. Repeat the same process for the other bottom corner. Having done this, then trim ⅕in (5mm) from both the side and the lower edges of the lining if you are doing a sewn-in lining, and place the valance fabric and the lining with their right sides together.

4 Next, align the side raw edges of the valance hem. Pin them firmly together. You will find that the lining fabric will overlap the valance fabric at the corners. Machine-stitch carefully down both sides of the valance, approximately ⅜in (10mm) in from the raw edges of the fabric.

5 Now stitch the bottom edge of the valance lining carefully to the valance hem approximately ⅜in (10mm) away from the raw edges of the fabric, in the same way as you did for the edges. Then snip off the two bottom corners of the valance lining diagonally with a pair of sharp scissors to reduce the bulk, making sure that you do not cut too close to the stitching. Having done that, turn the joined pieces right side out and press the seams. Turn the top of the valance fabric 1½in (40mm) to the wrong side. It should fold over at the top edge of the lining. Press, pin and sew the fabric neatly in place.

6 With the wrong sides facing each other, pin the heading tape firmly to the top edge of the valance. Next, turn under the side edges of the heading tape to align precisely with the fabric. Knot the cords of the heading tape firmly at one end. Then stitch this same short side, and then both long sides of the heading tape. At this stage, leave the cords free at the other end of the tape so that you can gather the valance. When you have gathered the valance to the right width, tie the loose cords neatly together. Finally, insert the curtain hooks into the slits in the tape at regular intervals, and hang the valance.

Blinds

Practical and economical, blinds are often chosen for their functional advantages. Because they do not obstruct the window area in the same way as draped or billowing curtains, they are the ideal choice for windows situated above a desk, work top or sink, or in a "working" area such as a bathroom or playroom. They are also particularly suitable for rooms which tend to be dark, as they do not cut out as much of the light when they are pulled up to the top of the window. You can add trimmings and decorations as you please.

Fabrics for blinds

Roman blinds hang flat when pulled down, but draw up into horizontal pleats. They should be made from a reasonably substantial fabric, but not one with a stiffened finish. Any good-quality, curtain-weight cotton is suitable. Austrian and festoon blinds have a gracefully swagged appearance. Both types look very pretty if made from fabrics such as lightweight voile, net, lace or fine cotton.

A cottage blind is ruched vertically across the window, covering half the window area. Light- or medium-weight fabrics are suited to this simple effect – attractive printed cottons and lightly embossed or textured fabrics for solid colour and pattern; sheers, nets and laces for translucency; broderie anglaise and other machine-embroidered fabrics for a pretty, fancy finish. A roller blind should be made from a firm fabric which hangs smoothly and rolls up evenly. Roller-blind kits are not expensive and easy to make up.

Choosing the right type of blind fabric
Light shining in through a window or darkness outside will alter the look of fabric used for blinds. See the effect of light and darkness on an all-over miniprint with a dark background (left), a plain cotton seersucker (centre), and a lightweight flocked voile (right).

EFFECTS WITH BLINDS

Blinds offer a range of stylish and versatile window treatments, whether used as the only window covering or teamed with curtains. The look can vary from plain and simple to exotic, according to the type of blind you prefer and your choice of fabric and trimmings. Choose the most appropriate style for the effect you wish to create – a Roman blind for a smart graphic effect; a frilled Austrian blind for a pretty, frothy look; a festoon blind for sumptuous elegance. For simpler styling, a permanent half-length cottage blind blocks a drab view or protects your privacy if the window is overlooked. A basic roller blind is just a flat length of fabric, but clever choice of colour and pattern or an inventive way with trimmings and edgings can enliven the plain construction of the blind. This type of blind is much more versatile than it appears at first sight.

Positioning blinds and measuring up

Roman, Austrian and festoon blinds are usually attached to a wooden batten, so that the screw eyes holding the cords which draw up the blind can be fixed to the underside of the batten. Roman blinds are attached directly to the front face of the batten, but Austrian and festoon blinds have a curtain heading tape which can be hung from a curtain track mounted on the batten, giving extra support to the weight of the fabric and making it easy to remove the blinds for washing or cleaning. It is also possible to buy a special blind track which incorporates the "eyes" for the cord system, thus making the batten unnecessary.

Blinds can be positioned inside or outside the window recess. If the blind is teamed with curtains, hang it inside the recess and make sure that it will not catch on the window fittings. A cottage blind is positioned on the window and need not extend beyond the frame. A roller blind hangs from brackets which you can fix to the frame or outside it.

The way you hang any blind may affect the finished size. Before you measure up and buy fabric, make sure that it is feasible to mount brackets or battens at the position where you want the blind to hang in relation to the window itself.

Calculating fabric amounts

For a Roman blind, add 1½in (40mm) to the width for the side hems and 4½in (110mm) to the length for the bottom and top turnings.

For an Austrian blind, measure the track length and multiply by 1½ to 2½, depending on the type of heading tape you have chosen. Make a small allowance for the side hems and joins in the fabric. For a festoon blind, calculate the fabric width as for the Austrian blind.

For a cottage blind, measure the area of window to be covered and add 1½in (4cm) to the width for the side hems. To the length, add enough to make a casing for the curtain wires or rods on which the blind is threaded.

For a roller blind, add ¾in (20mm) to the width for the side hems (ready-stiffened fabrics that will not fray need no hems) and add 12 to 13½in (30 to 35cm) to the measured length to allow for a lath channel and attachment to be fitted to the roller.

Tape requirements

To calculate how much tape is needed, make a scale drawing of the blind and work out how many vertical tapes should be evenly spaced across the width to draw it up neatly. You must make sure that you position tapes down either side of the blind close to the edge; while those in between should be spaced equally across the width of the gathered blind no more than 12in (30cm) apart.

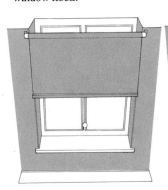

Roller blind
A roller blind can be either mounted inside the window recess, or outside, as shown here, when a batten is not required.

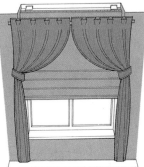

Roman blind
A Roman blind can look attractive when mounted within the window recess, with decorative tied-back curtains mounted outside.

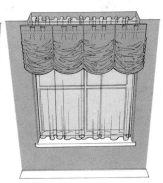

Net curtains
Fixed inside the window recess, they are effective when used in combination with an Austrian blind outside the recess.

Equipment for roller blinds

A roller-blind kit consists of a spring-loaded roller, a wooden lath or plastic bar for the bottom of the blind, a pull cord and the necessary fixings and screws. The roller can be made of either aluminium or wood. The fabric for the blind is often bought separately. Kits are sold in a range of sizes – buy one slightly larger than you need so that you can cut it down to the required dimensions.

Roller blind kit
These easy-to-use roller blind kits can be purchased at DIY shops. They come in several sizes, and it is best to buy one a little larger than you need.

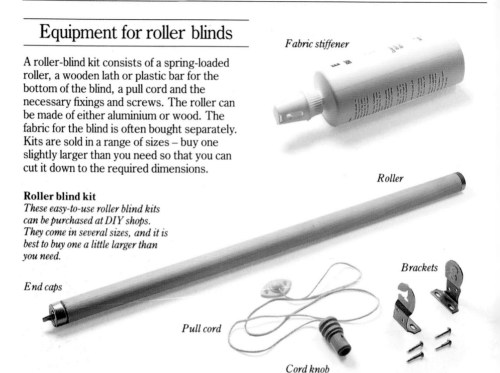

Fabric stiffener

Roller

Brackets

End caps

Pull cord

Cord knob

Fitting roller blinds

First check the roller length that you will need. Take into account the projecting pins that fit on to the ends of the roller – they usually take up about 1in (25mm) at each end. Depending on the design of the brackets, you may also need a little space to allow for the fixing screws.

When you attach the brackets to the frame, the one with the round hole should go on the right, the one with the slot on the left. Cut the roller to the correct length at the non-spring end. Make sure that you cut it square by measuring the length in several places, marking it all the way around, and using a fine-toothed saw, such as a tenon saw, for wood, or a hacksaw for aluminium.

Having cut it to the required length, smooth off the cut end with glasspaper and attach the fixing to the roller. On an aluminium roller this means simply pushing on the end caps.

To prepare the material, cut it to the right size, iron it flat and stiffen it. The easiest and quickest way to do this is to use an aerosol stiffener. If you prefer not to use aerosols because of the risk of environmental damage, make a solution of stiffener and water and soak the fabric carefully according to the manufacturer's instructions.

MEASURING FOR ROLLER BLINDS

First decide whether you want the blind to hang inside or outside the window recess. If you are going to fit it inside, measure the width of the recess and then subtract an amount to allow for the blind fixings on either side. If you are installing the blind outside the recess, allow for an overlap of at least 2in (50mm) on each side. Measure the length from where you want to fix the blind to the bottom when fully lowered. Finally, make allowances for the lath channel at the bottom, and the attachment at the top. These will add about 12–15in (30–35cm) to the measured length.

Assembling and fitting a roller blind

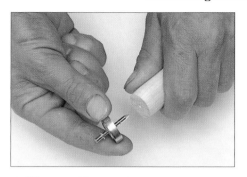

1 *When assembling a wooden roller, carefully drill a pilot hole for the fixing pin, push on the end caps and tap the pin home.*

2 *Mark the bracket positions on the window frame with a pencil, using a spirit level to ensure that the blind will be level.*

3 *Fitting the bar at the bottom of the fabric is usually simple. Cut it about ³/₈in (10mm) shorter than the blind and either glue it to the fabric or fit it into a pocket sewn along the bottom edge. Screw the holder for the pull cord to the centre of the bar.*

4 *With aluminium rollers, the material either fits into a slot in the roller or is secured with screw clips. With wooden rollers, the best method is first to glue the fabric to the roller to keep it in the right position and then to fix it permanently with tacks or staples.*

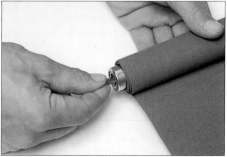

5 *When the material is attached, roll it up, put the roller on the brackets, and tension the spring so that it rolls and unrolls properly.*

6 *If the tension is wrong, unhook the non-spring end, turn the roller by hand to increase or decrease the tension, and refit it to the bracket.*

Roman blinds

A Roman blind hangs flat against the window when drawn down and folds into deep, horizontal pleats as it is raised. Roman blinds give an elegant, tailored look to the room, but are not difficult to make, particularly if you use a blind tape with woven-in loops or rings already attached. This fixes the size of the pleats, so if you wish to create deeper or narrower folds, you can machine-stitch plain tapes down the back of the blind and sew on small curtain rings by hand.

The geometric styling of the blind is particularly suited to strong colours and definite patterns, but when choosing patterned fabrics, bear in mind that the pleating will interrupt any large motifs or one-directional designs. All-over miniprints are ideal and you can find these in good, medium-weight cottons which are firmly woven and will fold crisply when drawn up. Plain, bold colours also create a good effect – clean lines are the essential feature here.

Before cutting out the blind fabric, work out the position for the top batten from which the blind will be hung. Measure the length from the top edge of the batten position to the required finished blind length. Then add the hem allowances to the length before cutting out. The cords are threaded across the top edge and then down the blind.

Calculating fabric amounts

Measure the window drop. Add 5½in (14cm) for hems and a little extra for making horizontal tucks in the fabric. Measure the width of the window area. Add 2⅜in (60mm) for side hems. Allow extra for seams if you are joining widths.

Roman blind
Choose fabric to reflect the mood of the blind. A small, geometric print goes well with the clear, uncluttered lines of the otherwise plain Roman blind.

FIXING TAPES TO A ROMAN BLIND

There are various types of blind tape but they all work on the same principle. The tape has rings or loops placed at regular intervals along it. A cord ties into the lowest ring or loop and threads up through the other rings or loops, which pull up to form the back folds of the blind when the cord is pulled. The tape shown on the right has loops ready fixed and these are suitable for both Roman and Austrian blinds (page 182).

Measure the width of the blind and divide the amount by 12in (30cm), rounding up or down to the nearest whole number. This will give the number of sections between the vertical tapes. Fold the blind into the appropriate number of sections and press in creases at folds as guide lines for the tapes. Cut the tapes to fit over the side hems and creases, making sure that each lower ring or loop is 4¾in (120mm) up from the edge.

Tie the cord firmly to the lowest ring or loop on the first tape. Thread the cord up through the ring or loops, then across the top to the side edge and down the length of the blind.

Make sure that the edge with the loose cord is the edge from which you wish to pull the blind. Thread cords through all the tapes in this way, each time taking the cord across the top edge and down the side edge of the blind. The tapes are stitched to the blind after you have folded and stitched the top, bottom and side hems of the roman blind, but before you have attached the fittings at the top and bottom of the blind. Make sure that the tops are firmly fixed at the bottom. This is where they take most strain.

Making up a Roman blind

1 *Cut the fabric to the required size. Turn a double ½in (12mm) hem to the wrong side along each side edge. Pin, tack and stitch. Turn a double 1in (25mm) hem along the top edge of the blind. Pin, tack and stitch. Fold and press the fabric at 10 to 12in (25 to 30cm) intervals across the width to provide guide lines for positioning the vertical tapes.*

2 *Cut strips of looped blind tape to the length of the blind plus ⅜in (10mm). Pin, tack and stitch the first strip close to the side hem, turning under ⅜in (10mm) at the top. Stitch the tapes down the back of the blind following the fold lines, making sure that all the loops in the tapes line up horizontally right across the width of the blind.*

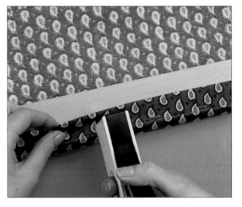

3 *Across the bottom of the blind, turn and press ⅜in (10mm), then fold up a 2in (50mm) hem. Pin, tack and stitch to form a casing hem. Slot the wooden lath through the casing and slip-stitch the hem ends together. To help form neat, tailored folds when the finished blind is drawn up into pleats, tack and stitch ⅛in (3mm)-deep horizontal tucks across the width of the blind to correspond to alternate rows of loops on the vertical tapes. Make the first tuck at the level of the second loop from the bottom of the blind (excluding the casing hem).*

4 *To make the tuck, fold and press the fabric wrong sides together and stitch ⅛in (3mm) from the fold. Press the folds accurately, following the straight grain of the fabric, to ensure that they will make clean, evenly spaced horizontal lines across the blind when it is hung. Cut the wooden batten to the width of the blind. Spread out the blind right side down and place the batten across the top edge. Turn the top hem over on to the broad side of the batten and staple or tack across the width. This completes the blind and it is now ready to be fitted.*

Austrian blinds

An Austrian blind creates remarkable impact with its loosely folded swags. The fullness comes from a gathered or pleated heading combined with the generous looping as the blind is drawn up. Light- and medium-weight cottons in bright colours or patterns have a sunny or vivid effect. A lightly textured or satinized surface provides an extra dimension, and sheers are also excellent, giving a beautifully softened look. Alternatively the blind can be made of a heavyweight fabric, which creates a more sculptured effect. The tapes should be about 12in (30cm) apart when the blind is gathered, although the distance can be varied to suit the shape and size of the window.

Calculating fabric amounts
Length: Measure the window drop. Add 2⅜in (60mm) for hem allowances.
Width: Measure the width of the window and multiply by 2 to 2½ to allow enough fabric width to form heading pleats. Add 1½in (40mm) for side hem allowances.

Austrian blind
Bright yellow, translucent fabric creates a sunny aspect, showing an Austrian blind to best effect. In contrast, the moulded effect of a heavier fabric can be emphasized if the material has a surface sheen.

Making up an Austrian blind

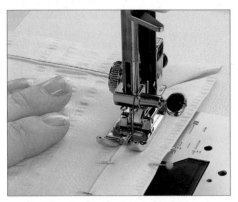

1 *Along the bottom and both sides of the fabric, turn a double ¾in (20mm) hem to the wrong side. Mitre the corners. Pin, tack and stitch the hems in place. Cut strips of looped blind tape to the length of the blind plus ⅜in (10mm). These strips of tape are to be positioned down the length of the blind at regularly spaced intervals of about 24in (60cm) across the width.*

2 *Make sure that there is a loop ⅜in (10mm) up from the bottom of each length of tape and that the strips are matched exactly, so that when in position the loops will line up horizontally across the blind. Fold the fabric vertically concertina fashion at approximately 24in (60cm) intervals across the width and press. The fold lines provide a guide for positioning the vertical tapes.*

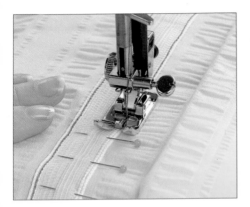

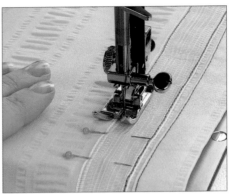

3 *If there are any joins in the fabric, arrange for the seams to be covered by the tape, but do not allow the spacing between the vertical strips to become irregular. Place the first length of tape down the length of the blind 1in (25mm) from the side edge, close to the side hem. Turn the end of the tape under for ³⁄₈in (10mm) at the hem edge, pin, tack and stitch down both edges of the tape, working both lines of stitching in the same direction so that the tape does not pucker. Continue stitching the tapes at regular intervals across the blind.*

4 *As the tapes are positioned, check that the loops are matched down each length to line up horizontally and conceal any seams under the tapes. Turn ³⁄₄in (20mm) of fabric to the wrong side across the top of the blind and press. Pin and tack the heading tape across the top of the blind to cover the raw edge of the turning. Stitch the heading tape in place. Then gather or pleat the heading tape until the blind is the width of the window. Thread the cords through the loops in the vertical tapes before mounting the blind in place.*

Adding a frill to blinds

To make the blind more opulent, a frill of purchased broderie anglaise edging or a fabric frill can be added to the side and lower edges. There are many types of ready-made fancy edgings available which need only be hand- or machine-stitched to a seamline or hem. They can be bought in most department stores.

First decide the required finished frill depth and trim this amount plus 1in (25mm) from the appropriate edges of the blind. For the frill length, allow 1½ times the length of the blind edges. For a double fabric frill, allow twice the required finished depth plus 1¼in (30mm) for the depth of the frill.

Cut and join enough strips to make the frill the length you require. Then gather up the edge of the frill so that it fits the blind, arranging extra gathers at the corners of the blind. With right sides facing, stitch the frill to the edge, taking ⅝in (15mm) seams. Finally, trim the seam to ⅜in (10mm) and zigzag-stitch the raw edges together.

Making the blind more opulent
The decorative styling can be further elaborated by the addition of a frill across the bottom of the blind, even running the length of both sides as well for a really sumptuous finish. Frills can be bought in different widths and small, delicate patterns or loosely structured, chunky designs. These ready-made decorative trims have a firm binding along one edge, which you can stitch to the fabric by hand or machine.

Festoon blinds

A festoon blind is similar to an Austrian blind, but although the swags are made by drawing up the fabric on a similar cording system, the festoon blind has additional ruching which keeps its decorative effect even when the blind is fully let down. This is achieved by using narrow curtain heading tape for the vertical tapes on the blind. The tape is drawn up to make even gathers down the length, which remain permanently in place. Small split curtain rings are then inserted at regular intervals in the curtain heading tape to accommodate the cording system.

The ruched finish works extremely well in light- and medium-weight fabrics – sheer, slightly textured or with a shiny surface. A translucent fabric creates romantic styling, and a lightweight blind can be teamed with heavily draped, floor-length curtains to create a luxurious effect. If the blind is used alone, to avoid covering a radiator beneath the window, for example, a heavier fabric and rich, strong colour emphasize warmth and privacy in the room when the blind is down, and enhance the shape of the window.

Calculating fabric amounts

Length: Measure the window drop and multiply by 1½ for medium-weight or 3 if you are using a lightweight fabric. Remember to allow an extra 2in (50mm) for the top turning and the frill seam.
Width: Measure the width of the window area and multiply by 1¼ for medium-weight or 1½

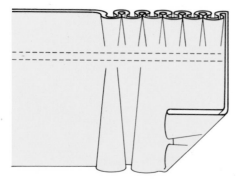

for lightweight and sheer fabrics. Add 1½in (40mm) for side hems and ⅜in (10mm) seam allowances if you are seaming more than one width of fabric together.

For the frill: You need enough 8in (20cm)-deep strips of fabric to make up one long strip 1½ times the width of the blind fabric. You can make the frill out of the same material as the blind, or buy a ready-made trimming.

Festoon blind
Made from a filmy, translucent material, festoon blinds can create a luxurious atmosphere. The fabric illustrated here filters the light coolly, which can be a boon on a hot summer day.

Double frill
The frill fitted to the festoon blind pictured above is a double frill. It is formed from a strip of fabric folded in half along its length. To finish the short ends neatly, fold the fabric in half lengthways with the right sides facing each other, tack and stitch across each end, then turn the material right side out once again, and press it carefully. Next, either hand-sew or machine-stitch two rows of stitches along the length of the fabric, and gather the material to the required length. Remember to allow some extra fullness at the corner, so that the frill will not look skimpy. The right side of the fabric shows on both sides of a double frill, making it suitable for fabrics with a different reverse side.

Making up a festoon blind

1 *Turn a double ¾in (20mm) hem down each side. To make the frill, fold the fabric lengthways, right sides together, with the raw edges matched. Stitch a ⅜in (10mm) seam across both short ends. Turn right side out and press. Work two rows of gathering stitches through both layers of fabric along the top edge of the frill. Pull until the frill equals the blind width. Then knot the threads.*

2 *Right sides together, align the raw edge of the frill with the bottom edge of the fabric. Stitch the frill in place. Press the frill seam upwards on to the wrong side. Fold the fabric at intervals of 10 to 16in (25 to 40cm) across the width and press. This provides guide lines for positioning the heading tape. The tape should be spaced evenly and positioned over the side hems and any seams joining fabric widths.*

3 *Cut the appropriate number of strips of tape to the length of the blind (excluding frill) plus ⅜in (10mm). Pin lengths of tape in position following the foldlines, turning under ⅜in (10mm) to neaten the ends at the seamline of the frill. Beginning with the tape at the side hem, tack and stitch each length of tape in place. Press the fabric from the wrong side, using a steam iron.*

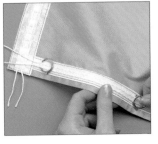

4 *Turn 1½in (40mm) of fabric across the top of the blind. Position heading tape to cover the raw edge. Stitch in place, but keep the gathering cords clear of the horizontal stitching line on the heading tape. Tuck the raw ends of tape under to neaten.*

5 *Slot small curtain rings into the vertical lengths of tape at intervals of about 8in (20cm). The top rings should be just below the heading and the bottom rings about 4in (100mm) from the bottom of the blind. Space them so that the rings line up horizontally.*

6 *Pull the cords to gather up the blind evenly to the required drop. Tie off the cords. Hand-stitch neatly just below each ring to secure the cords to the fabric. Gather the heading tape at the top of the blind to the required width. Thread the cords through the rings.*

TAPES FOR FESTOON BLINDS

Although festoon blinds do not require much fullness in width, they may have a good deal of fullness lengthwise. The tapes for festoon blinds should be about 12in (30cm) apart when the blinds are gathered, although this can be varied. On tapes with loops or rings attached, make sure that one is positioned near the lower edge and that they line up horizontally on each tape. Festoon blinds are gathered at the top with a heading tape. When this is gathered, the vertical tapes will hang more closely together. Attach the vertical tapes before fixing the heading tape.

Cottage blinds

This pretty half-length blind effectively disguises an ugly window, or blocks out an undesirable view, but it is a permanent feature, suitable for a bathroom or small landing window, for example, where you do not need to vary the amount of light entering. It can be mounted on curtain wire or on narrow, rounded or flattened curtain rod, threaded through a casing on the fabric at top and bottom and attached to the window frame on either side. A valance at the top completes the effect.

Calculating fabric amounts
This blind is made from one piece of fabric and does not require a tuck to be made for the wire. It is therefore ideal if you wish to use a patterned fabric.
Length: Measure the window drop. Add 1¼in (30mm) for the hem allowance and 2½in (65mm) for making the top casing.
Width: Measure the width of the window area. Add on 1¼ to 1½ times width for fullness and ¾in (20mm) for each side hem.

A traditional touch
The length of the valance can vary between a quarter to half of the blind's length.

Making up a cottage blind

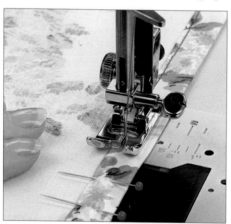

1 *Cut the blind fabric to the required size. Place the fabric face down and turn a double ⅜in (10mm) hem along both of the side edges of the blind. Pin, tack and stitch in place. With the fabric still face down, turn a double ½in (12mm) hem along the lower edge of the blind. Pin, tack and stitch in place.*

2 *Wrong sides together, turn under the top of the blind by ⅜in (10mm) then another 2in (50mm) to make a double hem. Press in the fold. Pin, tack and sew in place ¼in (6mm) from the inner edge. This will form the casing for the wire, which is inserted to make sure that the blind hangs evenly.*

3 *Measure 1¼in (30mm) down from the fold at the top of the blind. Pin, tack and stitch across the width of the blind at this point. Make sure that this line of stitching is parallel to the first line of casing stitching.*

4 *Trim the curtain wire to the correct length. It will need to be slightly shorter than the distance between the hooks so that it is held taut. Screw eyes into the ends of wire and thread the wire through the casing.*

MAKING AN UNLINED VALANCE

Traditionally, a cottage blind over the lower half of the window is given a finished look by the addition of a short valance at the top. If you choose a print fabric with a clearly defined border section, this border used as the valance makes a pretty link between the top of the window and the bottom of the cottage blind. The valance is traditionally unlined. It is cut to the same width as the blind, and its length may vary between a quarter to half of the blind length, depending upon the size of the window. Add on the same top and bottom hem allowances as on the blind. The valance is made in the same way as the blind. Position the hooks, which will hold the curtain wire, about 1¼in (30mm) down from the top of a recessed window. This will allow the self fabric frill at the top of the curtain to stand up above the wire on which the curtain hangs.

A cottagey print in glazed cotton is a highly suitable fabric choice; the treatment also lends itself to sheers or fancy fabrics such as Swiss muslin or broderie anglaise.

If you have chosen a plain fabric for your cottage blind, you may want to liven it up with extra trimming, and there is a wide range of fancy edgings – frills and embroidered trimmings, ribbons and laces – that can add an original and unexpected touch to the blind and to the valance. If you line the valance, choose a lining of a suitable weight, and check that it can be treated the same way as the fabric when washing.

ALTERNATIVES TO HAND-STITCHING

There may be occasions when you need to use a non-sew alternative to hand stitching. This may be for sheer speed, when you need to finish an item quickly and do not have time to hand stitch the hem, or as a temporary measure, which will later be replaced with stitching.

Fusible bonding is a web-like strip of adhesive, which is placed between the two fabric layers of a hem. The hem is then pressed to activate the adhesive which glues the hem in place. The bonding strip is about 1in (25mm) wide; when used at that width it will fasten the hem securely, but may also stiffen the hem. To avoid the stiffening effect, cut the bonding into ¼in (6mm)-wide strips and use these near the top of the hem allowance. This may not be quite as secure as the full width bonding when the item is laundered, but it will lessen the stiffening effects. Always try a test hem on spare fabric to check the finish, which may vary on different fabrics.

Tacking tape is a very narrow sticky tape which has adhesive on both sides. It is used purely as a temporary measure, to hold the fabric in place before stitching. It can be very convenient if you wish to hang curtains to test the length before stitching the hem. The tape can be used to hold the trial hem in place, and can then be adjusted to correct the hem level while the curtains are hanging. Tacking tape can also be used as an alternative to tacking where two wrong sides need holding together.

Trimmings for curtains and blinds

Curtains and blinds are often a major feature of the room, and it is as well to consider carefully the overall effect before applying any decorative details; if you overdo the trimming it may appear fussy or out of keeping with the rest of the décor once the curtains or blinds are in place.

Traditional styles, such as dense, floor-length curtains in velvet or an elegantly satinized finish, benefit from furnishing-weight braid trims, fringes or tassels, which look especially effective when applied to a matching valance.

A well-chosen border, frill or decorative edging can transform a plain blind into an interesting focal point, adding textural detail or contrast colour which can dress up an inexpensive fabric and provide the perfect finishing touch.

The clean lines of a Roman blind require an unfussy trimming, such as a deep fabric border or flat braid stitched to the sides and hem, or across the pleats where it must be perfectly aligned. The softer styling of Austrian and festoon blinds suggests ribbon trims, decorative tassels, bobbles or fringes to edge the bottom hem, or a softly ruched frill echoing the swagged effect of the blind. Cottage blinds can be smart and simple or heavily frilled and ornamented. Further ideas for decorating cottage blinds are given on page 187.

Trims and edgings for curtains

Tassels and fringes (right) make a luxurious finish for heavy, traditional-style curtains in fabrics such as velvet, chintz or damask. Many different styles are available in ready-made trims: silky textures or chunkier cotton trims; thick, short tassels or long and elegant fringes. These can be used on their own to make attractive tie-backs, or for edging on a wide, self-fabric tie-back. They also make a sculptured edging for valances or pelmets. Stiff pelmets can alternatively be decoratively finished with a neat wallpaper border, as illustrated above.

Trimmings for blinds

The crisp lines of a roller or Roman blind are suited to decorative braid trims (far left), embossed and subtly coloured, or sharply defined with bright motifs. Tasselled edgings (left) neatly finish the looped hem of an Austrian or festoon blind, complemented by silky pull cords hung with ornamental tassels, bobbles, or wooden acorns (below).

CHAPTER SEVEN

SOFT FURNISHINGS

Making your own soft furnishings can add flair and originality to the overall décor of your home. Bedding, table linen and cushions can be given a lift with frills, gathers, trimmings, pleats and flounces. Modern patterned fabrics can make otherwise plain furnishings look bright and cheerful, or they can be combined for a subtly co-ordinated effect. Techniques such as quilting, embroidery and appliqué can produce unique and beautiful household items which will be treasured in years to come, while being practical articles in day-to-day use.

Furnishing materials

The range of materials, trimmings and fabrics is bewildering, and it is best to think through the overall effect you want to achieve before buying. For example, if you are making sheets or duvet covers, consider the furnishings in the rest of the room. Are there patterned materials elsewhere which would make a plain fabric a good choice? Or are you confident that you can mix patterns to the best advantage? If the décor is already plain and simple, would a frill, flounce, or jazzy fabric give it more zest?

Basic bedlinen

The availability of extra-wide sheeting fabric has made it a very practical proposition to sew sheets, pillowcases and duvet covers in your own choice of colour and pattern. Sheeting looks cheerful in bright colours, stunning in rich, deep-dye hues, and fresh and restful in pastels or subtly subdued designs. Polyester/cotton blends are the most practical form

of sheeting. Pillowcases use little fabric, and this is one occasion when you can get away with using printed dress fabrics to create an attractive toning or contrasting pillowcase – or just add a pretty print frill or deep lace border to a plain-coloured sheeting pillowcase for a personal finish.

Bedcovers

Bedcovers range from the easy, informal throw-over cover or lightweight, quilt-style comforter to a neat, fitted cover with a deep flounce or formally tailored pleats.

Cotton and cotton/synthetic mixes are also a good choice for washable outer covers. For a more traditional effect there is a wide range of chintzes, brocades or glistening velvets; hard-wearing, informal styles come from brightly coloured canvases or various weights of corduroy. Linen and light wool fabrics are also a possibility, but check the cleaning instructions carefully. Practical, silk-look

Bedlinen
White bedlinen still has an inviting look despite the recent proliferation of fabric colours and patterns. Soft quilting and deep frilling with a discreet colour contrast creates luxurious styling by day or night.

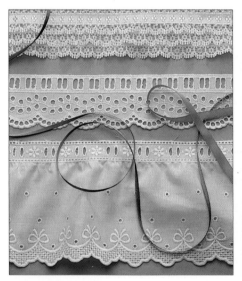

Trimmings
Lace, eyelet embroidery and shiny ribbons make beautiful decorations for traditional-style bedlinen in white or pastel colours, edging a pillowcase or a sheet turn-down.

synthetics can make a luxurious effect. Laces and sheers need simple styling – as a plain overthrow spread or fitted cover with a neat gathered frill.

Trimmings and fastenings for washable fabrics should also be washable, and colourfast. Check for possible shrinkage and deal with this before making up. If you plan to add self-fabric trimmings, wash all the fabric first. Braids, ribbons, lace or fringing should be washed before they are attached, unless you are sure that they are colourfast and shrinkproof.

Tablecloths and fabric napkins

These are not necessities of modern living, but they set a mood and style – bright and fresh, cool but decorative, elegantly luxurious – which can be enjoyed whether you are entertaining twenty people or dining alone. Alternatively, you may prefer to use table mats made from your own choice of fabric, or to combine mats with a tablecloth to create a fully co-ordinated effect. Table mats are simply constructed and can be made as plain or elaborately decorative as you wish.

For practical tablecloths choose washable fabrics – cotton/synthetic blends are also minimum-iron which is conveniently labour-saving. Plain colours lend themselves to smooth, easy styling and can be enlivened with decorative trimmings, appliqué and embroidery. A lawn, calico or other plain-weave cotton is a suitable choice, or a textured fabric such as seersucker, which adds interest to plain colouring.

Cushions

Cushions are for comfort and are the best means of highlighting and adding contrast to a room scheme. You can let your imagination run riot because they can be of any shape, with an outer cover of almost any fabric, and as plain or elaborately decorative as you wish.

The great thing about cushions is that you can plan them to co-ordinate with a new scheme of room decoration, or just make them up as you have time and simply add to your collection whenever an appealing small piece of fabric comes your way. A jumble of pretty cushions gives your familiar furnishings a whole new and different look.

Table linen
A cheerful co-ordinating print will enliven plain crockery and cutlery.

Cushion fabrics
Fabric remnants can be used for individual cushions, and careful choice of different, but complementary, fabric will give a lively effect.

VALANCES

A valance neatly and attractively covers the sides and foot end of the bed base (page 202). It can be designed to team up with the sheets and bedcover or to match the other soft furnishings in the room.

The valance can be made in one of three ways. A tailored valance with inverted pleats at the corners uses the least fabric and gives the made-up bed a crisp, smart appearance, a useful alternative to the overall fitted bedcover. Gathered or pleated valances are well suited to the decorative, less formal styling of a patterned quilt or comforter, or to the practical, unfussy look of a duvet.

Sheeting and medium-weight cottons or synthetic fabrics are good for gathers and fine pleats. Heavier chintzes and slubbed or textured-weave fabrics can be used, but these are best applied to the corner-pleated version of the valance, as they will look too bunchy if they are gathered into a flounce.

Types of material

Cotton is a natural fibre and is made into a number of fabrics. It can be blended with synthetic fibres. Cotton and cotton mixtures come with a variety of finishes, such as crêpe, chintz and seersucker, or with a pattern woven into the fabric – herring-bone or gingham, for instance. Cotton takes printed patterns well, and is easy to work with and to launder, although it may shrink when washed and fade in harsh sunlight.

Pure silk is luxurious but extremely expensive. Silk blended with other fibres is more reasonable, and 100 per cent synthetic silk substitutes cost a fraction of the price, while offering a comparable look. Moiré gives a wavy, watermark effect to silk, triacetate and acetate fabrics at the printing stage. It looks shiny and luxurious, although synthetic types tend to fray and are slippery to work with. Moiré must be dry-cleaned, or the pattern will disappear. Any cloth with a pile shorter than ⅛in (3mm) is known as velvet. It is available in cotton, silk, and synthetic fibres in a broad range of prices.

Unlike natural fibres, synthetics are all made entirely from chemicals. Different chemical combinations produce acetate, viscose, acrylic and polyester. They should not be confused with man-made fabrics, which may include natural, regenerated fibres as well as those made entirely from chemicals.

Quilted fabrics consist of light Terylene or polyester wadding sandwiched between a top layer and backing of fabric – usually cotton, silk and linen. Double-sided quilts are also available if you want to make a reversible quilt fabric. Quilts also make very good upholstery, curtain and bedcover fabrics.

Materials and trimmings
The silkiness of moiré, the richness of velvet, and simple cotton and synthetic prints cater for all tastes in home-made soft furnishings.

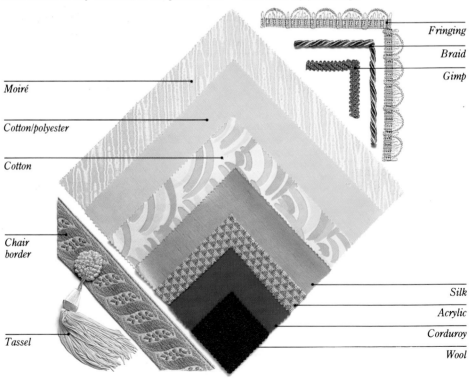

Moiré

Cotton/polyester

Cotton

Chair border

Tassel

Fringing

Braid

Gimp

Silk

Acrylic

Corduroy

Wool

Patterned fabrics

Patterns may be woven into or printed on the fabric, and you should see the effect of a drawn-out length from the roll. Remember, too, that the fabric may be seen under natural and artificial light. Check the pattern repeat and the wastage likely to be involved in matching the pattern if you are intending to make up a large item, such as loose covers.

Patterned fabrics are usually more practical than plain, since they do not show soiling so readily, but remember to buy enough fabric to allow for the matching of patterns. If you are unused to measuring up, ask the sales assistant to go over your calculations and make sure that the pattern matches are easily made without too much wastage. Fabric pieces left over can be used to make cushion covers and other small items.

Miniprints come in abstract, floral or geometric designs, printed as a small, all-over pattern. The majority are light- or medium-weight cottons or cotton/synthetic mixes, although you may find that heavier weights are sometimes available.

Geometrics range through circles, squares, diagonals and purely linear patterns. A close or fine-lined pattern may lose its identity at a distance and merge into a single shade, whereas bold, large-scale geometrics are likely to have a dramatic effect. These designs are available in all fabric weights and may be printed or woven, either in single-fibre or in fibre-mix fabrics.

Traditional patterns are often developed from historical sources, commonly chintzy florals, oriental influences and Art Nouveau or arts and crafts patterns of serpentine foliage. Medium-weight glazed and unglazed cottons, heavier cottons or sturdy linen union are available, with designs on a large or small scale.

Contemporary style is a term which covers a multitude of design ideas – these may be completely abstract, splashy patterns or improvisations on traditional themes. Some of these will in time become classics in their own right, but when making your choice, remember that this year's fashion may look depressingly out of place in two years' time. You will find contemporary designs in light and medium weight fabrics, in cotton, in pure silk, and also in synthetic materials.

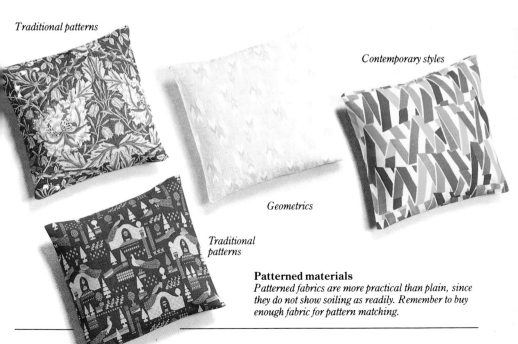

Traditional patterns

Contemporary styles

Geometrics

Traditional patterns

Patterned materials
Patterned fabrics are more practical than plain, since they do not show soiling as readily. Remember to buy enough fabric for pattern matching.

Bedding

The bedroom is a personal retreat, the place where individual preference for a type of decoration can be indulged. Fabric furnishings provide style and comfort, from the simplest pillowcase to a formal, fully fitted bedcover. But bedlinen should also be highly practical, to allow for frequent changing and washing. Fortunately, the great range of easy-care and washable fabrics offers plenty of scope for bright and colourful, sleek, or soft and luxurious effects. If, however, you want to make a once-for-all, sumptuous choice of fabric for the outer bedcover, you can move into the dry-clean fabric range to find special effects of pattern and texture on more exotic fabrics – such as silk, velvet or brocade.

Flat sheets

A flat sheet is useful whether your top cover is a duvet or fitted cover. It is simple to sew, bringing the satisfaction of a practical result for little effort. When calculating fabric amounts add the mattress length to twice the mattress depth; add 20in (50cm) for a 10in (25cm) tuck-in allowance at each end. For the width, add the mattress width to twice the mattress depth, then add 20in (50cm).

Making up a flat sheet

 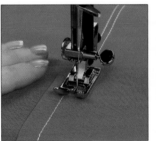 

1 *Cut the fabric and turn a double ½in (12mm) hem along both the long sides. Tack and stitch. Along one short edge turn a double 1in (25mm) hem. At the other short edge, turn under a double 3in (75mm) hem. Stitch ⅜in (10mm) from the fold.*

2 *Stitch again ½in (12mm) from the fold to form a narrow channel. This deeply hemmed edge forms the turn-down on a top sheet. If you are making a bottom sheet to be tucked in at both ends of the mattress, stitch a double 1in (25mm) hem at both the short edges of the fabric.*

3 *Using a long bodkin, carefully thread fine piping cord through the channel, across the full width of the sheet. Finally, secure the ends of the cord by stitching them firmly to the side hems, and neatly oversewing both the openings at either end of the channel. This completes the sheet.*

ALTERNATIVE FABRICS FOR SHEETS

If you have a taste for something a little different, look among the full range of suitable fabric weights for printed cottons, synthetics or even a washable cotton satin for a luxury effect. Handle the fabric before you buy it, to get a sense of its crease-resistance and durability.

Such fabrics will probably not be available in the width you need for full bed-size, so it will mean seaming sections together. Rather than joining two fabric widths, which will make a centre seam that falls down the middle of the bed, cut one section in half lengthwise and seam on either side of a central panel, so that the seamlines can be placed towards the edges of the bed.

To avoid showing the wrong side of a printed fabric at the turn-down of the top sheet, stitch a self-fabric or contrasting facing to create a neat, attractive finish.

Fitted sheets

A fitted sheet covers the mattress neatly and makes bedmaking quick and simple. Easy-care, purpose-made sheeting fabric is the most practical choice. You can adapt the technique to make a top sheet with fitted corners at the foot end of the bed only – plan the most convenient style for the size of your bed and its accessibility when it is necessary to change the bedlinen.

When calculating fabric amounts add the mattress length to twice the mattress depth; add 14in (36cm) for a 7in (18cm) tuck-in allowance at either end. For the width, add the mattress width to twice the mattress depth; then add 14in (36cm).

Making up a fitted sheet

1 *Cut the fabric to the required size. Then measure 14in (36cm) along the edge from each corner on all sides and mark these lines with pins. From the position of each pin, chalk a line on the fabric at right angles to the edge and mark clearly where the lines meet. This gives you the position of the edges of the bed.*

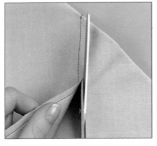

2 *With the wrong sides facing, fold one corner between the point where the lines intersect and the corner, so that the 14in (36cm) marker pins and chalked lines match. Pin together. Then stitch ³/₈in (10mm) inside the pinned line. Trim the corner of the fabric to within ¹/₄in (6mm) of the stitching line.*

3 *To complete the corner seam, press the seam open, then re-press, right sides facing and the seam at the edge. Pin, tack and stitch ³/₈in (10mm) from the fold, to enclose the raw seam edges and form a French seam. Repeat step 1, step 2 and step 3 to complete seams at each of the other corners.*

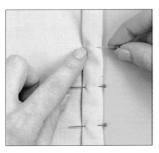

4 *Turn under ¹/₂in (12mm) all around the outer edge of the sheet. Then turn the fabric again to form a double ¹/₂in (12mm) casing hem. Pin the hem securely. Next, mitre the corners and slip-stitch the mitres carefully so that there is a clean channel inside the hem to thread the elastic through.*

5 *Measure 13in (33cm) along the pinned hem on either side of each corner seam; mark with pins. Stitch the casing hem along the straight edges and also around the corner section, leaving a gap of ¹/₂in (12mm) at each mark to thread elastic through. Cut four 9in (23cm) lengths of elastic.*

6 *Thread elastic into the casing hem at each corner with a bodkin. Pin elastic through the casing hem at each opening. Tuck the ends of the elastic inside the casing hem. Repin the elastic ends parallel to the edge so that you can machine across the ends. Stitch the elastic ends and openings securely.*

Plain pillowcases

The simplest type of pillowcase is made from a folded length of fabric with a fold-over flap on the inside which tucks over the inserted pillow. This type of pillowcase can be made in the same sheeting fabric as the sheets, or you may prefer a complete colour contrast. Plain colours can be enlivened with ribbon trims, appliqué shapes or embroidery to form designs at each corner or a pretty border along the short edge of the pillowcase. These trimmings can be stitched on before making up. When calculating fabric amounts, use a single piece of wide sheeting for each plain pillowcase. Measure the length of the pillow, double the measurement and add 8¼in (21cm) for the flap and hems. Measure the width and add 1¼in (30mm) for the seams.

Making up a plain pillowcase

1 *Cut the fabric to the required measurements. Along one short edge of the fabric piece, turn a double ¼in (6mm) hem on to the wrong side. Pin, tack and stitch.*

2 *On the other short edge, turn 2in (50mm) on to the wrong side and press. Turn in ⅜in (10mm) at the raw edge; stitch in place. This edge will be at the front.*

3 *Fold the narrow-hemmed edge to make a 6in (15cm) flap. Press and pin. Fold the fabric in half widthways, wrong sides together, aligning the wide-hemmed edge with the flap, and stitch the side edges.*

4 *Turn the pillowcase with right sides facing. Pin, tack and stitch the side edges ⅜in (10mm) from the first seam to enclose the raw edges. Turn the pillowcase right side out and press.*

Frilled pillowcases

Unlike a plain pillowcase, this is made with separate pieces for front and back, and the frill is another separate unit. The frill is made from a doubled-over fabric strip. You can use any printed cotton. Floral designs set off a pastel fabric, or use the same pattern with reversed colourways. When calculating fabric amounts, measure the length and width of the pillow. Add 1¼in (30mm) to each measurement for ½in (12mm) seam allowances all around. For the back, add 2½in (65mm) to the length and 1¼in (30mm) to the width. For the flap, allow the width of the front section, including seams, and a depth of 7in (18cm). Decide on the depth for the finished frill, double it and add 1¼in (30mm) for seams. Allow a total length twice the total measurement around the pillow.

Making up a frilled pillowcase

1 Turn a 2in (50mm) hem on one short edge of the back. Turn under ³⁄₈in (10mm) at the raw edge. Turn a double ¼in (6mm) hem on one long edge of the flap.

2 Seam strips of fabric to make a circular band for the frill. Divide it into four equal sections and mark with pins. Gather the frill separately in each section.

3 Mark the front piece of the pillowcase to match the sections on the frill. Stitch the frill in place. With right sides facing, align the hemmed edge of the back with the seamline on the front.

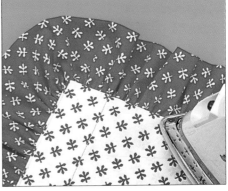

4 Place the flap right side down, matching the long raw edge of the flap with the raw edge on the front. Pin and tack all around the pillow, turn it over and stitch from the front on the frill seamline. Press.

Duvet covers

A duvet is designed to make life simpler, since it eliminates the more tedious aspects of bedmaking. Polyester/cotton sheeting is a suitable fabric. The basic duvet cover is very simply made and fastened with press-stud tape or touch-and-close fastening for quick removal. It consists of two rectangular fabric pieces, so you can make it all in one colour or pattern, or choose different fabrics for the two sides to create a toned or contrasting effect. If you want an unusual material for the upper side,

you can seam panels of standard-width fabric and cut a single width of sheeting for the lower side. Make sure that the fabrics are compatible for washing; wash the top fabric before cutting out to eliminate any shrinkage. This method also lends itself to a patchwork or a strip-pattern effect for the upper side.

Calculating fabric amounts

Length: Measure the duvet length, usually 79in (200cm), and add 2¾in (7cm) for the hem and the seam allowances.
Width: Measure the duvet width and add 1½in (4cm) for the seam allowances.

Making up a duvet cover

 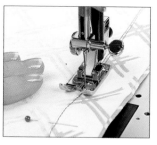 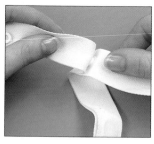

1 *Cut two pieces of fabric to the required size for your duvet. Turn a double 1in (25mm) hem along the bottom edge of both fabric pieces. Pin, tack and stitch the hems, then press them.*

2 *With right sides facing, pin and tack the hemmed edges together 12in (30cm) in towards the centre from each side, leaving a central opening. Stitch the tacked parts 1in (25mm) from the outer edge.*

3 *Cut a length of press-stud tape 1¼in (30mm) longer than the open section. Ensure that there is a stud close to each end so that the closure will not gape. Undo the press studs to separate the tape into two lengths.*

 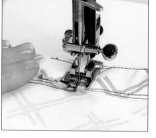 

4 *Pin one length of tape along one side of the opening, with ½in (12mm) of extra tape at each end. Tack and stitch using a zipper foot on the machine. Repeat on the other side, ensuring that the studs match along the length.*

5 *Fold the cover with right sides facing. Make a double row of stitches vertically across the sides of the opening to enclose the tape edges. Finish the stitching securely, as it will undergo wear and tear when the cover is changed.*

6 *Turn the cover to wrong sides facing and make a French seam around the three open sides. Pin, tack and stitch ¼in (6mm) from the raw edge. Trim the seam to within ⅛in (3mm) of the stitching. Turn to right sides facing and stitch.*

Fastenings

Fastenings are used mainly on items such as duvet and cushion covers, which must be removed for cleaning. There are many types of fastening and the choice is a matter of personal preference. For duvet covers there are two choices, a strip fastening or single fasteners.

Strip fasteners include press-stud tape, which comes with the press-studs ready fastened to a tape, and touch-and-close tape, which is just pressed together to fasten. Single fasteners include sew-on press-studs, circles of touch-and-close fastening and non-sew press-studs which just clip through the fabric. For cushions where the opening needs to be firmly and neatly fastened, a zip is the best choice.

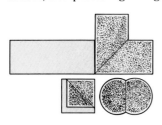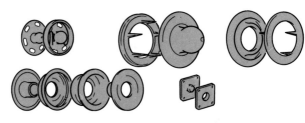

Touch-and-close fastenings
These are available in the form of circular spots, rectangles and strips. One half has fluffy loops and the other tiny hooks which adhere to the loops. They are available with an adhesive backing or to sew on.

Press-studs and poppers
Metal press-studs come in a range of sizes and in a black or silver-coloured finish. Small square white or clear plastic studs are less sturdy than metal poppers but handy where a small, flat fastening is needed.

Poppers are non-sew press-studs. Each half of the popper has a backing section which clips through the fabric to fasten the popper in place. They are more suitable for loosely covered items, since they will come apart if subjected to strain.

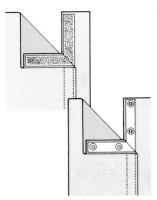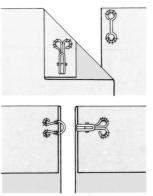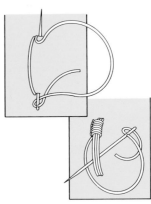

Fastening tapes
Touch-and-close tape and press-stud tape are ideal for fastening a duvet cover opening. Separate the two halves of the tape and stitch half to each edge of the opening along the long edges. Use a zipper foot on press-stud tape to pass by the studs. The ends of the tape are usually finished into the end of the opening and stitched across.

Lapped and abutted hooks
For overlapping edges, sew the hook on the inside of the overlapping edge of the fabric and the bar on the outside underlapping edge. For abutting edges, sew both the hook and eye on the inside of the fabric. The eye should extend slightly over the edge. These are versatile fastenings, which can be used in clothing as well as soft furnishings.

Making a thread eye
A thread eye provides a decorative alternative to a metal eye, but is not as strong. Mark the two points where the eye should start and finish and sew a few long stitches from one point to the other, keeping them fairly loose. Secure the ends. Then sew closely spaced blanket stitches over the strands of thread to form the eye.

Gathered valances

A gathered valance creates an informal style while providing a neat cover-up for the bed base. The skirt of the valance is sewn to a flat section of fabric that spreads across the bed base underneath the mattress. This can be made from the same fabric as the skirt or a co-ordinated material. For economy, if the base section of the valance will not show, an old sheet can be used, or a plain calico. Plain and patterned cottons are a practical choice for a gathered valance, while a basic style can be enlivened with trimmings or borders.

Calculating fabric amounts

Measure the mattress top and add 1⅜in (35mm) to the length and 1¼in (30mm) to the width. Measure the height from the floor to the top of the bed base and add 2½in (65mm). This gives the depth of the skirt. The total length of fabric needed for the skirt is four times the mattress length plus twice the width.

Making up a gathered valance

1 *Cut the main panel on the lengthwise grain. Curve the two base corners by drawing around the edge of a plate. Cut the curves. Cut strips of fabric to the depth of the skirt, giving them ½in (12mm) seam allowances.*

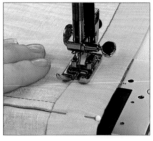

2 *Join the strips of fabric into one long strip using French seams. Turn under a double 1in (25mm) hem on the wrong side of the fabric at the lower edge of the skirt. Then pin, tack and stitch the hem of the skirt in place.*

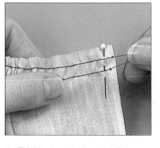

3 *Divide the total length of the skirt into six equal divisions and mark them with pins at the top. Work two rows of gathering stitches in each section. Pull up the threads to gather each section evenly and fasten them securely.*

4 *Measure the sides and bottom edge of the main panel and divide by six. Mark the six equal divisions with pins. Match the marks on the skirt to those on the main panel. Pull the gathers in each section until the lengths are matched. Pin, with right sides facing.*

5 *Tack and stitch the skirt to the panel ½in (12mm) from the edge. Trim down the seam to ⅜in (10mm) and stitch again close to the first line of stitching. Neaten the edges by working over them with machine zigzag stitch. Press the seam towards the main panel.*

6 *At the remaining raw edges of the main panel and valance (which will be placed at the top end of the bed), turn and press a double ⅜in (10mm) hem on to the wrong side of the fabric. Pin, tack and stitch this hem firmly in place. This completes the valance.*

Flounced bedcovers

A fitted bedcover with a deep flounce needs a firmly woven fabric which handles easily and has good draping qualities. Cotton with a satinized finish gives a slightly luxurious feeling, or you might prefer a light wool for comfort with a plain or slightly textured weave. Quiet, fresh pastels and cool, muted tones are suitable for this type of cover.

Main panel: Measure the length of the made-up bed top and add 8in (20cm) to allow for the height of the pillows; measure the width and add 1¼in (30mm) for the seam allowances.

Flounce: Measure from the top of the bed to within ⅜in (10mm) of the floor and add 2½in (65mm) for the seam and hem allowances. This makes the depth of the flounce. The full length of fabric needed is four times the length of the bed, plus twice the width, plus 1½in (40mm) for side hems at the bedhead end. Cut strips of fabric to the depth of the flounce and seam them together to make up this length.

Making up a flounced bedcover

1 Cut out the main panel on the lengthwise grain. Cut the lining to the same size. Curve the two base corners on both the fabric and lining by drawing around the edge of a plate. Trim the corners along the marked lines, making sure that the curves join into the straight edges in a smooth line.

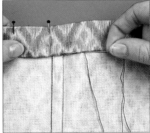

2 Cut the strips for the flounce and join them into one strip using French seams. Take ½in (12mm) seam allowances and match the pattern details on the seams. Turn a double 1in (25mm) hem on to the wrong side of the fabric at the lower edge of the flounce. Pin, tack and slip-hem in place.

3 Divide by six the length of the two long sides and lower edge of the panel. Mark with pins. Divide the flounce by six and mark with pins. Work two rows of gathering stitches along each section. Pull the gathers to match the divisions on the panel. Pin the flounce to the panel, right sides together.

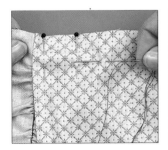

4 Stitch the flounce to the main panel ½in (12mm) from the raw edges. Trim the seam to ⅜in (10mm); stitch. Position the lining over the panel, wrong sides facing. Turn under the raw edge and tack.

5 Turn and press a double ⅜in (10mm) hem on to the wrong side of the cover across the side edges of the flounce and the tacked top of the main panel. Pin the hem and machine-stitch it in place.

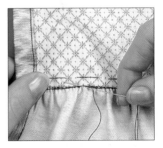

6 Turn under the sides and lower edge of the lining and pin it to the wrong side of the flounce, to cover the flounce seam. Tack the lining in place and secure the turned edges with hemming stitch.

Throw-over covers

A throw-over cover is almost as simple to make as a flat sheet, but clever choice of fabric can give a very rich effect. Medium-weight cottons are suitable, or, for a warm winter look, choose light wool, or figured fabric in glowing colours. When calculating fabric amounts, measure the bed with all the bedclothes in place, including pillows. Measure from the top of the mattress to the end of the bed, then the depth to the floor. Add 4in (100mm) for hems. Measure the width of the mattress and depth to the floor; double the depth. Add 4in (100mm) for hems.

Making up a throw-over cover

1 *Cut two widths of fabric and trim off the selvedges from both sides of each length. Cut one piece in half lengthways to make the side panels. Fold under a ½in (12mm) seam along the edge of one side panel and place it over the seam on one side of the central panel, matching any pattern. Ladder-stitch them together from the right side.*

2 *Repeat the previous step to attach the second side panel to the central panel, once again matching the pattern where possible. Machine-stitch the pieces together, making flat seams following the lines of ladder stitching. Neaten the raw edges of the seams and press open. Trim the side panels if necessary, allowing 2in (50mm) for the hem on each side.*

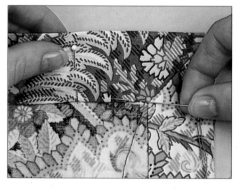

3 *Turn and press a 2in (50mm) single hem all around the edge of the cover, then fold in the raw edges ½in (12mm) and press. Mitre the corners by opening out the folded hem and cutting across the corner diagonally just outside the fold line. Fold the hem back in place once more and press.*

4 *Pin the hem in place and finish with hand stitching. Slip-stitch the edges of the mitred corner together and use hemming or blind hem stitch (page 167) to secure all four side hems. Finally, press the completed cover from the wrong side using a steam iron or a dry iron and a damp cloth.*

Comforters

A comforter is a lightweight quilt that can be used as a top cover over the other bedding, or if you combine it with a top sheet as a single covering for warm nights. You can make the two sides from different fabrics. It looks particularly attractive when teamed with a valance. When calculating fabric amounts, with bedding in place, measure from the head of the bed to just below the mattress at the foot. Measure across the bed and down to just below the mattress on either side. You need two panels of fabric and one panel of wadding to these dimensions. Allow an extra ¾in (20mm) on widths for joining sections. Allow extra fabric to make bias strips (page 171).

Making up a comforter

1 *Cut the wadding to length and stitch the sections together to make up the full width of the comforter. Overlap the edges of the wadding pieces and join them with a broad herring-bone stitch. Cut the fabric to the correct dimensions for the front and the back panels, joining the widths with flat seams if you find that this is necessary.*

2 *Spread out the back panel right side down and lay the wadding on top of it, matching the edges carefully. Then spread the front panel over the wadding right side up. Next, starting at the centre, pin and tack all three layers together across the width. When tacking, use large stitches and a contrasting coloured thread.*

3 *Continue pinning and tacking the layers, using rows of large stitching 10–12in (25–30cm) apart, working from the centre outwards on both sides of the first row of stitching. Take the tacking lines right to the edges of the fabric. When this is completed, tack all around the edges of the comforter ⅜in (10mm) from the raw edges.*

4 *Run 1in (25mm)-wide bias binding around all four sides of the comforter (you can also use self-fabric bias). Fold it over the raw edges of the joined fabric and wadding. Pin and tack, overlap the ends of the binding and turn in the raw edge. Stitch in place.*

5 *Remove the tacking threads and mark the positions for ties across the comforter with pins. To make a tie, thread a needle with embroidery cotton and make a short stitch through the layers of fabric, leaving a 2in (50mm) end of thread. Make a second stitch in the same place.*

6 *To complete the tie, knot the ends of the thread and trim them to equal lengths. Work right across the length and width of the comforter, tying the layers of fabric firmly together at the pinned marks. This completes the comforter and it is ready for use.*

Pleated bedcovers

A smartly tailored bedcover is cleanly styled and practical, concealing the bedding completely. Inverted pleats at the corners make it easy to lift and re-lay the cover, but on the bed it settles neatly into a crisp, boxy finish. The handsome styling depends upon choice of a fairly firm, crease-resistant fabric that folds elegantly into the pleats.

Calculating fabric amounts

Main panel: Measure the top of the bed with the bedding in place. Add 8in (20cm) to the length, for a tuck-in under the pillow, and 1¼in (30mm) to the width for seam allowances.
Skirt: The skirt is cut in three panels, one for each side and one for the foot of the bed. Measure from the top of the bed to within ⅜in (10mm) of the floor and add 2½in (65mm) for the seam and hems. This gives the depth of the skirt panels. For the side panels, measure the length of the bed and add 16in (40cm) for the corner pleats and pillow tuck-in. For the foot panel, measure the width of the bed and add 16in (40cm) for the corner pleats.

One-room living
This is a useful style if you live in a single room or studio apartment. The bed is neat and unobtrusive when it is fully covered during the day, and if you remove the pillows the bed can effectively be turned into a sofa for daytime use.

Making up a pleated bedcover

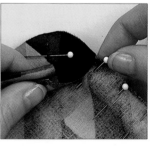

1 *Cut the panel on the lengthwise grain of the fabric. If the fabric pieces have to be joined to give sufficient width, use French seams to eliminate the raw edges on the wrong side. Draw a line at 45° from each of the base corners. Curve the corners slightly. With tailor's chalk, mark the position of the corner pleats on the line ½in (12mm) from the raw edges.*

2 *Cut out the panels for the skirt and join them into one long strip. Be sure to join the side and foot panels in the correct sequence. Make French seams taking a ½in (12mm) seam allowance. Turn a double 1in (25mm) hem on to the wrong side of the fabric at the lower edge of the skirt. Pin, tack, then hem the skirt by hand. Then press the hem with a hot iron.*

3 *Mark the centre of the top edge of the foot panel with a pin. Having done this, mark the centre of the foot edge of the main panel in the same way. Next, with right sides facing, and matching the two pinned marks accurately, firmly pin the foot panel of the skirt to the edge of the main panel, right up to the pinned marks at the lower corners of the main panel.*

4 *Starting at the top end of the main panel, pin the skirt panels to the main panel, down to the pinned marks at the base corners. The surplus fabric in the skirt at each corner will be used to form the inverted pleats.*

5 *Fold the surplus fabric into a pleat at each corner, matching the centre of the pleat to the mark at the corner of the main panel. Clip into the seam allowance of the pleat so that it will turn easily around the corners, tack and stitch.*

6 *Tack and stitch the skirt in place. Neaten the raw edges of all the seams with machine zigzag stitch. Along the top edge of the cover, turn a double ³⁄₈in (10mm) hem. Pin, tack and stitch the hem in place. Press the finished cover.*

Types of pleating

Pleats give a tailored, slightly severe air to a furnishing, but make a neat and tidy finish. Pleats can be formed either side-by-side or spaced further apart in groups. There are several types of pleats: the simplest and easiest to make are knife pleats, where the folds of fabric face in the same direction; there are also box pleats, where the folds are turned away from each other; finally, there are inverted pleats, where the folds are turned towards each other. These are the ones used in the pleated bedcover illustrated opposite.

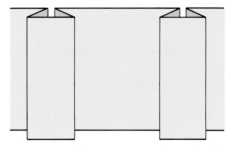

Box pleats
Each of the pleats has two folds which are turned away from each other. The back folds are facing and may meet on one line.

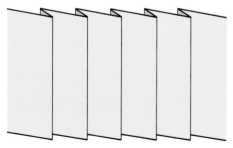

Knife pleats
Each pleat has one fold which is aligned with another line. All the pleats face in the same direction. Knife pleats are the simplest and easiest type of pleats, both to make and to maintain. An example of a knife pleated frill is shown on pages 224–5.

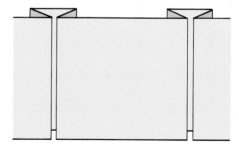

Inverted pleats
Each pleat has two folds which are turned towards each other and meet on one line. Back folds face away from each other. Inverted pleats, because they are hidden by the way the material falls, make a neat, unfussy finish.

Decorative finishes

Making your own soft furnishings is an opportunity to put your design skills to work, not only in the choice of fabric but also in terms of the details which make the project representative of your personal style and taste. In addition to the sewing methods involved in making the main item, there are many techniques of decorative stitching and applied decoration which can extend the range of your ideas for soft furnishings. Patchwork and appliqué are simple to learn and can produce original effects by allowing you to mix colours and patterns as freely as you wish on a small or large scale.

Patchwork quilts

Patchwork consists of a mosaic of small pieces of material joined together to form a pattern. To create an artefact of beauty and neatness, the choice of fabrics and shapes, and the accuracy of joins, must all be carefully considered. With patchwork thorough planning at the outset is a must.

For beginners, it is advisable to limit the number of fabrics you use, until you get a feel for mixing colours and patterns together. A chequerboard effect using only two different fabrics can have remarkable impact if you select the combination carefully. Colours can be highly contrasted or subtly moody; you can set off a discreet geometric pattern against a floral miniprint, with colour links between the two. Use fabrics of the same basic weight to avoid puckering at the seams. As you gain more confidence with this technique, you can develop the patchwork patterning more freely.

Traditional, hand-stitched, "pieced" patchwork requires a methodical approach and is best used for relatively small items such as table mats, cushions and decorative panels. However, compared to machine patchwork, it is easier to work more complex designs, with diamonds, hexagons, stars and fan shapes. You can plan out the colours and patterns before you begin, or let the work grow piece by piece into the jewelled effect of mixed fabric patterns often seen in antique patchwork.

The fabric pieces are tacked to templates of paper or thin card with the edges turned on to the wrong side. With two pieces together, right sides facing, the edges are slip-stitched to create a firm, neat seam. The templates can be removed when individual shapes are completely surrounded by others and stitched on all sides.

Quilted table mats
Patchwork techniques can be adapted to regular shapes if the edges are accurately matched.

As with machine patchwork, fabrics should be of a similar weight, and if the finished item is to be washable, all must be shrink-resistant and colourfast. Printed cottons make beautiful patchwork and accommodate small shapes and intricate designs. Co-ordinated fabric ranges offer plenty of scope for patchwork designs, but there is great pleasure in selecting and combining fabrics from personal taste, and all sorts of scraps and offcuts can be given useful life in this way.

Quilting

In items such as table mats and oven gloves, quilting provides the necessary thickness and an attractive finish for plain or patterned fabrics or patchwork pieces. Polyester wadding is sandwiched between two layers of fabric and the quilted pattern is machine-stitched through all three layers. You can work the quilting and then bind the raw edges of fabric and wadding. Alternatively, treat the front piece of fabric and the wadding as one thickness, tacking them together, and seam them to the back section on three sides; then turn out to the right side and neaten the remaining seam.

Diagonal quilting adds interest to a plain fabric or simple geometric. Patchwork quilted along the lines of the template shapes has a very decorative, neat effect. A similar technique is used in quilting the outlines of a fabric design, such as a large floral print; stitch around the edges of the main motifs to create a lightly raised relief surface.

Appliqué

Appliqué consists simply of applying one piece of fabric to another larger piece, and there are several ways in which an appliqué motif can be stitched to the base fabric.

The motif may be a single piece of fabric, or constructed from any number of pieces which are tacked down in place to form the design and then secured with finished stitching. The stitching is worked around all the edges of the appliqué, whether they are raw edges or neatened with a narrow turn-in. Closely worked machine zigzag stitch secures an appliqué motif in place, so that the fabric cannot fray or tear. If you use straight stitch, turn under the raw edges. Otherwise, the outlines can be overstitched by hand.

As with patchwork, it is necessary to select the fabrics carefully, matching them for weight to avoid straining or puckering, and compatibility for washing or dry cleaning. Appliqué designs worked in small pieces of plain-coloured fabrics have an attractive appearance particularly effective for borders and corners of sheets and pillowcases, but make sure that the colours are fast, or the first wash will ruin your work. Avoid loose weaves which will eventually fray, however carefully stitched to begin with. You can also use embroidery stitches to make patterns.

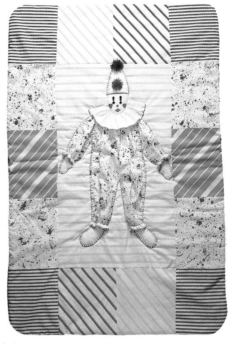

Combined techniques
Fresh, bright colours and textural detail make a decorative cot cover. A simple block patchwork provides the background with a jolly clown motif appliquéd at the centre. Both the patchwork cover and the appliqué detail are padded; the clown's frilled collar and pompon hat add three-dimensional interest.

Table linen

Table linen includes tablecloths, mats and napkins. These are all easy and quick to make, and it is simple to add a personal touch to a complete set. It is more economical to make your own than to buy these items, and you also have a wider choice of materials and combinations of fabrics.

Table linen needs to wear well and come up fresh when washed, but you may also wish to make beautifully decorative cloths for side tables or for the main table when it is not in use for dining. You can add a range of attractive and easy-to-sew trimmings, but ensure that they are compatible when washing.

Types of fabric

Printed cottons offer a wide range of different effects, from small, busy, all-over patterns in cool morning colours to rich, dark, swirling designs subtly glowing in a room lit for a leisurely evening at home. Gingham is a lively choice for the kitchen, the woven white-and-coloured checks pretty but informal; you can choose a tiny dogtooth or broad chequerboard effect in fresh green or yellow, strong blue or red, brown or black. PVC-coated fabrics are a useful option for wipe-clean kitchen cloths, available in plain colours and a variety of attractive patterns.

The crisp and heavy textures of linen are pleasantly traditional, especially the natural creamy colours, lending themselves to discreet embroidered or cutwork borders and corner motifs. Pure linen needs extra care, but linen/synthetic mixes or linen-look fabrics are easier to handle.

Plain fabrics and woven-in patterns are suitable for matching napkins, and also for making table mats, which may be designed for use with other table linen or to be placed directly on the table-top. As table mats are made from a double layer of fabric, you can choose one-sided prints if preferred. Medium to heavy, hard-wearing materials are a good choice for mats in everyday use – fabrics such as denim, canvas or hessian, which are available in a range of colours and light or dark neutral tones. Brightly coloured binding or a patterned braid edging lightens the purely practical emphasis. To make a thick mat you can insert a layer of wadding, or you can use ready-quilted fabric instead.

Decorative effects

For decorative purposes, lace makes an ideal throw-over cloth, perhaps draped on a floor-length cover of velvet or a rich silk or taffeta underlayer. Layered cottons look attractive as a daytime cover-up for a round table, in co-ordinated prints or contrasting colours, depending upon the effect you want to create. The top cloth should be considerably shorter than the lower layer and can also be a different shape. This treatment lends itself to decorative edgings such as scallops, braids, ribbons, cutwork embroidery or appliqué, to emphasize the layered effect. When adding trimmings, make sure that you match the weight of the trimming to the fabric weight, or you may get a distorted effect.

Co-ordinated table linen
Co-ordinating table linen will enhance any table. Matching quilted mats and napkins in bold, bright colours will complement modern tableware; or, for a more traditional setting, choose plain white with a little surface texture to form the perfect backdrop for elaborate tableware.

Design details

By making your own table linen, you can set the mood and atmosphere of your meal, whether for a leisurely summer breakfast or for an elegant dinner party. The choice of fabric should flatter your tableware and blend in stylishly with other furnishings, and small design details such as the trimmings and edging for tablecloths, place mats or napkins can make all the difference, lending a personalized touch that makes even the most basic table linen extra special.

Pick up cues on colour and detail from the existing elements of your table. An attractively patterned dinner service may suggest an unusual colour combination; gleaming silverware and delicate china look good against spotless white or subtly creamy table linen enhanced by the most discreet trimming such as a narrow satin binding, lace edging, or toning embroidery at borders and corners. Modern cutlery and sturdy china benefit from bold colours and equally modern fabric designs. Dark hues and large-motif patterns can create a dramatic setting.

Borders and edgings
A neat, attractive way to create unusual styling for a tablecloth is to add a deep border in a co-ordinated or contrasting fabric. Wide strips of fabric stitched around the edges of the cloth can be doubled over with mitred corners. Plain colour with a strong abstract or geometric border creates a good effect, while pretty flowered fabrics gain an eye-catching finish when edged with an all-over miniprint in co-ordinated colours.

Measuring up

Unless you are copying the size of an existing cloth, the basic measurements you need are the size of the table-top and the required drop from the edge of the table downwards. To judge a good length for everyday use, sit at the table on a chair in regular use and measure from the edge of the table to your lap. A little below lap-length – usually a drop of about 10–12in (25–30cm) – is about right to avoid a skimpy appearance. The drop should hang gracefully even if it is short; too little fabric will stand out awkwardly from the table-top. For a full-length cloth, measure from the top of the table to within ⅜in (10mm) of the floor.

When calculating the full amount of fabric needed, add twice the drop to the table length and width, or to the diameter of a round table, and add hem allowances. The hem is most easily kept to a narrow depth for convenience

in sewing, but you can make it deeper to add more weight, which helps the fabric to hang elegantly, especially on a floor-length cloth. Alternatively you can bind the edges of the cloth, so that no hem allowance is needed. This is effective on a round cloth, where a bias binding accommodates the curves neatly.

A tablecloth should be made from a single width of fabric, but if you need to seam widths together, make a central panel with equal side panels. This applies to rectangular and round cloths, but remember that you should never have a seam across the centre of the table.

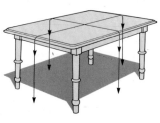

Calculating fabric amounts
Add twice the calculated drop to the width and length of the table.

Rectangular tablecloths

Whether your table is square or oblong, a tablecloth gives a clean, finished effect, for daytime freshness or evening elegance. Basically, it is simply a hemmed rectangle of fabric, but the hem is neatened with mitred corners, a technique which, once learned, is useful for a number of soft furnishings projects to give a professional touch.

Plain or printed cottons are a practical choice of fabric. If you are making up the cloth from seamed panels, you have the option to use one fabric for the central panel and a co-ordinated colour or pattern for the outer panels, rather than the same fabric throughout. The traditional choice of white makes a crisp base for your table settings, and gives a sparkling effect for a dinner party, but you may prefer a darker colour or busy pattern for daytime use.

Calculating fabric amounts
Measure the length and width of the table-top. To each measurement add twice the drop from the edge of the table. Add 2⅜in (60mm) to the length and width for the hem. For a large table, you may need to join widths of fabric. If so, allow twice the length. Also allow extra fabric for positioning and matching any pattern.

Making up a rectangular tablecloth

1 *Cut the fabric to size, or join widths (page 211). Along each edge of the fabric, turn ½in (12mm) on to the wrong side and press. Fold over ½in (12mm) again to make a double hem and press.*

2 *Open out one fold. Cut diagonally to within ¼in (6mm) of the point at the inner fold. Refold the fabric and match the cut edges. Match the folded edges and pin them together to keep them level.*

3 *Pin and stitch a narrow seam along each diagonal cut. Stitch the seam ¼in (6mm) from the raw edge, with the stitching line passing through the inner corner point. Press the seams. Turn the corners out.*

4 *Refold the double hem. The diagonal seam forms a neat mitre. Stitch all around the edge of the tablecloth. At each end of the stitching line, pull the threads through to the wrong side. Fasten off.*

Round tablecloths

A round tablecloth is cut from a square of fabric: the fabric is folded in four and cut using a paper pattern of a quarter-circle. For everyday use a short cloth is neat and stylish, but a round cloth looks particularly elegant in a floor-length version, especially when made of a medium-weight fabric.

Fresh cottons are a good choice for informal styling, while all-over flower prints and random abstracts with small motifs minimize problems of pattern matching if you need to join widths of fabrics. For a more formal effect, choose a plain-weave linen or linen-look fabric, or a lightly textured weave. Round cloths lend themselves particularly to a decorative layered style. Choose co-ordinated or contrasting colours and patterns and simply cut two paper patterns to make a floor length underlayer and a top cloth with a half-length drop.

Calculating fabric amounts

Measure the diameter of the table-top. Add twice the depth of the drop plus 1¼in (30mm) for hem allowances. A round tablecloth creates the best effect if cut from a single width of fabric, but if you need to join widths, use the method for the rectangular tablecloth.

Making up a round tablecloth

1 *Measure the radius of the table-top. Hold the measured point on the string at one corner of the paper. Move the pencil to draw a quarter-circle on the paper. Cut along the pencil line.*

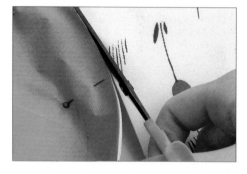

2 *Fold the fabric in four. Pin on the paper pattern, aligning the straight edges of the paper with the folded edges of the fabric, then cut. Stitch around the outside edge of the cloth ½in (12mm) in from the raw edge.*

3 *Press the edge on to the wrong side all around the cloth along the stitched line. The stitching will tend to roll over naturally just inside the fold, giving a good, smooth curve.*

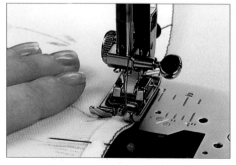

4 *Turn under the raw edge to make a double hem. Pin and tack. Stitch all around the hem, keeping the stitching line close to the inner fold. Remove the tacking and press.*

Table mats and napkins

Place mats and mats for serving dishes can be as plain and practical or as decorative as you wish, made as a basic rectangle or with neatly rounded corners. A quilted effect can be stitched by hand or machine, with a layer of polyester wadding sandwiched between two pieces of fabric, or you have the option of a very handy short-cut, using ready-quilted fabric and simply binding two layers together. Fabric mats are not entirely heat-proof, so do not put down dishes straight from the oven without slipping a cork or plastic mat underneath the fabric one, but they provide sufficient insulation to protect the table-top from most warm plates.

If you are making a tablecloth, buy an additional length of fabric for a set of matching napkins; otherwise, this is an opportunity to use up offcuts of fabric and remnants of cottons which are too small to be of use for any major projects. Make them co-ordinate or contrast with the tablecloth or place mats.

Napkins
Lacy edging in cool pink adds an attractively restrained touch of colour for white linen napkins. The delicacy of the lacy edges gives a dainty finish to offset fine chinaware, or perhaps gleaming glassware and silver cutlery.

Making up a table mat

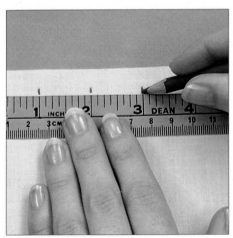

1 *Cut two pieces of the chosen fabric to the required size. With a hard pencil or tailor's chalk, mark evenly spaced lines about 1in (25mm) apart along one of the shorter sides. Draw parallel lines from short side to short side. Then cut the wadding to exactly the same size as the fabric.*

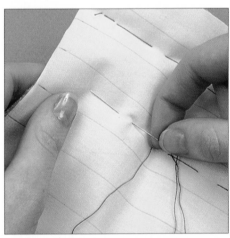

2 *Sandwich the wadding between the wrong sides of the two pieces of fabric. Next, holding the three rectangles firmly between your finger and thumb, pin them together carefully. Then stitch rows of neat, even tacking stitches between alternate drawn lines as shown in the picture above.*

 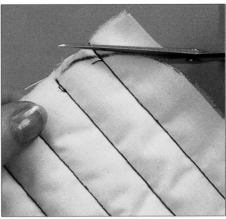

3 *Using the pencilled or chalked lines as guide lines, sew several parallel rows of long machine stitches from one short side of the rectangle to the other. Do not sew them too close together, or the result will look cramped and fussy. You might also like to use a contrasting thread for working the quilting stitches, which can produce a very attractive effect.*

4 *Cups, saucers and plates can all be used as a guide to round the corners of the table mat. Decide how tight a curve you require and place the cup, saucer or plate on the first corner. Draw around it with tailor's chalk and repeat the same process for each corner. Having done this, cut along the curved lines. Then, finally, trim the corners neatly.*

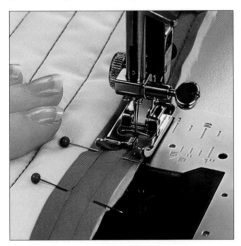 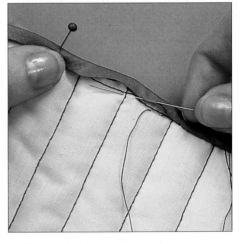

5 *To give a neat and stylish finish to the table mat, it is a good idea to edge it with binding. If you have used a contrasting colour for the quilting stitches as suggested above, it is a good idea to use binding which is of the same contrasting colour to give a unified look to the finished article. Open out one folded edge of the binding. Pin the binding around the mat with the right sides facing and the raw edges level. Stitch it in place along the crease on the binding as shown in the illustration above.*

6 *Fold over the edge to the wrong side. Press and stitch the binding in place. On the right side, machine-stitch on the inside edge of the binding to strengthen the mat around the edge. Napkins can then be easily made with any offcuts. Cut out identical 18in (45cm) squares. Fold and press a double ¼in (6mm) hem on all four edges of the napkin, taking care to fold in all the corners neatly. Pin, tack and stitch the hemmed edges close to the inner fold. Press each napkin carefully with a hot iron.*

Embroidered table linen

A craft long associated with home sewing, embroidery adds delicate detail to beautiful table linen. There are literally hundreds of different embroidery stitches that can be used singly or combined to build up pretty edgings, intricate corner motifs, deep borders and scattered colour detail. Embroidering your own table linen is an opportunity to give elegance and originality to the atmosphere in which you dine.

Outline and filling stitches, cutwork embroidery, cross stitch and drawn thread work offer a range of decorative possibilities for application to a variety of fabrics. Embroidery requires patience and skill – a good effect depends upon neat, even stitching – but it is a rewarding craft, and beautifully embroidered items often become treasured family heirlooms.

To make a design for embroidery, you can use commercially available transfers which are ironed on to the fabric or traced over using dressmaker's transfer paper to leave a faint colour outline on the fabric. Alternatively, draw up your own designs or trace attractive motifs from books or magazines, or even from the pattern of a favourite fabric. Flower patterns, small animal motifs and abstract symbols such as Greek keys or linked circles are traditionally popular embroidery motifs, but with a little invention you can adapt any type of form or symbol to a line drawing which forms the basis of a stitched motif.

Embroidery threads are available in glowing colours and subtly graded tones; stranded thread allows you to vary the thickness of the stitch and creates a smooth, silky finish, while the heavier cotton perlé yarn has a lightly textured sheen that is suitable for medium-weight fabrics.

Crewel work embroidery has a striking character all its own, although it is more usually used on heavier fabrics because the fabric weight must give firm support. Therefore, this technique is better suited to cushions or curtains rather than to the lighter fabrics used for table linen. Crewel-type stitches radiate from the centre of the motif

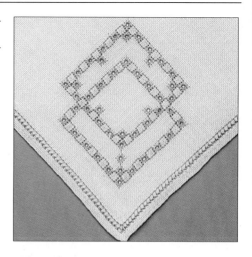

Drawn thread work
Drawn thread work is used to create borders or blocks of pattern. A good effect of subtle texturing is obtained by using an embroidery thread in a colour close to that of the fabric. A busier appearance can be achieved by the use of a definite contrast between the thread and the fabric colours, and you can combine different threads in alternate or complex stitching. However, it is as well to limit the number of colours, or the overall shape of the design will become very confused.

A corner motif
An embroidered corner motif is attractively framed in a scalloped and pointed edging. Clear colours and the fresh contrast of pink and yellow against green on a natural linen background create an informal but eye-catching design. Discreet, self-coloured stitching secures the edges of the fabric. The design is traditional but not old-fashioned.

outwards, filling the shape solidly. Long stitches tend to pucker and distort the fabric, so make sure that you judge the direction of the stitching carefully.

Satin stitch is one of the most common filling stitches in embroidery, for small blocks of colour. The stitches should be even, closely spaced and not too long and the finished effect is a flat colour area with an attractive surface sheen. The stitching is worked diagonally across the shape, rather like pencil or crayon shading in a drawing.

Outline stitches range from simple running stitch or back stitch to fancy linear effects such as chain stitch or feather stitch. Subtle colouring sometimes needs some outline detail to make the pattern more distinct.

Embroidered edgings give a well-finished look when interior detail is also embroidered. Bold outlines and strong colours match up to modern styles of furnishing; though there is a special charm to the traditional embroidery designs, it is an immensely adaptable craft which need never look old-fashioned.

Cutwork embroidery
The intricacy and delicacy of cutwork embroidery makes it appear quite a complex technique, but it depends upon a basic type of stitching and careful organization of the design. This consists of outlines which are worked solidly with close blanket stitch. The inner sections are then cut away using an extremely sharp pair of scissors. The design must be carefully worked out so that no element becomes detached from its neighbours when the open areas are cut. The cut areas should be kept fairly small, or the fabric is weakened and does not retain a crisp finish. The main character of the design depends upon the balance between open and solid areas. Cutwork is especially suited to table linen. The fabric should be firmly woven and not too heavy, but not so lightweight that the stitching can cause distortion. Interwoven shapes and floral designs have always been particularly suitable types of design for cutwork.

Cross stitch
A remarkably simple but versatile technique, cross stitch provides a range of decorative effects, from single motifs and narrow edgings to deep, complex borders or even embroidered pictures. It is essential to use a base fabric in which threads can be counted to regulate the stitching, such as even-weave linen or heavy cotton. Special fabrics are also available with a grid-like weave of tiny holes, or you can follow the woven pattern of a finely checked fabric.

Cushions

Unlike the sofas and chairs on which they sit, cushions can simply be moved to another room if you get tired of them, or you can make up a different type of cover for little extra investment, so it is worth trying out ambitious design ideas on this small scale. At the least you will end up with some unusual and individual focal points in your room which will give zest to the overall décor, and at best it may get your confidence up to put a larger project into action. Cushions of all shapes and sizes will add comfort and a warm welcoming atmosphere. Fabric remnants can be used for individual cushions, and careful choice of different, but complementary, fabric will give a lively effect. The cushions can be made plain or trimmed with piping, a frill, tassels and even appliquéd lace fabric.

Cushion pads

Ready-made pads for round and square cushions and bolsters are readily available in a range of standard sizes, and you will also find pads for neat little neck cushions and some decorative shapes such as hearts and fans. But you can make up a cushion pad to any shape you please, just by seaming up a calico or other plain-weave cotton inner cover and stuffing it with a suitable synthetic wadding or with natural down.

Make up a paper pattern before cutting the fabric, to guarantee that the shape works out as you expect. Straight-sided shapes are easily constructed – an L-shape, triangle or cube, for example. Use dinner plates or other circular objects as guide lines for curves and draw any irregular shaping freehand, going over the line until it looks right.

Synthetic wadding is available in various types and qualities, usually of polyester or acrylic, both of which are fully washable. The best grades are siliconed for extra softness and there are special "firm-fill" grades which may be a good choice for an unusual shape of cushion. Check the washing instructions on the particular type you choose and make sure that it is compatible with the pad cover fabric. Some fillings, such as down, are expensive, others, such as foam, are cheaper.

Down is light, soft and resilient, an expensive choice, but you will find that a little goes a long way. It is an appropriate filling for a cushion to be covered with a light and luxurious fabric such as silk. Feathers are less expensive than down but also less resilient.

Foam fillings are not as soft or flexible, whether you use a block of foam or foam chips, but they are good for informal styles which will have to withstand some rough and tumble, in a child's bedroom or playroom, for example, or for use with garden furniture. Polystyrene beads are tiny balls of white polystyrene. Although they are lightweight they are not soft, and are best used for informal shapes and floor cushions.

Cushion fillings
There are various types of cushion filling. Make sure that you suit the type of filling to the use of the cushion. Some fillings, such as down, are more luxurious and suited to expensive fabrics and tailored cushions.

Other types of filling, such as foam filling, provide a cheap, sturdy alternative for less formal cushions such as those for children's rooms. Shown here from left to right: down, foam filling, synthetic wadding, polystyrene beads.

Cushion trimmings

Trimmings range from neat piping inserted into outer seams to fringes, lace frills, braids, tassels or quilted appliqué motifs. Decorative trains may be plain or multi-coloured, discreetly woven or heavily embossed. Hand-stitched to the outer edges of the cushion cover, they define the outline of the shape while disguising the seam-lines.

A very simple method of enlivening the basic rectangular cushion is to add a contrast edging stitched to the outer seams of the cover, or a heavy braid border sewn to the front of the cushion, aligned to the seam or with a self-coloured margin on the cushion edges. A self-fabric border can also be created by making up the cushion cover a little larger than the pad and stitching 1½ to 2in (40 to 50mm) inside the seamlines all around. Lace makes an attractive appliqué design on the body of the cushion, and embroidery for borders and corners can also be appliquéd to the front section, particularly effective on a translucent fabric over a solid colour background. Pretty handkerchieves or scarves can be converted into cushion covers, stitched to a backing fabric in which the zip is inserted.

Plain ribbons make pretty edging. Plaited ribbons make an inner border for cushions or place mats, while woven into a block, they form a colourful panel which can be set into a cushion cover. Lengths of narrow satin ribbon can be stitched to sheer fabric to disguise the lines of seams and hems.

If you are machine-stitching ribbons to a flat piece of fabric, start at the same end when you machine down each side, otherwise there is a tension between the lines of stitching which pulls the ribbon out of shape and causes unsightly puckering.

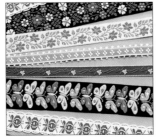

Cushion edgings
A small selection of braids, ribbons and furnishing trims suggests the range of possibilities for supplying an otherwise plain object with additional colour, texture and pattern, using simple applied decorations.

Fabrics

Crisp cottons are a good choice if you are adding self-fabric frills to round or square cushions. For bolsters and boxed cushions you should use firm and hard-wearing fabrics, though bolsters are traditionally given a rich effect with satin or satinized fabric covers drawn up with silky tassels and cords. As you do not need a great length of fabric for cushions, it is a good opportunity to use luxury fibres, fancy weaves and unusual hand-printed patterns, which can give a real lift to the room in general if you have decided on a plain and economical choice for the fabric used to cover the sofa and chairs.

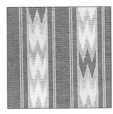

Patterns and textures
Decorative cushions can be made from any fabric, but boxed cushions and bolsters should be covered in a firm, fairly heavy furnishing fabric. Lightly embossed and textured designs offer a number of different ideas for a co-ordinated look. Plain-coloured piping creates a smart effect if the colour is chosen to make a link between variations in the colourways of the fabric as shown above, or in the patterns.

Piping

Piping is made by covering a purchased piping cord with bias strips. This is then stitched into a flat seam to give cushions and other furnishings a smart, tailored and professional finish. The piping cord is available in different thicknesses for large and small items. Although it is most commonly used to outline the seaming around cushions and loose covers, it will also form an attractive edging on duvet covers and pillowcases, and also in the seaming of bedcovers. Piping can be made either from matching or from contrasting fabric, and, as the strips are cut diagonally on the fabric, you will find that striped and checked fabric can be used for special effect.

Covering piping cord

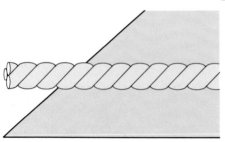

1 *Piping cord first has to be covered with bias binding. Press the bias binding strip flat, right side down, and place the piping cord in the middle.*

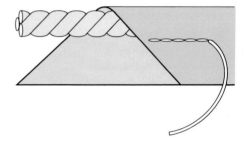

2 *Wrap the binding around the cord, wrong sides facing. Tack the front and back together. Using a zipper foot, stitch close to the piping cord.*

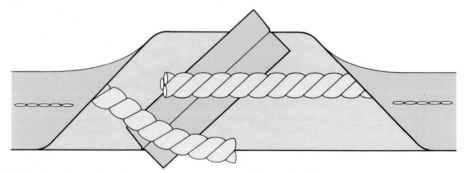

To join two pieces of cord
Join the bias binding strips with a flat seam along the grain (above). Trim the edges. Unravel the ends of piping cord and trim to different lengths. Overlap the ends by 1in (25mm) (below). Wrap the binding around the piping cord and complete stitching the cord.

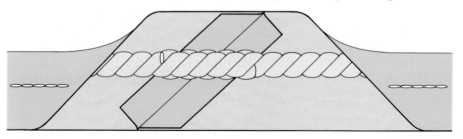

Inserting the piping

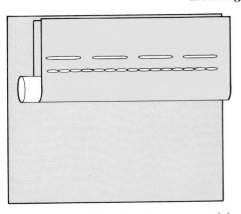

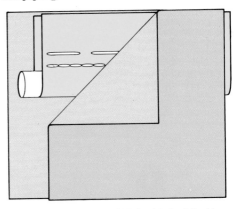

1 *The piping cord is sewn into the seam as you stitch the main seamline. To begin with, place one piece of fabric with the wrong side facing downwards. Then lay the piping cord on top of it so that the raw edges of the binding are facing outwards. Make sure that the raw edges of the binding material properly match the raw edges of the piece of fabric. Then tack the piping carefully in place.*

2 *Place the other piece of fabric with the right side down on top of the first piece of fabric and the binding. Make sure that both the raw edges of both pieces match. Using a zipper foot on the machine, stitch the four layers together on the seamline. Remove the tacking stitches. Then turn the material right side out. You will find that the piping cord makes a decorative edging along the seam.*

Shaping bolsters
Bolsters can benefit from being edged with piping, as it helps to retain the shape. Wash the piping cord before you cover it if it is not a pre-shrunk type. Allow it to dry thoroughly or it will shrink when you wash the cover itself. Note that 3ft (1m) of narrow material makes approximately 73ft (24m) of 1½in (40mm) piping.

A neat finish
Piping is particularly effective on a round cushion to give it a neat, firm edging. If you are using covered piping (opposite), you will find it is far less time-consuming if you make a continuous length and cut it as you need it. Measure the length around the articles first to ensure that you make enough.

Square cushions

The simple symmetry of a square lends itself to a wide range of fabrics and treatments. If you have a plain sofa, select a lively range of well-co-ordinated, patterned fabrics; on patterned upholstery you can choose rich, plain colours and add luxurious fringing, silk cord edging or fancy braids. Piped edges give a smart effect, or to soften the shape, insert a pleated or gathered frill in the seams.

The neatest and most secure way of fastening a square cushion cover is by a zip placed across the back of the cushion. Alternatively you can insert a zip in the side seam, or use press-stud tape or touch-and-close fastening in one side of the cover, but there is inevitably a slight distortion of the edge with these methods. Square cushion pads are available in a range of sizes, but it is a simple matter to seam and fill your own if you want a particular size of pad, perhaps to fit comfortably into an upholstered armchair.

Calculating fabric amounts

Front cover: Measure the length and width of the cushion pad. Add a ½in (12mm) seam allowance all around.

Back cover: You will need to cut two pieces of fabric for the back of the cushion so that you can add the zip. Divide the area of the cushion pad in half widthways and add a ½in (12mm) seam to the centre edges of both halves.

Themes and variations
The square cushion is one of the most varied and versatile furnishings in your scheme of decoration.

Cushions can either blend subtly with other fabrics, or provide bright splashes of colour, and they are an opportunity to use edgings, piping or frills.

Making up a square cushion

1 *Mark the square for the top of the cover and the two rectangles for the back on the straight grain. If the pattern needs matching, mark out one back piece and use this as a guide for the second back piece. Cut out the three sections.*

2 *Place the two back rectangles with the right sides facing. Tack a flat ½in (12mm) seam along the centre edges. Stitch for 2in (50mm) in from each end, leaving the centre of the seam open for the zip. Press the seams with a hot iron.*

3 *Insert the zip into the opening with the wrong side of the fabric to the right side of the zip. The open section of the seam should cover the zip teeth. With the fabric placed right side up, tack and sew the zip firmly in place.*

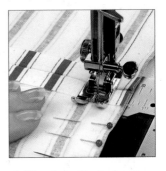

4 *Stitch the fabric and zip as close to the teeth of the zip as possible, and make sure that the stitching is evenly spaced. Carefully press the seams around the zip. Then open the zip, making sure that the fabric does not catch the teeth of the zip, and that the ends of the zip itself are stitched firmly.*

5 *For a piped edging, place the covered cord on the right side of the front fabric. Match the stitching to the seam ½in (12mm) in, and align the raw edges of the piping with the raw edges of the cover. Pin. Unpick a few inches at each end of the piping, join the fabric and cord ends and restitch. Tack in place.*

6 *Place the cushion back on the cushion front with the right sides facing and edges level. Stitch seam all around. If the edge is piped, use a zipper foot, keeping the stitching close to the cord. Press the seam open. If using heavyweight fabric, clip the corners to minimize bulk. Turn the cover right sides out.*

FRENCH SEAMS

This seam gives a very neat, strong finish with no stitching line or raw edges showing on the right side of the fabric. With the wrong sides of the fabric together, and raw edges matching, stitch a flat seam ¼in (6mm) from the fabric edge.

Trim the edges to ⅛in (3mm) and press. Turn the fabric back on itself so that the right sides are facing and the seam is on the fold, and tack the two layers together. Stitch another seam ⅜in (10mm) down from the first seam, enclosing the raw edges. Remove the tacking and press and turn the seam to the wrong side. This gives you a very narrow seam which is useful if you need to strengthen a fine fabric or a fabric that frays easily. With fabrics such as lace, the seams will be highly visible and, however neat they are, you may wish to hide them. In this case, line the material or hide the seams with an appliqué trim.

Round cushions

Frilled, piped, fringed, braided, ribboned – like square cushions, the basic round cushion shape can be enlivened in any number of different ways, most simply by the choice of beautiful fabrics for the outer covers.

Round cushion pads are sold in various standard sizes. If you are using a smooth or shiny fabric, choose a firm cushion pad and make sure that the cover fits the pad closely, otherwise the edges will not stay crisp and any unevenness will be emphasized.

The circles for the front and back of the cover are cut from squares of fabric – you can make a paper pattern as a cutting guide or draw directly on the fabric with a tailor's chalk pencil. The cover is fastened with a zip, and it is easier to sew a zip across the back of a round cushion than to insert it in the edge.

Calculating fabric amounts

Measure the diameter of the cushion pad; add a 1¼in (30mm) seam allowance. You will need to cut a circular paper pattern of this diameter to be used directly for the front cover.

Frill: First decide the required finished depth of

Variations on a theme
A group of plain, round cushions can be made up from a number of different fabrics with a unifying element, such as colour or shape.

frill. For a double frill cut the fabric strips to twice the required depth plus 1¼in (30mm). For a single frill, cut to the required depth plus 1in (25mm). For the frill length, measure around the cushion pattern ½in (12mm) in from the edge. For a knife-pleated frill, as shown, allow twice the length around the cushion. Divide the length of the frill by the width of the fabric to find how many strips are needed. Multiply the number of strips by the depth of the frill to work out the extra fabric needed.

Making up a round cushion

1 *Draw a circular paper pattern of the required diameter. Cut out the paper pattern and fabric circle for the front cover. Using the same circular pattern, rule a line across the pattern where the zip is to be placed in the back of the cover.*

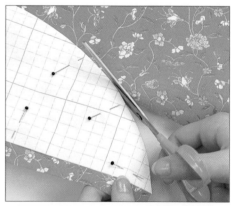

2 *The line should be 5¼in (13cm) longer than the length of the zip. Cut the paper pattern along the line. Pin the top section of the back cover pattern to the fabric. Allowing ½in (12mm) for the zip seam allowance on the straight edge, cut out the fabric.*

3 Pin the bottom section of the paper pattern to the fabric, again allowing for the zip seam, and cut out the fabric. Right sides together and raw edges matching, pin and tack the straight edges of the back cover together. Sew 2½in (65mm) from either end along the seamline. Press the seam open. Remove the tacking.

4 With the fabric right side up, insert the zip into the opening. The wrong side of the fabric should face the right side of the zip, and the open section of the seam should cover the zip teeth. Tack the zip in place. Sew down both sides and across each end of the zip, keeping as close to the teeth as possible. Open the zip.

5 Pin the front and back circles together with a ½in (12mm) seam. To add a frill, align the raw edge with the raw edge of the front cover. Sew in place. Tack the right side of the back cover to the other right side of the frill, with a ½in (12mm) seam.

6 Stitch the front and back covers together, sandwiching the frill in place if inserted. Notch the seam to minimize bulk inside the cushion. Turn the cover right side out through the zip opening and insert the cushion pad. Close the zip.

CIRCULAR FRILLS

A frill can make an otherwise plain round cushion into an original and decorative article. It has the advantage of being easy to make. To make a circular frill, cut out a circle of fabric, and then cut out a smaller circle from its centre. Clip the fabric around the inner edge of the circle; these small cuts will allow the fabric to be straightened out later on. Cut through from the outer edge of the fabric to the inner edge and flatten out the inner edge in to a straight line, so that you produce fullness on the outer, longer edge. Stay-stitch (small machine stitch) the inner edge of the frill.

With the right sides facing, pin and tack the inner clipped edge of the frill to the fabric. Machine-stitch along the seamline and then turn back the frill so that the stitching is hidden. Press carefully. If you make a frill from a different fabric, ensure that they are compatible for washing.

Boxed cushions

Often made for a particular purpose – to fit a special chair or window seat – boxed cushions give a smart effect and are sturdy and practical.

You can use a suitable cushion pad, or cut any shape you require from a thick foam block; this enables you to make regular geometric or irregularly shaped cushions, using the dimensions of the block to make a paper pattern before cutting out the fabric. The cover is opened and closed with a zip in the side gusset, and you can pipe the seams to make a neat, strong finish.

Covers for boxed cushions need to be firm and close-fitting. Medium-weight cottons are highly practical, creating crisp lines and even seams. There is a wide choice of bold, plain colours, and patterns from traditionally pretty to powerfully abstract. The fabrics may have a matt or glazed surface, a textured weave or subtle figuring.

Calculating fabric amounts
Measure the length and width of the top of the cushion pad; to each measurement add 1¼in (30mm) for seam allowances. Allow for two pieces of fabric this size, for the top and bottom of the cushion cover.

The gusset is made from four strips of fabric. Measure the depth of the pad and the width on each side. For three sections of the gusset, add 1¼in (30mm) to the length and width for ½in (12mm) seam allowances all around. For the back section, add seam allowances all around and add 1¼in (30mm) to the depth for the zip opening.

Round boxed cushions
When making a round cushion you will need to make a different type of gusset to accommodate the zip. The gusset for a round cushion is made from two seamed strips, one shorter section enclosing the zip. When attaching the gusset to the top and bottom cover pieces, ease the edge of the gusset on to the curve of the flat fabric, pin and tack to check the fit before machine-stitching all around the cover. To ensure that the seams do not pull when the cover is turned out to the right side, clip V-shaped notches in the seam allowances at regular intervals around the edge of the fabric.

Making up a boxed cushion

1 *Cut the back gusset piece in half lengthwise. Place the halves right sides together and tack a short seam on either side ½in (12mm) from the long raw edges. Each seam should be 2in (50mm), leaving a central opening for the zip. Press open the seam. Insert the zip in the back gusset. Secure each end of the zip with a short line of vertical stitching.*

2 *Seam the four gusset pieces firmly together at the short edges. Place them with their right sides together and stitch them carefully with a ½in (12mm) seam. Make sure that you leave ½in (12mm) unstitched at the top and bottom of each seam, but finish the stitching line securely. Then press the seams open on the wrong side with a hot iron.*

3 *Right sides facing, stitch the top edge of one section of the gusset along one edge of the top cover piece, taking a ½in (12mm) seam. At the gusset seam, leave the needle in the fabric and raise the machine foot, turn the fabric and align the next section of the gusset on the cover piece. Lower the machine foot and continue stitching. Work all four sides in this way.*

4 *Clip the seam allowances diagonally across each corner close to the stitching. Open the zip. Stitch the lower edges of the gusset to the bottom section of the cover. Clip the corner seams and press all the seams towards the gusset. Turn the cover out to the right side, through the open zip. Ease and straighten out the seams and push out the corners.*

Zips

Zips are especially suitable as fastenings for cushions. They are neat and are more secure and less visible than poppers or hooks. They are available in a wide range of colours and are made of both plastic and metal. It is better to use a metal zip if the cushion pad is a tight fit in the cover, since a plastic zip is more likely to pull apart under the strain.

INSERTING A ZIP OFFSET

A zip is inserted offset so that it is better concealed from view. Leave an opening as described previously. Position the zip over the seam opening so that the teeth of the zip are in the centre of the right seam allowance. Pin and tack one side of the tape in position ⅛in (3mm) from the teeth of the zip. Close the zip and tack the other side of the tape through the other seam allowance near the opening. Turn the fabric right side up and, using the zip foot attachment, top-stitch through all layers of the material, seam allowance and tape. Stitch as close as possible to the ends of the zip. Remove the tacking. This is by far the neatest way to insert a zip, and is particularly suitable for cushions and other soft furnishings where you want to disguise the zip.

Inserting a zip

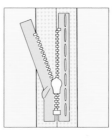

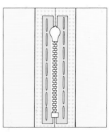

1 *Stitch a seam, leaving a gap. Centre the zip over it. Tack one side.*

2 *Close the zip. Tack the other side of the zip close to the teeth.*

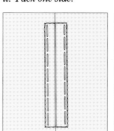

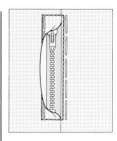

3 *Turn right side up and stitch the fabric, seam and tape.*

An offset zip
This is placed to one side of the opening.

Bolsters

An elegant addition to a sofa, a window seat, or a chaise longue, bolsters can be a noticeable and attractive feature of your room that can be styled, varied and decorated to create any mood you choose.

Your choice of fabric for bolster covers can make them roughly practical or luxuriously opulent, from matt-surfaced, textured weaves to shiny satin finishes with silky cords and floppy tassels.

There are three basic designs for bolster covers – fully fitted with flat ends; fitted with gathered ends; or a bag-like cover which pulls up with a drawstring at either end. The long, firm lines of a bolster lend themselves particularly well to directional designs such as stripes or trellises.

If you choose a heavily patterned fabric, it is best made up in the fitted style with a zip closure, so that the pattern is evenly stretched around the bolster shape.

The gathered and drawstring versions can be informally styled in cottons and textured synthetic mixes, more formally finished in traditional chintzes or figured fabrics, or given a touch of glamour by a fabric with a definite surface sheen, which catches the light down the rounded length of the bolster and gives greater emphasis to the decorative effect of the gathers.

Although the simplest ones to make are those with no additional features, the steps opposite also show how to cover and attach the buttons for a bolster with a gathered end. Bolsters can also benefit from the use of piping (page 220), since it helps to retain the shape against wear and tear.

You can also use a bolster as an attractive part of a group of scatter cushions of various shapes and sizes.

Calculating fabric amounts

The steps below and opposite show the making of a gathered bolster cover, which is made from a rectangle of fabric.
Length: Measure the length of the cushion pad plus the diameter of the circular end. Add 1¼in (30mm) for the seam allowances.
Width: Measure around the circumference of the cushion pad; add another 1¼in (30mm) for the seam allowances.

Making up a bolster

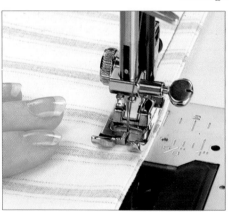 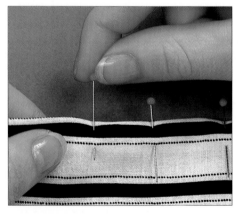

1 *Cut out a rectangle of fabric to the required size for the main body of the bolster. Fold it with right sides together and with the long edges accurately matched. Pin, tack and stitch the long edges together, making a French seam. Then turn the fabric tube right side out and press the seam on the right side with a warm iron.*

2 *Having done that, turn under a generous ½in (12mm) hem at each end of the fabric, and pin it firmly in place. Then tack each hem securely, using a contrasting colour thread, as shown above. Finish the tacking with a double stitch and then make sure that you remove all the pins.*

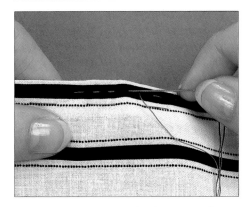

3 *At each end of the bolster, hand-sew a row of gathering stitches. Take care to position this stitching close to the fold and keep the stitches even. Insert the bolster cushion pad into the tube of fabric. Make sure that the cover fits snugly around the shape and is not loose along the body of the pad.*

4 *Adjust it so that the projecting ends of fabric are equal. Pull up the gathering threads to bring the edges of the cover in to the centre. Adjust the gathers to distribute them evenly from the centre. The hole left at the centre will be covered by the button. Fasten off the gathering threads with back stitch.*

Covering the buttons

Cut a circle of fabric generously larger than the button. Fold it over the top section of the button and push the edges of the fabric inside the button top. Use your finger to push the fabric on to the hooked spikes inside the button top; attach the fabric first at two opposite edges, then again at the other two opposite edges. Finally, work around the button, hooking in the remaining fabric smoothly.

Using double thread, pass the needle through the bobble of the tassel so that the thread end is hidden inside. Secure the thread with two small back stitches on top of each other. Take a stitch through the centre of the button covering the fabric, then one through the top of the tassel. Stitch securely and finish the thread end. Stitch buttons at each end of the bolster, concealing the gathered edges.

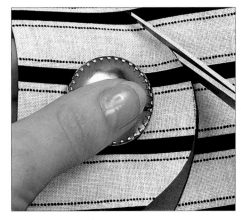

Bolster buttons
You can buy the special buttons for a bolster cushion, as shown above. The fabric must be cut a good deal larger than the button. Push the fabric on to the spikes inside the button.

OVERLOCKING SEAMS

Overlocking is a way of enclosing the raw edges of a seam, thus hiding any frayed ends. It works best on lightweight fabrics. Pin the two pieces of fabric together, right sides facing and raw edges matching. Stitch a flat seam and press. Trim the top seam to ⅛in (3mm). Turn the edge of the other seam allowance under ⅛in (3mm) and press. Turn it again, bringing the folded edge to the seamline, so that the trimmed edge of the top seam is enclosed. Press. Hand-stitch the seam to the fabric. You may find it worthwhile to invest in an overlocking machine (page 145).

Shaped cushions

Once you have mastered the principle of cushion-making, you can consider decorative, unusual "fun" shapes based on flowers, fruits, animal motifs and so on.

The steps below and opposite show the construction of a triangular cushion pad and cover. Draw up a paper pattern of the shape and make a second outline to allow for ½in (12mm) seams all around each piece. Measure the pattern for the cushion across the widest and longest sections.

If you are making the cover from fabric which just covers the width of the cushion, buy twice the length. If you can get two pattern pieces from the width, you need only the length of the cushion itself.

If the fabric has a pronounced directional pattern or large motif, allow extra if you want both sides of the cushion to include the same area from the repeats of the fabric design. Add an allowance for gusset strips if necessary.

Make your own shapes
Plain cushions do not have to be round or square – they can be triangles or diamonds, L-shaped or oval – or you can let your imagination wander into the range of slightly more complex shapes, such as hearts or fans. Any shape can be worked out as a paper pattern which can be used to make up your own cushion pad and a suitable cover.

Making up a shaped cushion pad

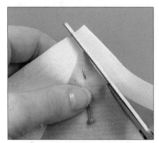

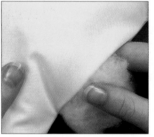

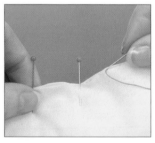

1 *Draw a paper pattern for the cushion shape and add on a ½in (12mm) seam allowance all around. If the shape is symmetrical, you can construct a pattern for half the shape and cut it out on a fold of the fabric, cutting through both layers away from the folded edge. The shape is then perfectly symmetrical when the fabric is opened out. Pin the paper pattern to the fabric and cut out the shape. Position the pattern separately for the front and back if the fabric has a definite design.*

2 *Pin the two pieces of fabric right sides together and stitch around the edges taking a ½in (12mm) seam allowance, and making sure that you leave an opening at least 6in (15cm) long so that you can insert the filling. If the shape has a distinct point or a sharply curved section, you will find that it is best to place the opening along a relatively straight part of the seam opposite this point. Then you can push the filling firmly into the shape and it will not be distorted when it comes to closing the opening.*

3 *To give the seams extra strength, work a second row of stitching along the seamline on top of the first row. Then insert the filling through the opening in the seam. Make sure that you work it well into the contours of the shape and also make sure that it is distributed evenly so that the cushion pad is firmly filled out but not lumpy. To close the opening in the seam, turn in the seam allowances neatly and pin the two sides of the gap together. Slip-stitch the seams by hand as invisibly as possible.*

Making up a shaped cushion cover

1 *Using the same pattern as for the pad, cut pieces of fabric for the top and bottom of the cushion cover, but this time take a seam allowance of ³/₈in (10mm) beyond the edges of the paper pattern. The outer cover needs to be larger than the pad to allow it to be inserted.*

2 *Put the pieces of fabric right sides together and pin. Stitch around the edge, taking a ¹/₂in (12mm) seam allowance and leaving an opening in one side large enough for insertion of the pad. It is a good idea to make a row of stitching to strengthen the seams.*

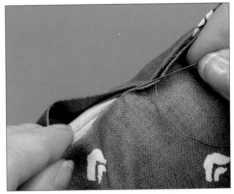

3 *Turn the cushion pad out to the right side, pushing out the seams to achieve the correct shape. If necessary, cut diagonally across the corners to reduce the bulk of material. Then press the cushion cover, and try to ensure that the seamlines are even.*

4 *Insert the cushion pad through the opening in the cover. Tuck in the raw edges neatly along the opening and slip-stitch them together as illustrated. This completes your shaped cushion. You can insert piping or frills as with any other cushion.*

FABRICS FOR SHAPED CUSHIONS

As with the more conventional cushion shapes, if the pad is well constructed and evenly filled, you can choose any type of fabric for the outer cover to suit the style of the design. It can also be fun to try and match the fabric to the shape of the cushion – red for a heart shape, for example, or use a grey, textured fabric for an elephant shape. In addition, any decorative edging, such as piping or a frill, can be inserted in the seams, but stitched to one side of the cover only at the opening in the seam. Ribbons, tassels, lace edgings and covered buttons are other types of decoration you may want to consider when making up shaped cushions – use your imagination!

GLOSSARY

Anti-condensation paint
Provides an insulating film
between a cold surface and a
humid atmosphere, and so
reduces condensation.

Architrave The moulding around
a door or window.

Basting A long stitch used to
hold fabric in place prior to the final
stitching. Also known as tacking.

Batten A sawn strip of wood
fixed to the wall or ceiling to
support shelves or blinds.

Berber A type of carpet, made
from undyed sheep wool, with a
denser, looped pile.

Bias strips Lengths of fabric cut
diagonally across the warp and
weft threads of the fabric. They
are used to bind edges and cover
piping cord.

Binder bars Aluminium strips
used to hold carpet taut and
prevent it from fraying.

Buckram A strong, coarse
cotton or linen cloth, impregnated
with gum or other stiffening
agents. It is used to stiffen fabric
cornices and pelmets.

Butt joint Made by pushing one
strip of wallpaper up against
another to form a slight ridge. This
disappears as the paper dries, and
ensures there is no gap between
the strips.

Cavity wall A hollow wall, made
of two layers of plasterboard
supported by wooden joists.

Colourways The colour or
combination of colours used in a
fabric. Most fabrics have the same
design produced in a number of
different ways.

Cove A strip of material fixed to
the angle between the ceiling and
the wall. Used to hide cracks and
provide a neater finish.

Cutting-in brush The slanting
angle of the bristles means that
the paint can be taken neatly right
to an edge, such as a skirting
board or the glass in a window
frame, without smudging.

Cutwork A decorative technique
in which a motif or pattern is
outlined in close blanket stitch and
the fabric is then cut out in various
sections of the design.

Dowel A small wooden peg which
slots into holes in two pieces of
wood, forming a joint.

Dress fabrics Those produced
for the purpose of making clothing.
Many are less durable than
furnishing fabrics and are not fade-
resistant in sunlight.

Dressing A substance applied to
fabric to improve its feel or
appearance. When used to
enhance fabric of an inferior
quality, the dressing may rub off or
be removed when it is washed.

Dry-strip paper Wallpaper that
can be peeled off the walls without
using water.

Edgings These are decorative
trimmings that are used to finish
the edge of an item. They may be
made from fabric, such as a frill, or
purchased, such as lace or eyelet.
Edgings have one finished edge
and one raw edge, by which they
are attached to the hem.

Eggshell paint Has a matt
finish, used for interiors and for
some decorative finishes.

Embossed wallpaper A heavy
wallpaper designed to be painted
over. It has a texture pressed into
it in a range of patterns.

Emulsion paint A water-based
paint with a matt or sheen finish,
used for interior painting jobs on
walls and ceilings. It is an easy
paint to apply and dries quickly.

Enamel A hard-wearing, high-
gloss top coat paint.

Even weave Fabric that has
warp and weft threads that are
identical in thickness and provide
the same number of threads over a
given area, enabling stitches to be
worked by counting the threads.

Facings Used to finish edges in
places where hems are unsuitable,
such as a scalloped edge. The
facing is made from a separate
piece of fabric, cut to the same
shape as the edge to be finished,
and stitched to it.

Figurative designs Those
which include life-like shapes
within the pattern. The figures
may represent birds, trees,
flowers or scenery.

Figured weaves Those which
have figurative designs woven into
the fabric. The different areas of
the design may be woven in
different colours or with a
contrasting texture.

Flock wallpaper A fine pile is
added to selected areas of the
paper or vinyl base to produce a
flocked pattern.

Foamed polyethelene A
lightweight material resembling a
printed fabric. Pasted to the wall,
it is warm to the touch, washable,
and easy to strip.

Glasspaper Otherwise known as
sandpaper. Sheets of paper used
for abrading.

Gloss paint A hard top coat paint
with a high finish, used for both
exterior and interior wood and
metal. It is solvent-based.

Grippers Plywood strips with
nails punched through them, fixed
around the edges of the room with
the nail points up, to grip carpet
and hold it taut across the room or
in place on stairs.

Grout A powder, mixed with water, applied to the spaces between tiles to seal them. It is also called grouting.

Interlining A fabric which is placed between the main fabric and the lining to strengthen or stiffen the fabric, to give it extra body, or to provide more insulation. On fabric cornices and tie-backs the interlining is placed between the fabric and the buckram stiffening to mask the coarse weave of the buckram and give a softer, more pleasing feel to the finished side of the fabric.

Jigsaw A versatile power saw. It will make straight, curved, or scroll cuts in timber, boards, metals, plastics and other materials. The vertical blade cuts by moving rapidly up and down.

Joist A beam made of timber, steel or reinforced concrete. Used as a support for floors and roofs.

Knot Part of the pattern of the grain of wood. Knots should be covered with stopper before painting or varnishing.

Lathes Thin strips of wood which are inserted into the casings at the lower edges of Roman blinds to keep the fabric stiff and straight.

Lining paper A plain paper applied to uneven walls or ceilings to provide a smoother surface for paint or paper.

Masonry paint A tough, weatherproof paint used for external decorations.

Matt finish A finish for paint, tiles or fabric without any sheen or reflecting properties.

Mercerized fabric Fabric which has been treated under tension with caustic soda which causes the fibres to swell. It gives the fabric extra lustre, and makes it softer to the touch.

Mosaic tiles Small ceramic tiles that are supplied fitted to a mesh backing for easy fitting.

Orbital sander A machine with a rectangular pressure pad which vibrates very rapidly. Sheets of abrasive paper are fixed to it.

Parquet panels Polished wooden blocks fitted together to form a high-grade floor.

Pattern repeats The places where exactly the same motif is repeated again in the same position farther down the fabric or wallpaper. The length of a pattern repeat is the distance between these places.

Plumb and bob line A piece of cord with a weight attached used to ensure straight lines.

Polyurethane seal A synthetic, transparent seal, used to protect wood or cork.

Primer Applied to wood to seal the pores and provide a stable base for undercoat.

Quadrant tiles Round-edged slivers of tiling used for borders on corners, such as window sills.

Returns The side edges of a cornice between the front edge of the cornice, or pelmet, and the window or wall.

Sander There are industrial sanders for hire, and also hand sanders, both used for stripping timber floors and doors before staining or varnishing.

Scraper A metal implement used to remove paintwork.

Sculptured pile A woven or tufted carpet made up of a mixture of cut and looped pile.

Seal A transparent liquid applied to wood to protect the surface.

Self fabric The fabric that has been used for the main part of the soft furnishing item.

Selvages The finished-off edges of fabric which run down both sides of the length of fabric.

Shag pile A luxurious carpet with a pile of 1in (25mm) pile.

Shavehook For removing softened paint from wooden mouldings around doors and windows. They are available with triangular, pear-shaped and combination edges.

Sheen finish A paint finish midway between matt and gloss. Also called silk finish.

Stain For colouring wood. There are oil-based, spirit based and water-based varieties, used for different types of wood.

Straight grain This runs along the warp threads, parallel to the selvages in woven fabrics.

Stripper There are peel-off, chemical and heat-based types of strippers. They are used for stripping paint from wood and metal surfaces.

Sub-floor A floor laid under the surface flooring to provide a smooth, firm surface.

Textured paint Available both ready-to-use and in powdered form. Some leave a pattern automatically when applied, others are textured by hand after they have been applied.

Thixotropic paint Non-drip, gloss paint.

Toggles Enable fixtures to be secured to low-strength plasterboard and panelling.

Tongue-and-groove boards Wooden boards with a groove at one edge and a "tongue" or protrusion at the other. These enable the boards to be slotted into one another.

Underlay The layer of material, usually rubber or felt, laid down before the carpet proper is laid.

Warp threads Those which run lengthways, parallel to the selvages in woven fabrics.

Weft threads Those which weave under and over the warp threads and run across the fabric between the selvages.

INDEX

Figures in italic refer to illustrations.

ACKNOWLEDGMENTS

Editor: Eileen Cadman
Editorial assistant: Joanna Swinnerton
Designer: Ron Samuels
Design assistant: Mark Davies
Illustrators: David Ashby, Kuo Kang Chen, Kevin Maddison,
Fraser Newman, Les Smith
Studio: Del & Co.

Dorling Kindersley
Managing editor: Jemima Dunne
Managing art editor: Derek Coombes
Editorial assistant: Tom Fraser
Designer: Rachel Griffin
Production: Helen Creeke

Contributor: Elaine Brumstead

Photography
(t=top, b=bottom, l=left, r=right)
Jon Bouchier: half title page, title page, 8t and bl, 9t and br, 10tl and bl,
11tr and br, 12t and bl, 13t and br, 17, 18, 19, 26, 27, 28, 30, 32, 33, 39,
41, 42, 43, 45, 51, 58, 59, 60, 61, 62, 63, 65, 66, 67, 68, 69, 70t, 78–9,
87, 88, 89, 90, 91, 92, 95, 96, 97, 103, 104, 105, 109, 111, 112, 113, 114,
124, 125, 126, 127, 128, 129, 131, 132, 133, 136, 137, 140, 141,
151, 168, 178, 179, 194.
Camera Press: 83tl, 83b, 110b, 118tl and r, 139tl.
"Coverplus" (Woolworth's): 23br.
Mark French: 195, 214t, 216, 217.
Stephen Oliver: 6–7, 14–5, 46–7, 74–5, 98–9, 134–5, 142–3, 190–1.
Steve Tanner: 8br, 9bl, 10tr, 11tl, 12br, 13bl, 145, 146–7, 148, 149, 150,
155, 156, 157, 160, 161, 162, 163, 164, 165, 166, 169, 170, 173, 174, 175,
176, 180, 181, 182, 183, 184, 185, 186, 187, 188, 189, 192, 193, 196, 197, 198,
199, 200, 202, 203, 204, 205, 206, 207, 208, 209, 210, 211, 212, 213, 214bl and br,
215, 218, 219, 222, 223, 224, 225, 226, 227, 228, 229, 230, 231.
Elizabeth Whiting Associates: 22, 23t and bl, 44br, 54, 55, 70bl and br,
82l, 83tr, 107, 110t, 118bl, 138, 139tr, 153.

For their generous assistance in supplying articles for the photographs on
pages 6–7, 46–7, 74–5, 98–9, 134–5, 142–3 and 190–1, the authors and
publishers would like to thank the following:

Amtico: vinyl tiles.
William Armes Ltd: sisal, coconut, seagrass and woven plastic Danycord matting.
Laura Ashley: bedlinen, cushions, bolster, tablecloths, lace napkin,
wallpaper, wallpaper border, stencil, stencil brush, paints.
Astrohome Ltd: black and silver shelving.
Black and Decker: electric drill, Super Powerdriver, electric sander and heat gun.
C. Brewer & Son Ltd: white metal shelving, wallpapering tools and brushes, tiling tools.
Dixon Wallcoverings Ltd: textured wallcoverings.
Nairn Flooring: linoleum.
Nice Irma: rugs.
Wincanders (Great Britain) Ltd: woodblock flooring.
World's End Tiles: floor and wall tiles.